AND I LIVE ON

edited by Anne-Marie de Brouwer,
Sandra Ka Hon Chu, Eefje de Volder &
Samer Muscati

photographs by Samer Muscati

THE RESILIENCE OF RWANDAN GENOCIDE

foreword by Patricia Viseur Sellers

AND I LIVE ON

SURVIVORS OF SEXUAL VIOLENCE

And I Live On: The Resilience of Rwandan Genocide Survivors of Sexual Violence.
Edited by Anne-Marie de Brouwer, Sandra Ka Hon Chu, Eefje de Volder & Samer Muscati.
Photographs by Samer Muscati.
Foreword by Patricia Viseur Sellers.
Publisher Willem-Jan van der Wolf.
Cover photographs by Samer Muscati.
Front: Marie Louise Niyobuhungiro; back: Faustin Kayihura and his wife.
ISBN: 978-94-6240-600-1

This book is published by:
Wolf Legal Publishers (WLP)
Talent Square 13
5038 LX Tilburg
The Netherlands
www.wolfpublishers.com
info@wolfpublishers.nl
Tel: +31 - 13-5821366

To those persevering through the aftermath of sexual violence, to those who continue to suffer from it around the world, and to those who provide them solace.

"History will judge us harshly if, once aware of the nature and scope of this violence, once outraged by its injustice, we do not choose to act against it."

JAN EGELAND

Former UN Under-Secretary-General for Humanitarian Affairs and Emergency Relief Coordinator

CONTENTS

FOREWORD

DID TWENTY-FIVE YEARS, or one thousand and three hundred weeks, or nine thousand and one hundred days really steal by since the genocide against the Tutsi cursed through Rwanda's Kigali, Cyangugu, Taba and Butare? We remain alive, still breathing, still stunned, often muted. At times, we divert our eyes when recalling the horrific ghastliness of those one hundred days. We shiver, once again, when deciphering the sheer magnitude of the deaths, rapes, mutilations and the utter human loss.

Did we, the "international community" (decode: non-Rwandans) really survive our psychic wounds? Didn't we apply a soothing international legal balm to redress the machete gashes and support the national *gacaca* courts' healing prescriptions? Do we feel better as we readily refer to the splendid roads and infrastructure network built by Rwandans subsequent to the genocide? Is our solace palpable, although a little strained, when reciting that, now, Rwandan women constitute the majority of parliamentarians, even more than in Sweden? Do we tend to highlight the absence of blue plastic bags stuck in trees due to the Rwandan revival of the sustainable paper sack?

When the international community failed to invoke its preventive, international law to guard against any attempt, conspiracy, or direct and public incitement to commit genocide, it faltered. It inflicted a self-wound as well as allowed the unleashing of a gruesome, genocidal torrid upon Rwandans. The very doctrinal premise of genocide is *not* to allow the destruction of racial, ethnic, national or religious groups—groups that constitute "protected components" of the international community. Humanity's composition, as expressed by our communal belonging to religions, races, nationalities or ethnicities broaches the sacred within international criminal law. Genocide represents a *jus cogens* value that we, as an international community, by our inaction renounced in Rwanda in 1994. That gnawing unease is our own unattended psychic wound.

I suggest that now, even more than two decades later, we direct our bewilderedness to the first-line survivors (decode: Rwandans) of the genocide. This 2nd edition of *The Men Who Killed Me* entitled *And I Live On: The Resilience of Rwandan Genocide Survivors of Sexual Violence*, gives voice to the persistence of life. Lives traversed by genocide, and ultimately strengthened; life as a wily act of fortitude. Life constructed, in part, by rejecting any permanence that the inhumanity of sexual violence, as an act of genocide, could inflict. Turn to these words of females and males who emerged from the crucible and survived, with and by their persistent humanness. In this edited volume, members almost lost to the international community bear essential words that confer their mettle, encouragement and their aliveness.

Turn around slowly, and listen deeply. We possibly might be able to survive, to regain our voice and our essence, intact.

PATRICIA VISEUR SELLERS
Special Advisor on Gender to the Prosecutor of the International Criminal Court
Former Gender Legal Advisor for the International Criminal Tribunal for Rwanda

February 4, 2019

INTRODUCTION

LIKE ALL BOOKS, this one began with an idea. As colleagues in 2006 at a women's rights organization in The Hague, Anne-Marie and Sandra worked closely on a variety of issues related to sexual violence in conflict. Rwanda became a frequent topic of conversation as our friendship grew. The country known as the "land of a thousand hills" had, in effect, become Anne-Marie's second home; not only had she visited and worked in Rwanda over the years, but she had developed a deep friendship with a young Rwandan woman who had survived traumatic sexual violence during the 1994 genocide against the Tutsi. At the time, the issue of sexual violence in conflict consumed less public attention: over ten years would pass before the 2018 Nobel Peace Prize was awarded to Dr. Denis Mukwege and Nadia Murad for their heroic efforts to end the use of sexual violence as a weapon of war. We discussed the possibility of creating a venue for Anne-Marie's friend and others like her to bring forth their experiences.

In Rwanda, between 250,000 and 500,000 women and girls, as well as an unknown number of men and boys, were raped over the span of 100 days in 1994. In the years that followed, the consequences touched every aspect of survivors' lives, as they desperately tried to carry on. Despite numerous accounts of the genocide, including coverage about perpetrators standing trial before the International Criminal Tribunal for Rwanda, the voices of rape survivors were notably absent.

In 2007, Anne-Marie and Samer, a fellow human rights advocate and photographer, visited Solace Ministries, a survivor-run grassroots organization in Kigali that works with widows and orphans of the genocide, offering them food, housing, medical care, counselling, education, income-generating projects and spiritual care. We were amazed by both the strength of the women and men we met, and the invaluable support they provided for each other as survivors with a common bond. We decided then that we would do whatever we could to allow them to share their struggles more widely, so the world would know their stories and their resilience. Samer suggested that photographs would bring another dimension to survivors' accounts of their experiences.

And so the first iteration of *The Men Who Killed Me* was conceived. The process involved working remotely on the book from the Netherlands and Canada and returning to Rwanda in 2008 to interview the 17 courageous survivors featured in the first edition. Throughout the interviews, the remarkable staff of Solace Ministries were on hand to assist with translation and, if necessary, with counselling. Once the interviews were complete, Samer travelled across Rwanda photographing survivors in their homes and the areas where they experienced the genocide. In April 2009, 15 years after the genocide, *The Men Who Killed Me* was published. In 2011, the book was also published in Dutch.

The impact of the book has been indelible. By featuring rarely conveyed narratives and photographs of survivors of genocide-related sexual violence, readers were exposed to the brutal reality of the sexual violence perpetuated against women, girls, men and boys during the genocide against the Tutsi, which took on a myriad of cruel forms. The book also illustrated the protracted aftermath of genocidal sexual violence, and the manner in which sexual violence was used as an effective tool of genocide to destroy the Tutsi population.

The authors' proceeds from book sales were donated to the survivors in the book via Mukomeze (Kinyarwanda for "empower her"), a foundation that supports those raped during the Rwandan genocide. Founded in 2008 and run by volunteers including Anne-Marie and her colleague Eefje, Mukomeze works in close cooperation with Solace Ministries. The book proceeds and Mukomeze's sponsorship program enabled many survivors to rebuild some aspects of their lives.

Survivors also conveyed to us that their participation in *The Men Who Killed Me* gave them a sense of catharsis. To share their accounts of the genocide, and to have their suffering recognized, was a healing experience for many. It also offered the survivors an opportunity to appeal to the world to take steps to prevent these atrocities from recurring. At the same time, the survivors were proud to learn that their stories had attracted a global audience, inspiring readers around the world to share their own experiences of sexual violence, and that their testimonials had taken on new creative forms, including as a theatre production (in Halifax, Canada), as a component of university courses (in Winnipeg, Canada), as a Gregorian chant honouring female victims of violence (in Nijmegen, the Netherlands) and as photography exhibits (including at the International Criminal Court in The Hague, the Netherlands and in Toronto, Canada). Survivors felt these were all important platforms to commemorate stories of sexual violence in Rwanda and other conflicts worldwide.

But their stories are obviously not over. Ten years after the publication of *The Men Who Killed Me*, readers expressed an interest in learning how the survivors' lives had unfolded. With two exceptions, the survivors also expressed a desire to chronicle the trajectory of their lives since we first interviewed them. Two survivors also requested pseudonyms to protect their privacy. Sadly, four survivors—Adela Mukamusonera, Immaculée Makumi, Françoise Mukeshimana and Françoise Kayitesi—had passed away from poor health, largely related to the trauma they experienced during the genocide. This is a heart-breaking reality of conflict-related sexual violence that warrants our attention. Their children, who we interviewed, elaborate on this and also recount the tremendous impact of their mothers' deaths on their lives. The other survivors continue to struggle, haunted by a persistent array of challenges that include making ends meet, providing for their children's education, and grappling with many health complications that are a result of the sexual violence they endured during the genocide. But on the whole, their lives have changed for the better, made possible by their resilience, perseverance, industriousness, empathy and compassion as well as the sustained medical, psychosocial, spiritual and economic support that they received.

To document these developments, Anne-Marie, Eefje and Samer returned to Rwanda in 2018 to interview and photograph the remaining eleven survivors and four children of those who had passed away. Supporting them were law students and research associates from the University of Toronto's International Human Rights Program at the Faculty of Law. Sandra joined the team in the following months transcribing, editing and reviewing the testimonials with the survivors, aided by the staff of Solace Ministries, to ensure they accurately and sensitively captured their stories. Other parts of the book were also revised to include developments in support of Rwandan genocide survivors of sexual violence as well as a chapter on the work of Solace Ministries and Mukomeze in this area.

So often, narratives of genocide are limited to the violence that was inflicted over a deadly, discrete period. Rarely are we provided with a glimpse into the worlds of survivors living with the genocide's legacy decades after a conflict. The first book was a vital documentation of the sexual violence that plagued Rwanda during the genocide. With the 25th anniversary of the genocide, this edition showcases survivors' extraordinary strength, courage, resilient outlook and ability to forgive and live alongside *génocidaires* in the face of seemingly irreparable harms. As with the first book, proceeds will go to the survivors so they can continue to heal, rebuild their lives, and support themselves and their loved ones. In line with survivors' plea to raise public awareness of the genocide so that history is never repeated, we will also produce educational materials on conflict-related sexual violence, justice and reconciliation, and make these available online as an interactive platform for students, researchers and practitioners of all disciplines.

Survivors of sexual violence are an enduring testament to our collective abandonment of them. But they also represent the promise of transformative change. There is, indeed, life after death. As one survivor pronounced: "My hopes for the future are bright." We share her optimism.

Our heartfelt thanks to the survivors and their families for honouring us again with their testimonials, and to the staff of Solace Ministries for their unwavering support, without which this initiative would not have been possible. The survivors featured in this book have profoundly changed our lives. We hope that their stories will do the same for you.

ANNE-MARIE DE BROUWER
SANDRA KA HON CHU
EEFJE DE VOLDER
SAMER MUSCATI

February 25, 2019

Family photos of children who perished during the violence of 1994 on display at the Kigali Genocide Memorial

RWANDA
National capital
Prefecture capital
Town, village
DEMOCRATIC
REPUBLIC OF
CONGO
WESTERN
PROVINCE
NORTHERN
SOUTHERN
PROVINCE
Nyabarongo
Buta
Kidaho
Ruhengeri
Busogo
Kora
Mutura
Kagali
Goma
Gisenyi
Nyundo
Kabaya
Nemba
Rushashi
Ngaru
Ngororero
Kiyumba
Bulinga
Mabanza
Kibuye
Gitarama
Birambo
Bwakira
Gishyita
Rwamatamu
Masango
Ruhango
Gatagara
Kaduha
Nyanza
Rwesero
Karaba
Rusatira
Gisakura
Kamembe
Rwumba
Gikongoro
Karama
Bukavu
Cyangugu
Cyimbogo
Karengera
Kitabi
Nyakabuye
Bugumya
Butare
Ruramba
Gisagara
Bugarama
Busoro
Munini
Runyombyi

UGANDA
Kagitumba
Rwemhasha
Lubirizi
Nyagatare
Muvumba
Mulindi
Gatunda
Gabiro
Ngarama
Byumba
EASTERN
PROVINCE
Kinyami
Rutare
Muhura
Murambi
Rukara
KIGALI
Gikoro
Rwamagana
KIGALI
Kicukiro
Bicumbi
Kayonza
Butamwa
Kigarama
Bugesera
Kibungo
Rilima
Rukira
Gashora
Sake
Rusumo
Bare
Kirehe
Nemba
Ngenda
Kagera
River
UNITED
REPUBLIC OF
TANZANIA
BURUNDI
AFRICA
RWANDA
0 10 20 30 40 50 km
0 10 20 30 40 50 mi

1

THE ROOTS OF SEXUAL VIOLENCE IN RWANDA

"It has probably become more dangerous to be a woman than a soldier in an armed conflict."

PATRICK CAMMAERT

Assistant Secretary-General, Head of UNMHA

A statue of Mary overlooks victims' clothing inside the former church at the Nyamata Genocide Memori

IN THE ONE HUNDRED DAYS of genocide that ravaged the small Central African nation of Rwanda from April until July 1994, about one million Tutsi and moderate Hutu were killed,[1] and an estimated 250,000 to 500,000 women and girls as well as an unknown number of men and boys were raped.[2] According to a United Nations (UN) report, rape was the rule, its absence the exception.[3] Sexual violence occurred everywhere, and no one was spared. Grandmothers were raped in front of their grandchildren; girls witnessed their families being massacred before being taken as sex slaves; boys were raped by women; fathers were forced to have sex with their daughters. Many women were murdered following rape. Almost all of the women who did survive the genocide were victims of sexual violence or were profoundly affected by it.[4]

Twenty-five years later, the impact of the sexual violence endured by survivors continues to be monumental, threatening their daily survival. An astounding 70 per cent are living with HIV.[5] Recognizing this, the UN General Assembly passed a resolution in 2004 affirming that survivors of sexual violence are among those who face the greatest hardship in post-conflict Rwanda.[6] Gender inequality and gender-based violence existed in Rwanda prior to the genocide,[7] but the events of 1994 provided a backdrop for rape to be perpetrated against Tutsi women and their sympathizers on a mass scale. The ideology of Hutu power was underscored through the dehumanization of Tutsi women.

THE GENOCIDE IN Rwanda was one of the most ruthless and effective of all time. Ostensibly sparked by the death of Hutu President Juvénal Habyarimana, whose plane was shot down by unknown assailants above Kigali airport on April 6, 1994, the event was preceded by a complicated and bloody history between Tutsi and Hutu.

When Belgian colonialists arrived in Rwanda in 1916, they favoured the Tutsi minority over the Hutu majority. The Belgians classified the Tutsi by their physical traits and viewed them as more similar to Europeans and, therefore, deemed them to be more intelligent. The clergy in Rwanda were complicit in creating and maintaining divisions between Tutsi and Hutu.[8] Tutsi were awarded better jobs and had greater educational opportunities, a distinction reinforced by the development of separate educational systems. In the early 1930s, to solidify the division between Tutsi and Hutu, the Belgians produced identity cards classifying individuals according to their ethnic group: Hutu, Tutsi or Twa.[9] These identity cards, still in use in the 1990s, led many Tutsi to their death by readily identifying them to the *génocidaires*.

The ethnic classification between Tutsi and Hutu was imposed despite their many commonalities. The two groups speak the same language, Kinyarwanda. They share a similar culture, and intermarriage was common between Tutsi and Hutu. The distinction between Tutsi and Hutu is more accurately defined as one of fluid socioeconomic class than of ethnicity. Traditionally, Hutu were farmers and Tutsi were wealthier cattle herders. Hutu who accumulated wealth were often reclassified as Tutsi, and Tutsi bereft of property could be reclassified as Hutu.[10]

Resentment among the Hutu about the special treatment of Tutsi festered over the years. It culminated in a series of killings of Tutsi, beginning in 1959 with the unexpected death of the ruling Tutsi king, and continuing through Rwandan independence from Belgium in 1962, after a popular uprising drove out the Tutsi elite and installed a Hutu-dominated government. Between 1959 and 1973, more than 700,000 Rwandan Tutsi were exiled to neighbouring countries.[11] Tutsi refugees were barred from returning, despite many peaceful efforts to do so. Some joined the Rwandan Patriotic Front—the RPF, commonly referred to as the *Inkotanyi*—a political and military movement formed by Tutsi refugees in Uganda to demand Rwandan unity. On October 1, 1990, the RPF, seeking to pressure the ruling Rwandan government into a power-sharing agreement, invaded Rwanda from Uganda. They were repelled by troops from France and Zaire sent to reinforce the Rwandan government.[12] Tutsi living in Rwanda were blamed for the RPF attack, and the Rwandan government massacred about two thousand of them across the country in apparent retaliation.[13]

When President Habyarimana's plane was shot down on April 6, 1994, he was returning to Rwanda from peace negotiations with the RPF in Tanzania. The president was killed instantly, and with him, all hope for peace. Habyarimana's death served as a pretext for Hutu extremists to launch their one hundred days of genocide. Previously prepared execution lists were circulated showing the names of Tutsi and moderate Hutu (Hutu who were opposed to the oppression of Tutsi). The most influential, educated and wealthy among these people were the first to be killed. Even influential Hutu were not spared if they posed a threat to the extremists. Most notably, moderate Hutu Prime Minister Agathe Uwilingiyimana was assassinated at the Kigali UN compound on April 7, 1994, after which her corpse was sexually abused.

Eradicating the Tutsi became the calling of Hutu extremists. They taunted their victims with threats to "return" them to Ethiopia, where the Tutsi allegedly originated; because they were perceived to have lighter skin and narrower noses and chins, Tutsi were accused of being "of European stock." Within hours of Habyarimana's death, Hutu began killing and raping Tutsi, with the aim of complete annihilation. With the prospects for peace extinguished, the RPF invaded Rwanda. After ensuring that nationals of Western governments had safe access out of the country, the world stood by silently and watched one of the worst massacres in human history.[14] The genocide ended only when the RPF overthrew the Hutu regime in July 1994.

THE SEXUAL VIOLENCE in Rwanda during the genocide was extreme in its brutality and systematic in its orchestration. Victims were selected predominantly on the basis of their gender and their Tutsi ethnicity. Age did not play a role in who was attacked: Tutsi women and girls of all ages were raped. The targeting of Tutsi girls and women was spurred in part by anti-Tutsi propaganda preceding the 1994 genocide, which alleged that the minority Tutsi population was a threat to the Hutu community. Radio and newspapers, to which most Rwandans had access, both played a major role in the genocide. To desensitize the Hutu masses, hate radio station Radio Télévision Libre des Mille Collines (RTLM) continuously referred to Tutsi as cockroaches and snakes.[15]

In the December 1990 issue of Kangura, an influential Rwandan newspaper, the sexuality of Tutsi women was one focus of the Hutu "Ten Commandments." In four of the "commandments," Tutsi women were portrayed as tools of the Tutsi community and as sexual weapons who would be used to weaken and ultimately destroy Hutu men.[16] Newspapers also featured cartoons that portrayed Tutsi women, including the moderate Hutu Prime Minister Agathe Uwilingiyimana, as sexual objects.[17]

Perpetrators often referred in the midst of rape to the supposed beauty and arrogance of Tutsi women; hate propaganda alleged that Tutsi women looked down on Hutu men and thought they were "too good" for them. Rape thus served as a means to degrade and subjugate Tutsi women. Sexual violence was also directed at Hutu women considered moderates: women who were married to Tutsi men, protected Tutsi individuals or were politically affiliated with Tutsi. Though much less frequently, sexual violence was perpetrated against Hutu women and girls with no affiliation with the Tutsi population—crimes made possible by the prevailing chaos during the conflict. Men, primarily of Tutsi ethnicity, were also sexually assaulted, often by the sexual mutilation of their genitals, which were sometimes displayed in public. In some cases, Tutsi men and boys were forced to rape Tutsi women, forced to have sexual intercourse with dead animals or were raped by Hutu women. Women and girls were subjected to the full range of sexual atrocity. This included rape, gang rape, sexual slavery, forced incest, forced marriage, and amputation or mutilation of victims' breasts, vaginas and buttocks, or of features considered to be Tutsi, such as small noses or long fingers.[18] Even pregnant women were not spared.

An expert panel has reported that some HIV-positive perpetrators intentionally tried to transmit the virus by raping Tutsi women.[19] In the eyes of the Hutu perpetrators, infecting a Tutsi woman with HIV served as an effective means to infect her future sexual partners and any children she bore as well as to eventually kill her and leave her dependents without her support.[20] Some women abducted to be the personal slaves, or "wives," of Hutu men were forced to remain with their rapists after the genocide, in some cases moving to neighbouring countries with their captors.

At the time of the genocide, Rwanda's twelve prefectures were subdivided into communes, sectors and cells, with cells being the most decentralized territorial unit of local government. Sexual violence took place in every part of the country, though the majority of cases occurred in the southern part of Rwanda, probably because these regions were among the last to fall under the control of the invading RPF.[21] Rape did occur inside victims' or perpetrators' houses, but more often it was committed in plain view of others, at sites such as schools, churches, roadblocks and government buildings. Many women were also raped in the bushes where they had hidden to avoid being discovered. Frequently, rape victims' corpses were left spread-eagled in public view, as a reminder of the brutality and power of the genocide's perpetrators. In addition to the sexual violence they endured, many women witnessed crimes such as torture and murder committed against their loved ones. Many of them lost their houses and property.

The perpetrators of sexual violence were mostly members of the Hutu militia, the *Interahamwe*. But rapes were also committed by Presidential Guards, military soldiers of the Rwandan Armed Forces (FAR), the Rwandan police and civilians, as well as by international soldiers—most notably the French, who were stationed in the southwest of the country under a UN mandate to supposedly establish and maintain a "secure humanitarian area" called Opération Turquoise.[22] Many government officials and leaders of the militia and the military were complicit. They knew that rape was being committed, and there is evidence that leaders encouraged or ordered their men to rape Tutsi women or condoned the commission of sexual violence by not intervening.[23] Hutu women from all walks of life also perpetrated sexual violence by raping boys and men, by violating Tutsi women with objects and by facilitating or ordering their rape.[24]

Compared with conflicts in other places, the sexual violence in Rwanda is notorious because of the organized propaganda, which contributed significantly to fuelling sexual violence against Tutsi women, the very public nature of the rapes and the level of ruthlessness directed toward women.[25] Today, shockingly, despite the many documented horrors during the genocide, there is a continuous denial of what happened during those one hundred days in Rwanda and a resurgence of genocidal ideology in Rwanda and other countries.[26]

RAPE AND OTHER forms of sexual violence during conflict have historically been viewed as a private matter, seen as collateral damage inconsequential to the larger considerations of wartime politics or justified as an inevitable consequence of war, a necessary bounty for fighting men. However, following the genocide against the Tutsi in Rwanda in 1994 and the wars in the former Yugoslavia (1991–2001), numerous accounts brought to the fore the pervasive degree of sexual violence committed against women and girls. The use of rape in war had finally captured the world's attention, and sexual violence was transformed in people's understanding from the private actions of individuals to a public and political tool of aggression.

But despite the brazen nature of the sexual violence committed in Rwanda and the former Yugoslavia, such crimes were by no means new. During almost every conflict in the world, sexual violence has been perpetrated in various ways, often with complete impunity. Although sexual violence during conflicts has been documented as both widespread and systematic, perpetrators of these crimes have rarely been held accountable for their actions. Even today, it is common to hear the assertion that those who were raped and survived are "lucky" they were not killed, and there is a broad perception that rape is somehow a lesser crime not worth investigating.

Traditional attitudes toward women's rights tacitly condone violence against women. A culture of pre-existing gender inequality that turns a blind eye to sexual violence in the family helps create an environment for targeted violence against women during armed conflict. Social norms crumble during conflict: tolerance to violence increases, and communities begin to accept violence as a legitimate way of expressing anger and resolving issues. The environment during armed conflict is devoid of the social safety mechanisms that normally inhibit extreme and exaggerated forms of gender-based violence. When societies collapse, some men perceive a licence to rape. Sexual attacks in such situations may be crimes of opportunism, made possible by the breakdown of the usual protection mechanisms. In cases where a conflict pits one group against another, sexual violence may target one particular group of women and girls.

Like sexual violence against women and girls, sexual violence against men and boys has a long history and is more common than previously presumed; yet attention to and recognition of this phenomenon is fairly recent.[27] While some of the motivations underpinning sexual violence against men and boys are distinct from those underpinning sexual violence against women and girls,[28] they are both often driven by a desire to humiliate, disempower or degrade victims.[29]

IN THE CONSERVATIVE social and cultural climate of Rwanda, women and men find it extremely difficult to speak openly about sexual violence.[30] The stigma and discrimination experienced by rape survivors is compounded if they are living with HIV. In the immediate years following the genocide, a significant number of persons living with HIV in Rwanda had no access to antiretroviral (ARV) treatment, so for many, HIV-positive status meant certain death.[31] Although today most women aware of their HIV status receive free ARV treatment and have begun to speak more openly about their experiences during the genocide, people living with HIV still suffer discrimination.[32] Twenty-five years later, the devastating consequences of sexual violence on survivors remain palpable. At the same time, tremendous strides have been made in addressing survivors' many needs. The Rwandan government, non-governmental organizations and the international community have undertaken a host of initiatives and programs to support survivors, many with promising and impressive outcomes, particularly in the realms of HIV and healthcare, justice and reconciliation, socio-economic support, and survivors' healing process.[33]

Much has been written about the use of rape and sexual violence during the Rwandan genocide, but survivors themselves have been notably absent from the discussion. The survivors who tell their stories in this book hope to change that.

A flower blooms in front of a memorial wall with names of the dead inscribed at the Kigali Genocide Mem

NOTES

1. Republic of Rwanda, National Commission for the Fight against Genocide, online: <https://cnlg.gov.rw>. While it is difficult to estimate the actual number of people killed during the genocide, numbers cited in various reports vary from 500,000 to more than one million deaths.
2. African Union, *Rwanda: The Preventable Genocide* (July 2000), at para 16.20 [African Union, *The Preventable Genocide* (2000)]. A 2007 study estimated the number of women raped during the Rwandan genocide to be just over 350,000, and most of them were Tutsi. The study emphasized that this number was very likely an underestimate (Catrien Bijleveld, Aafke Morssinkhof and Alette Smeulers, "Counting the Countless: Rape Victimisation During the Rwandan Genocide," *International Criminal Justice Review* 19(2) (2009), pages 208–224).
3. UN Commission on Human Rights, *Question of the Violation of Human Rights and Fundamental Freedoms in Any Part of the World, with Particular Reference to Colonial and Other Dependent Countries and Territories: Report on the Situation of Human Rights in Rwanda, submitted by Mr. René Degni-Segui under paragraph 20 of resolution S-3/1 of 25 May 1994* (E/CN.4/1996/68), 20 January 1999, at para 16.
4. African Union, *The Preventable Genocide* (2000), *supra* note 2, at para 16.20.
5. Amnesty International, "Rwanda: 'Marked for Death,' rape survivors living with HIV/AIDS in Rwanda" (5 April 2004), at page 3 [Amnesty International, "Marked for Death" (2004)].
6. UN General Assembly, *Resolution 59/137 of 10 December 2004 on Assistance to Survivors of the 1994 Genocide in Rwanda, Particularly Orphans, Widows and Victims of Sexual Violence* (A/RES/59/137), 10 December 2004.
7. For example, see Human Rights Watch, *Rwanda: Human Rights Developments* (1992), online: <http://www.hrw.org/reports/1992/WR92/AFW-07.htm#P451_159300>; Human Rights Watch, *Rwanda: Human Rights Developments* (1994), online: <http://www.hrw.org/legacy/reports/1994/WR94/Africa-06.htm> [Human Rights Watch, *Human Rights Developments* (1994)]; Amnesty International, "Marked for Death" (2004), *supra* note 5, at page 2; Christopher C. Taylor, "A Gendered Genocide: Tutsi Women and Hutu Extremists in the 1994 Rwanda Genocide," *POLAR* 22 (1999), pages 42–54. For a discussion on the position of women in pre-genocide Rwanda more generally, see John Eriksson, "The International Response to Conflict and Genocide: Lessons from the Rwanda Experience," Joint Evaluation of Emergency Assistance to Rwanda (March 1996), online: <https://www.oecd.org/countries/rwanda/50189495.pdf>.
8. Stephanie Nieuwoudt, "Rwanda: Church Role in Genocide under Scrutiny," *Institute for War and Peace Reporting* (1 December 2006), online: <https://iwpr.net/global-voices/rwanda-church-role-genocide-under-scrutiny>.
9. The Twa, also referred to as "pygmies," are considered to be the first inhabitants of Rwanda and make up less than 1 per cent of the total population (almost thirteen million in 2019). The Tutsi account for about 14 per cent of the total population in Rwanda, and the Hutu about 85 per cent. Today, division on the basis of ethnicity is no longer made. See, CIA World Fact Book, *Rwanda*, (2019), online: <https://www.cia.gov/library/publications/the-world-factbook/geos/rw.html>.
10. Mahmood Mamdani, *When Victims Become Killers: Colonialism, Nativism, and the Genocide in Rwanda* (Princeton: Princeton University Press, 2001), at page 70.
11. Kigali Memorial Centre, *Path to a "Final Solution"* (last accessed 27 August 2008), online: <http://www.kigalimemorialcentre.org/old/genocide/rwanda/political.html>.
12. For example, see Linda Melvern, "France and Genocide: The Murky Truth," *The Sunday Times* (8 August 2008), online: <https://www.thetimes.co.uk/article/france-and-genocide-the-murky-truth-8v22codqrtb>.
13. Human Rights Watch, *Human Rights Developments* (1994), *supra* note 7.
14. For a personal account of the international community's indifference at the height of the

Rwandan genocide, see Romeo Dallaire, *Shake Hands with the Devil* (Toronto: Vintage Canada, 2004). See also Samantha Power, *"A Problem from Hell": America and the Age of Genocide* (New York: Perennial, 2004).

15. For example, see Russell Smith, "The Impact of Hate Media in Rwanda," *BBC News* (3 December 2003), online: <http://news.bbc.co.uk/2/hi/africa/3257748.stm>; Yaroslav Trofimov, "As Horror Recedes in Time, Rwanda Still Restrains Press," *Wall Street Journal* (30 April 2004), online: <https://www.wsj.com/articles/SB108327587506997851>.
16. Four of the Ten Commandments dealt specifically with Tutsi women: (1) "Every Hutu should know that a Tutsi woman, wherever she is, works for the interest of her Tutsi ethnic group. As a result, we shall consider a traitor any Hutu who: marries a Tutsi woman; befriends a Tutsi woman; employs a Tutsi woman as a secretary or a concubine"; (2) "Every Hutu should know that our Hutu daughters are more suitable and conscientious in their role as woman, wife, and mother of the family. Are they not beautiful, good secretaries and more honest?"; (3) "Hutu women, be vigilant and try to bring your husbands, brothers and sons back to reason"; and (4) "The Rwandese Armed Forces should be exclusively Hutu. The experience of the October [1990] war has taught us a lesson. No member of the military shall marry a Tutsi."
17. In the December 1993 issue of *Power*, a Hutu publication, Tutsi women were portrayed as seductresses and RPF allies who were having sex with the Belgian UN peacekeepers of UNAMIR, considered by the Hutu to be RFP supporters. Another cartoon featured Prime Minister Agathe Uwilingiyimana in various sexual poses with other politicians. During the genocide, Hutu extremists shot the prime minister, and exposed her naked lower torso with a beer bottle protruding from her vagina. See Jean-Pierre Chrétien, *Rwanda: Les Médias du Génocide* (Paris: Karthala, 2005), pages 336 and 368.
18. Human Rights Watch, *Shattered Lives: Sexual Violence during the Rwandan Genocide and its Aftermath* (September 1996).
19. African Union, *The Preventable Genocide* (2000), *supra* note 2, at para 16.19.
20. Françoise Nduwimana, "The Right to Survive: Sexual Violence, Women and HIV/AIDS," *International Centre for Human Rights and Democratic Development, Rights and Democracy* (2004), at page 18.
21. For example, the RPF overtook the following areas on the following days in 1994: Mulindi and Nyagatare (April 8), Byumba (April 21), Rwamagana (April 27), Rusumo (April 29–30), Kigali airport and Kanombe military camp (May 22–23), Nyanza (May 29), Kabgayi (June 2), Gitarama (June 13), Butare (July 3), Kigali (July 4), Ruhengeri (July 14), Gisenyi (July 17). See Phillip Green, "Map of RPF advance into Rwanda (April–July 1994)," at page xii, in Linda Melvern, *A People Betrayed: The Role of the West in Rwanda's Genocide* (London: Zed Books, 2000). See also National Service of *Gacaca* Jurisdictions, *Summary of Persons Prosecuted of Having Committed Genocide* (last accessed 27 October 2008), online: <http://www.inkiko-gacaca.gov.rw/pdf/abaregwa%20english.pdf>. This overview reveals that the majority of identified perpetrators are from the Southern Province (353,297, or 43.2% of 818,564). On January 1, 2006, the twelve prefectures of Rwanda were abolished and replaced with five provinces. The Southern Province includes the former prefectures of Gikongoro, Gitarama and Butare.
22. Opération Turquoise existed between June 23, 1994 and August 21, 1994, and a subsequent report by the government of Rwanda brought to light evidence of French involvement in the raping of Tutsi women (Republic of Rwanda, *Commission Nationale Indépendante Chargée de Rassembler les Éléments de Preuve Montrant l'Implication de l'Etat Français dans la Préparation et l'Exécution du Génocide Perpétré au Rwanda en 1994* (Kigali, 2007)).
23. A notorious example is Mayor Akayesu from Taba commune in Gitarama prefecture, who was sentenced at the International Criminal Tribunal for Rwanda to life imprisonment. Among his convictions were rape and sexual violence amounting to genocide and crimes against humanity (*The Prosecutor v. Jean-Paul Akayesu* ICTR-96-4-T (Judgment, 2 September 1998).
24. African Rights, *Rwanda—Not So Innocent: When Women Become Killers* (Kigali, 1995). Some 3,000 women accused of participating in the genocide were imprisoned in Rwanda in

2002 (Nicole Itano, "3,000 Rwandan Women Await Trials for Genocide," *Women's Enews* (20 December 2002), online: <https://womensenews.org/2002/12/3000-rwandan-women-await-trials-genocide>). One notable example of a woman who allegedly ordered Hutu men to rape Tutsi women is Pauline Nyiramasuhuko, the former Minister of Family and Women's Development, who stood trial at the International Criminal Tribunal for Rwanda in Tanzania. Nyiramasuhuko was the first woman to be indicted by an international criminal tribunal. In addition to other charges, she was charged with rape amounting to genocide, a crime against humanity and a war crime. She was convicted of the latter two, and on December 14, 2015, she was sentenced to 47 years' imprisonment.

25. See testimony of Binaifer Nowrojee, expert witness before the International Criminal Tribunal for Rwanda, in *The Prosecutor v. Théoneste Bagasora and others: Transcripts*, ICTR-98-41-T (Judgement, 12 July 2004), at page 34.
26. More than a decade following the genocide, genocidal ideology was still being taught in a number of schools in Rwanda. See "Rwanda 'Still Teaching Genocide,'" *BBC News* (17 January 2008), online: http://news.bbc.co.uk/2/hi/africa/7194827.stm>. In June 2008, Rwanda adopted a new law that criminalizes the spreading of "genocide ideology," and convictions carry a harsh range of sentences that include life imprisonment. See Human Rights Watch, *Law and Reality: Progress in Judicial Reform in Rwanda* (July 2008), online: <https://www.hrw.org/reports/2008/rwanda0708/index.htm>. The spread of genocidal ideology remains an issue 25 years following the genocide ("Genocide Ideology Remains a Threat to Rwandans: Official," *The New Times* (9 April 2018), online: <https://www.newtimes.co.rw/rwanda/genocide-ideology-remains-threat-rwandans-official>).
27. United Nations Office for the Coordination of Humanitarian Affairs (UN-OCHA), *The Nature, Scope, and Motivation for Sexual Violence against Men and Boys in Armed Conflict*, in UN-OCHA, *Use of Sexual Violence in Armed Conflict: Identifying Gaps in Research to Inform More Effective Interventions* (OCHA - Policy Development and Studies Branch, Pretoria, South Africa, 2008), pages 1–13 and background papers; Sandesh Sivakumaran, "Sexual Violence Against Men in Armed Conflict," *The European Journal of International Law* 18(2) (2007), pages 253-276; Lara Stemple, "Male Rape and Human Rights," *Hastings Law Journal* 60 (2009), pages 611-615 [Stemple, "Male Rape and Human Rights" (2009)]. Sexual violence against men in conflict and other tense situations has been reported in at least 25 regions in the last three decades alone with different forms of intensity: Argentina, Burundi, Central African Republic, Chechnya, Chile, DRC, East Timor-Indonesia, El Salvador, Greece, Guatemala, Iran, Iraq-Coalition, Iraq-Kuwait, Kenya, Liberia, Northern Ireland, Peru, Rwanda, Sierra Leone, South Africa, Sri Lanka, Sudan, Turkey, Uganda, the former Yugoslavia, and Zimbabwe.
28. Sandesh Sivakumaran, "Prosecuting Sexual Violence against Men and Boys," in Anne-Marie de Brouwer *et al.* (eds.), *Sexual Violence as an International Crime: Interdisciplinary Approaches* (Intersentia, Cambridge/Antwerp/Portland, 2013), pages 79-97.
29. *Ibid*; Stemple, "Male Rape and Human Rights" (2009), *supra* note 27, pages 614-615.
30. Usta Kaitesi, *Genocidal Gender and Sexual Violence: The Legacy of the ICTR, Rwanda's Ordinary Courts and Gacaca Courts*. Cambridge, Antwerp, and Portland (Intersentia, 2014).
31. According to the World Health Organization (WHO), an estimated 7,800 Rwandans died of AIDS in 2007, out of approximately 150,000 HIV-positive Rwandans (UNAIDS/WHO, *Epidemiological Fact Sheets on HIV and AIDS: 2008 Update* (last accessed 30 November 2008), online: <http://www.who.int/globalatlas/predefinedReports/EFS2008/full/EFS2008_RW.pdf>.
32. See further the chapter "Life after 'Death'" in this book.
33. *Ibid*.

Crosses for genocide victims buried at a graveyard at the École Technique Officielle memorial site near Kig

SEXUAL VIOLENCE IN CONFLICTS AROUND THE WORLD

Map of sexual violence in conflict-affected countries since 1945 (based on UK Parliament, "Sexual Violence in Conflict: A War Crime" (2016))

SEXUAL VIOLENCE IN conflict continues to take place in every corner of the world. Such violence includes rape, sexual slavery, enforced prostitution, forced pregnancy and enforced sterilization.[1] Depending on the circumstances, sexual violence can be a war crime, a crime against humanity or an act of genocide. The true magnitude of sexual violence in situations of conflict may never be fully known. Many survivors feel discouraged from reporting these crimes due to stigma, lack of socioeconomic supports, or a real or perceived lack of justice.[2] In many cases, victims are also killed. Notwithstanding these difficulties with reported numbers, recent studies have shed light on the widespread nature of sexual violence in conflicts.[3] The following list details specific cases of conflict-related sexual violence from around the world to demonstrate the pervasiveness of this crime.

EUROPE: During World War I (1914–1918), rape, forced prostitution and other forms of sexual violence were perpetrated against women in Belgium and France, largely by the German army and the armies of other Axis powers.[4] In World War II (1939–45), rape and other forms of sexual violence, including enforced prostitution and enforced sterilization, were committed on a large scale in Europe. German soldiers raped Russian and Jewish women and girls, and Russian soldiers raped German women and girls on a massive scale.[5]

ASIA: During World War II (1939–1945), between 20,000 and 80,000 girls and women were raped in Nanjing, China, after the city fell to the Japanese Imperial Army in 1937.[6] Sexual mutilation and murder following rape were common, and up to 200,000 women were forced into sexual slavery by the Japanese Imperial Army in different countries in Asia.[7]

COLOMBIA: During Colombia's civil war (1964–2016), the Revolutionary Armed Forces of Colombia (FARC) and state-based paramilitaries committed sexual violence against more than 24,000 women and men.[8]

BANGLADESH: During Pakistan's invasion of Bangladesh in 1971, Pakistani forces raped at least 200,000 women.[9]

CAMBODIA: Between 1975–1979, approximately 250,000 Cambodian women and men were forced into marriage during the rule of the Khmer Rouge regime.[10]

PERU: During Peru's civil war (1980–2000), more than 538 cases of sexual violence against women and girls were registered with the Truth and Reconciliation Commission in Peru.[11]

SRI LANKA: In the aftermath of the civil war (1983–2009), Sri Lankan state security forces in the military zones committed sexual violence against ethnic Tamils perceived to be associated with the insurgent group.[12] Men, women and children who were in police custody, or who lived near the military zone, reported being raped and sexually abused.[13]

UGANDA: The rebel group Lord's Resistance Army (LRA) abducted between 60,000 and 80,000 children from northern Uganda during the 1987–2006 conflict with the government. Boys were used as child combatants and girls were often forced to be "wives" to the soldiers as soon as they attained puberty.[14]

LIBERIA: Toward the end of the Liberian civil war (1989–1994), 49% of women between the ages of 15 and 70 reported having experienced at least one act of physical or sexual violence at the hands of a soldier or fighter.[15] 32.6% of male combatants surveyed reported being subjected to sexual violence, largely perpetrated by soldiers or rebels.[16]

HAITI: Between 1991–1994, during the reign of General Raoul Cédras, who ousted Haiti's then democratically elected president in 1991, the Commission Nationale de Vérité et Justice documented 140 cases of "political rape" (i.e., rape perpetrated against women because of their husbands' alleged political affiliation) but estimated that, in view of non-reporting and other circumstances, the actual number of cases could be as much as twelve times higher.[17]

SIERRA LEONE: Between 1991–2001, as many as 64,000 internally displaced women were subject to war-related sexual violence.[18]

BOSNIA-HERZEGOVINA: During the 1992–1995 Bosnian war, an estimated 20,000 to 50,000 women were raped, representing about 1-2% of the total pre-war female population.[19] Men detained in concentration camps were also sexually assaulted, as reported by 80% of males in held in Sarajevo Canton.[20]

KOSOVO: During the war of 1998–1999, thousands of Albanian women and girls living in Kosovo were victims of sexual violence.[21]

DEMOCRATIC REPUBLIC OF THE CONGO (DRC): Between 1998–2003, tens of thousands of women and girls were raped or otherwise subjected to sexual violence during the conflict in the DRC.[22] Between 2005–2007, more than 32,000 cases of rape and sexual violence were registered in the province of South Kivu alone.[23] In a 2010 study of sexual violence in Eastern DRC, rates of reported sexual violence were 39.7% among women and 23.6% among men.[24] In 2017, renewed political unrest resulted in over 6,000 cases of sexual violence, mainly in the Irumu territory.[25]

TIMOR-LESTE: During the 1999 siege, the Indonesian military and local militias committed sexual violence against hundreds of girls and women.[26]

CENTRAL AFRICAN REPUBLIC (CAR): Following a failed coup attempt in 2002, the Presidential Guard and the National Army committed more than 1,000 documented cases of rape.[27] Since 2012, tensions arising from the instability of the Seleka rebel group have resulted in more cases of sexual violence. In 2017, the UN documented 308 reported incidents of conflict-related sexual violence committed by various forces, including the Seleka and opposition groups.[28]

SUDAN: Between 2003–2008 alone, government forces and government-backed Janjaweed militias committed widespread rape and sexual violence in Darfur as a deliberate strategy to terrorize the population.[29] From October 2004 to February 2005, Médecins Sans Frontières treated approximately 500 rape survivors in Darfur, but the total number of cases is likely much higher.[30] According to a Human Rights Watch report, Sudan's army committed organized mass rapes against more than 220 women in the rebel-dominated village of Tabit in 2014.[31]

BURUNDI: Between 2004–2007, the Seruka centre of Médecins Sans Frontières Belgium registered 5,466 cases of sexual violence, an average of 1,366 victims each year and 27 victims each week.[32] In the post-electoral political crisis of 2015, state security forces and members of the Imbonerakure (the ruling party's youth league) committed sexual violence against perceived government opponents.[33]

KENYA: In the aftermath of the post-election crisis (December 2007–June 2008), Kenya experienced a 7,500% increase in the incidence of sexual violence against women, along with a catastrophic breakdown in the health support system for rape victims.[34]

NIGERIA: Since their emergence in 2009, Boko Haram insurgents have inflicted sexual violence against thousands of Nigerian women and girls. In 2014, Boko Haram abducted 276 schoolgirls, and subjected them to forced marriage and sexual servitude.[35] In 2017 alone, the insurgents perpetrated nearly a thousand cases of sexual violence, including rape, sexual slavery and forced marriage.[36]

SYRIA: In the context of the 2011 uprising that led to an ongoing civil war, government forces and militias perpetrated sexual violence against women, girls and occasionally men during ground operations, house raids at checkpoints and in detention.[37]

SOUTH SUDAN: After obtaining independence in 2011, South Sudan spiraled into an ethno-political conflict in 2013, during which state-led troops and opposition forces raped, abducted and sexually abused women and girls.[38]

In 2018 alone, more than 1,150 cases of conflict-related sexual violence were documented.[39]

IRAQ: In 2014, the attack by the Islamic State in Iraq and Syria (ISIS) on Iraq's Sinjar district marked the beginning of the genocide against the Yazidis in the area. ISIS captured thousands of Yazidi women and girls, selling many of them to foreign fighters as sex slaves. Out of the total 6,417 Yazidi women, men and children reportedly captured by ISIS during the attack, half remain missing as of 2018.[40]

SOMALIA: Ongoing civil conflict in Somalia has displaced thousands of women and left them vulnerable to sexual violence at the hands of armed assailants, African Union Mission in Somalia troops, Al-Shabab insurgent forces, the Somali National Army and the Somali Police Force. In the first eight months of 2014, more than 2,850 cases of sexual and gender-based violence were documented in Mogadishu alone.[41] In 2017, the UN verified 330 cases of conflict-related sexual violence were uncovered.[42]

UKRAINE: Between 2014–2017, instability in the region leading to Russia's occupation of Crimea resulted in widespread hostilities, especially near the contact line. Government forces and armed groups sexually assaulted both men and women in detention in order to punish, humiliate or extract confessions.[43]

MYANMAR: Since the mass expulsion of the Rohingya people in August 2017, members of the Myanmar Armed Forces, local militia and civilians perpetrated widespread rape and sexual violence as part of a government strategy for eradication. These attacks took place in at least 19 different villages in Burma's Rakhine State, and more than 2,750 victims of sexual and gender-based violence have received humanitarian assistance upon fleeing the country.[44]

NOTES

1. *Rome Statute of the International Criminal Court* (17 July 1998), UN Doc A/CONF.183/9, Articles 7(1)(g), 8(2)(b)(xxii), 8(2)(e)(vi). See also UN, *Report of the Secretary General on Conflict-Related Sexual Violence* (23 March 2018), UN Doc S/2018/250, online: <https://www.un.org/sexualviolenceinconflict/wp-content/uploads/reports/sg-reports/SG-REPORT-2017-CRSV-SPREAD.pdf> [*Report of the Secretary General on Conflict-Related Sexual Violence* (2018)].
2. *Report of the Secretary General on Conflict-Related Sexual Violence* (2018), *supra* note 1.
3. For example, a recent study found that, over the span of two decades – between 1989 and 2009 – armed groups perpetrated sexual violence in the majority of the 129 active conflicts around the world, and sexual violence became more prevalent in the early 2000s (Dara Kay Cohen and Ragnhild Nordas, "Sexual Violence in Armed Conflict: Introducing the SVAC Dataset, 1989-2009," 51(3) *Journal of Peace Research* (2014), pages 418-428).
4. Kelly D. Askin, War Crimes against Women: Prosecution in International War Crimes Tribunals (The Hague: Martinus Nijhoff Publishers, 1997), page 42.
5. *Ibid*, pages 52–61, 71–73, 88–91. Soviet Red Army soldiers are estimated to have raped two million German women and girls by the end of World War II. See Antony Beevor, "They Raped Every German Female from Eight to 80," *The Guardian* (1 May 2002), online: <https://www.theguardian.com/books/2002/may/01/news.features11>.
6. Iris Chang, The Rape of Nanking (US: Ingram Publisher Services, January 2012); Yoshimi Yoshiaki, Comfort Women: Sexual Slavery in the Japanese Military During World War II (Columbia University Press, September 2002).
7. Ustinia Dolgopol and Snehal Paranjape, Comfort Women: An Unfinished Ordeal (Geneva: International Commission of Jurists, 1994).
8. Joe Parkin Daniels, "Colombia's hidden victims finally get their day in court," *The Guardian* (21 November 2018), online: <https://www.theguardian.com/global-development/2018/nov/20/colombia-sexual-violence-court-farc-tribunal>. See *Report of the Secretary General on Conflict-Related Sexual Violence* (2018), *supra* note 1, paras 31-34.
9. Gendercide Watch, "Case Study: Genocide in Bangladesh, 1971," online: <http://www.gendercide.org/case_bangladesh.html>. See also Nilanjana S. Roy, "Bangladesh War's Toll on Women Still Undiscussed," *New York Times* (24 August 2010), online: <https://www.nytimes.com/2010/08/25/world/asia/25iht-letter.html>.
10. Amnesty International, "Making Violence Against Women Count: Facts and Figures – A Summary" (5 March 2004).
11. Truth and Reconciliation Commission of Peru, *Final Report of the Truth and Reconciliation Commission of Peru: The Factors which made the Violence Possible* (2003). See also Jelke Boesten and Melissa Fisher, "Sexual Violence and Justice in Post-Conflict Peru," *United States Institute of Peace*, Special Report 310 (7 June 2012), online: <https://www.usip.org/publications/2012/06/sexual-violence-and-justice-postconflict-peru>.
12. Human Rights Watch, *"We Will Teach You a Lesson": Sexual Violence against Tamils by Sri Lankan Security Forces* (26 Feb 2013), online: <https://www.hrw.org/report/2013/02/26/we-will-teach-you-lesson/sexual-violence-against-tamils-sri-lankan-security-forces>.
13. *Ibid.* See also International Truth and Justice Project, *Unstopped: 2016/17 Torture in Sri Lanka* (July 2017), online: <http://www.itjpsl.com/assets/ITJP_unstopped_report_final.pdf>; International Truth and Justice Project, *Unsilenced: Male Survivors Speak of Conflict-Related Sexual Violence in Sri Lanka* (September 2018), online: <http://www.itjpsl.com/assets/ITJP_unsilenced_report-final.pdf>.
14. Jeannie Annan and Morah Brier, "The Risk of Return: Intimate Partner Violence in Northern Uganda's Armed Conflict", *Social Science and Medicine*, Vol 70(1), 2010, page 152.
15. Shana Swiss et. al, "Violence against women during the Liberian civil conflict," *Journal of the American Medical Association* 279, 1998, pages 625–629.

16. Kirsten Johnson et al. (eds.), "Association of Combatant Status and Sexual Violence with Health and Mental Health Outcomes in Postconflict Liberia," *Journal of the American Medical Association*, Vol 300(6), 2008, page 676.
17. Commission Nationale de Vérité et Justice, *Si M Pa Rele: 29 Septembre 1991–14 Octobre 1994* (Port-au-Prince: Ministère National de la Justice de la République d'Haiti, 1996), page 84.
18. Marie Vlachova and Lea Biason (eds.), Women in an Insecure World (Geneva: Geneva Centre for the Democratic Control of Armed Forces, 2005).
19. UNICEF International Child Development Centre, Women in transition, monee project, cee/cis/Baltics Regional Monitoring Report No. 6 (Florence, 1999), page 85.
20. Zeljka Mudrovcic, "Sexual and Gender based Violence in Post-Conflict Regions: The Bosnia and Herzegovina Case," in *The Impact of Conflict on Women and Girls*, UN Population Fund, 2001. See also, Lara Stemple, "Male Rape and Human Rights," *Hastings Law Journal*, 60(5), 2009.
21. Human Rights Watch, *Federal Republic of Yugoslavia—Kosovo: Rape as a Weapon of "Ethnic Cleansing"* (1 March 2000). See also Karen McVeigh, "After two decades, the hidden victims of the Kosovo war are finally recognized," *The Guardian* (3 August 2018), online: <https://www.theguardian.com/global-development/2018/aug/03/after-two-decades-the-hidden-victims-of-the-kosovo-war-are-finally-recognised>.
22. Human Rights Watch, *Seeking Justice: The Prosecution of Sexual Violence in the Congo War* (7 March 2005).
23. John Holmes, "Congo's Rape War," *Los Angeles Times* (11 October 2007), online: <http://articles.latimes.com/2007/oct/11/news/OE-HOLMES11>.
24. Kirsten Johnson et al. (eds.), "Association of Sexual Violence and Human Rights Violations with Physical and Mental Health in Territories of the Eastern Democratic Republic of the Congo," *The Journal of the American Medical Association*, Vol 5 (2010), pages 553-561.
25. *Report of the Secretary General on Conflict-Related Sexual Violence* (2018), *supra* note 1, paras 36-41.
26. Galuh Wandita, Testimony to the Truth and Friendship Commission on Rape and Sexual Violence in the context of the Popular Consultation in East Timor 1999 (March 2007).
27. Katy Glassborow, "CAR Case to Focus on Sexual Violence," *Institute for War and Peace Reporting* (24 May 2007).
28. *Report of the Secretary General on Conflict-Related Sexual Violence* (2018), *supra* note 1, para 27. See also Human Rights Watch, "Killing Without Consequence: War Crimes, Crimes against Humanity, and the Special Criminal Court in the Central African Republic" (5 July 2017), online: <https://www.hrw.org/report/2017/07/05/killing-without-consequence/war-crimes-crimes-against-humanity-and-special>.
29. Human Rights Watch, "Five Years On: No Justice for Sexual Violence in Darfur" (6 April 2008).
30. Médecins Sans Frontières, "The Crushing Burden of Rape: Sexual Violence in Darfur" (8 March 2005), page 2.
31. Human Rights Watch, "Sudan: Mass Rape by Army in Darfur" (11 February 2015), online: <https://www.hrw.org/news/2015/02/11/sudan-mass-rape-army-darfur>.
32. ACAT Burundi and OMCT, *NGO Report on Violence Against Women in Burundi (CEDAW, 40th Session): Executive Summary*, (Geneva, 2008), page 3.
33. Human Rights Watch, *World Report 2017: Burundi* (2018), online: <https://www.hrw.org/world-report/2018/country-chapters/burundi>.
34. See Kyle Kinner, "A Paradigm Shift in Prevention," *Caucus for Evidence-Based Prevention Newsletter*, 13(1), 2008.
35. *Report of the Secretary General on Conflict-Related Sexual Violence* (2018), *supra* note 1, paras 93-95. See also, "7,000 women, girls abducted as sex slaves by Boko Haram, says UN report," *The Guardian* (14 January 2016), online: <https://guardian.ng/news/7000-women-girls-abducted-as-sex-slaves-by-boko-haram-says-un-report/>; "A timeline of Nigeria's abducted Chibok schoolgirls," *News 24* (27 February 2018), online: <https://www.news24.com/Africa/News/a-timeline-of-nigerias-abducted-chibok-schoolgirls-20180227>.

36. *Report of the Secretary General on Conflict-Related Sexual Violence* (2018), *supra* note 1.
37. *Ibid*, paras 75-78. See also UN, *"I Lost My Dignity:" Sexual and Gender-based Violence in the Syrian Arab Republic* (8 March 2018) UN Docs A/HRC/37/72/CRP, at paras 9-50; Bethan McKernan, "Inside Assad's prisons: horrors facing female inmates in Syrian jails revealed," *Independent* (28 August 2017), online: <https://www.independent.co.uk/news/world/middle-east/assad-prisons-women-syria-female-inmate-treatment-conditions-exclusive-life-jails-a7899776.html>.
38. *Ibid*, paras 65-68. See also Human Rights Watch, "Soldiers Assume We are Rebels" (1 August 2017), online: <https://www.hrw.org/report/2017/08/01/soldiers-assume-we-are-rebels/escalating-violence-and-abuses-south-sudans>.
39. Office of the Special Representative of the Secretary-General on Sexual Violence in Conflict, "Remarks of the Special Representative of the Secretary-General on Sexual Violence in Conflict, Pramila Patten, to the Security Council on South Sudan" (18 December 2018), online: <https://www.un.org/sexualviolenceinconflict/statement/remarks-of-the-special-representative-of-the-secretary-general-on-sexual-violence-in-conflict-pramila-patten-to-the-security-council-on-south-sudan-18-december-2018/>.
40. International Federation for Human Rights, "Iraq, Sexual and Gender-Based Crimes Against the Yazidi Community: The Role of ISIL Foreign Fighters" (October 2018), online: <https://www.fidh.org/IMG/pdf/irak723angweb.pdf>; Human Rights Watch, "Iraq: ISIS Escapees Describe Systematic Rape" (14 April 2015), online: <https://www.hrw.org/news/2015/04/14/iraq-isis-escapees-describe-systematic-rape>; Paul Wood, "Islamic State: Yazidi women tell of sex-slavery trauma," *BBC News* (22 December 2014), online: <https://www.bbc.com/news/world-middle-east-30573385>.
41. UN, *Report of the Secretary-General on Conflict-Related Sexual Violence*, UN Docs S/2015/203 (23 March 2015), para 44.
42. *Report of the Secretary General on Conflict-Related Sexual Violence* (2018), *supra* note 1, paras 62.
43. Office of the UN High Commissioner for Human Rights, "Ukraine conflict: End impunity for sexual violence, UN report urges" (16 February 2017), online: <https://www.ohchr.org/EN/NewsEvents/Pages/DisplayNews.aspx?NewsID=21187&LangID=E>. See also UN, *Report on the Human Rights Issue in Ukraine*, UN Docs, A/HRC/37/CRP.1 (15 March 2018).
44. *Report of the Secretary General on Conflict-Related Sexual Violence* (2018), *supra* note 1, para 55-59; Human Rights Watch, "All of My Body Was Pain: Sexual Violence against Rohingya Women and Girls in Burma" (16 November 2017), online: <https://www.hrw.org/report/2017/11/16/all-my-body-was-pain/sexual-violence-against-rohingya-women-and-girls-burma>. See also Dania K. Putri, Mukwege Foundation, "The world remains silent while Rohingya women are subjected to rape in Myanmar" (January 2017), online: < https://www.mukwegefoundation.org/2017/01/the-world-remains-silent-while-rohingya-women-are-subjected-to-rape-in-myanmar/>.

2

TESTIMONIALS

MARIE LOUISE NIYOBUHUNGIRO

BORN: 1975 (day and month unknown) *
BIRTHPLACE: Shyorongi, just outside Kigali

TESTIMONIAL: Kigali, 2008

PEOPLE THINK I am crazy because I am always crying, and I do not blame them for thinking so. I am always angry, and I do not sleep at night. I hoped secretly that I would die during the genocide, but being among other survivors within a survivors' organization has brought me comfort and hope. I feel like I have a family now, and I am very grateful for that.

Before the genocide, we were a family of eight children—five girls and three boys. I was the fourth child in the family. My father was a teacher, and my mother was a farmer. We lived in Shyorongi, just outside Kigali. There were many Tutsi families in Shyorongi; we had only one Hutu neighbour. Although he was our neighbour, that Hutu hated us, especially my father, because we were Tutsi. In 1991, my father was poisoned, and I suspect that the Hutu neighbour who hated him so much did it. When my father started to feel sick, he went to a traditional clinic. After his death, my mother asked the people at the clinic what my father had died of, and they told her that he had been poisoned. Today, our former Hutu neighbour and all his family are in prison for crimes they committed during the genocide.

Our mother told us that, in 1959, another Hutu had set fire to my mother's house and then accused my father of doing it. When my mother told us her history of discrimination for being Tutsi, she would also tell us not to dismiss

* Some Rwandans do not know their specific birth date because the dates are not recorded, especially in rural areas.

it as a tale. And years later, what we thought to be just a part of history became our reality.

On April 6, 1994, when President Habyarimana died, the local authorities ordered my family to go back to our house. We had been walking outside. But we did not feel secure in our house, and we went to pass the night on our cassava plantation instead. The next morning, we went to our uncle's house, which was about a thirty-minute walk from our house. The *Interahamwe* surrounded my uncle's house a few hours later. As the killings hadn't started yet, the militia were just trying to frighten us. When the *Interahamwe* got tired of this and left, we ran to the Catholic church of Mboza, which was about fifteen minutes' walking distance from my uncle's house. Almost three hundred Tutsi had found refuge in the church.

We arrived at the church at about ten in the morning, and a few minutes later the *Interahamwe* and FAR soldiers started shooting. They had guns and shot all the men, including my uncle. I fell, and some dead bodies fell on top of me. I was all covered with blood. I heard screams and babies crying, but I was unconscious for most of the time the attack was continuing. The next day, they came back to kill those who were not yet dead. There was blood all over me, and the killers thought that I was dead, too, so they left me there, lying among those dead bodies. Once I had regained consciousness, all I could see were a lot of bodies lying around the church. The stench of blood was thick in the air. Except for one of my sisters, all my other relatives died during this attack at the church. Out of three hundred people in the church, only five had survived. I felt completely empty. I had no thoughts and felt nothing, nothing at all.

After the *Interahamwe* left the second time, I left the church. My sister and I went in different directions, because we felt that even if one of us was killed, the other one might have a chance to survive. I fled in the direction of a nearby forest and ran into an *Interahamwe* on the road, who asked me where I came from. I recognized him as a fellow churchgoer named Ntirenganya. I told him that I had lost my way and was just wandering around. He said that he had finished killing for the day, so others would kill me, not him.

After that close encounter, I spent three days hiding in the bushes. On the fourth day, I went to the house of another uncle, who had not yet had an opportunity to flee, because his wife had just given birth. He and his wife had already been warned by their neighbour, an *Interahamwe*, to leave their house immediately; they would not have much longer to live otherwise. Together with my uncle's relatives, I left his house that night. But, at the gate in front of his house, we ran into a group of *Interahamwe* militia. They took the girls among us and brought us to a nearby roadblock in order to kill us.

Every FAR soldier or *Interahamwe* we met on the way made an insulting speech or had a rod to beat us with. One of them said that the girls should be brought to the Twa, who were often ridiculed in Rwanda and considered stupid and worthless. At some point, a FAR soldier picked me out of the group and took me to a nearby bush. I don't know what happened to the other girls I was with.

This soldier raped me. After he was done with me, he took me to a house and told the owners of the house to keep me safe, so that he could rape me every time he came. He told them if anything happened to me he would kill them. Every time he came to the house after that, he took me to the forest to rape me. Over five days, I was raped five times a day. The rapist didn't say anything to me. In the forest, the local people often saw me being raped by this man. The local people, an *Interahamwe* militia man and other Hutu would watch the soldier rape me and did not even raise their little finger to stop it. They didn't care, because I was Tutsi. They were silent. The FAR soldier who did this to me was so old—about forty—and so savage. It was the very first time I saw what a man was capable of doing.

After those five days, the old man brought me to a lady called Mukandoli, who was an *Interahamwe* too, and I stayed there. She didn't care about my situation. She didn't say anything, except when she sometimes ordered me to go out and farm. I stayed with this lady for one week. Then another FAR soldier came and told Mukandoli that his colonel wanted me.

When I arrived at the FAR camp, the colonel had the "manners" to ask me if I wanted to sleep with him. But I knew that whatever answer I gave, the outcome would be the same, and that I would end up in his bed if he had one. I said no and ran into the bushes. His soldiers spent the whole night looking for me, but they didn't find me.

A little later, I saw a house and entered it. The house appeared to be an *Interahamwe*'s harem, full of Tutsi women and girls. There were about ten teenage girls in the house, all between about sixteen and twenty years old. The FAR soldiers who were looking for me found me there and took me back to the colonel. On the way back, they asked me to sleep with them. I told them I could do that the next day. While they were still discussing this, I managed to escape, and I walked all the way to Ruhengeri, which was already under the control of the RPF.

For two weeks, I hid myself during the day and walked during the night. I ate nothing and hid in the bushes. When the RPF went to Kigali, I followed them. I walked just behind them, back to my place of birth. I occupied a house that belonged to owners who had fled the country, because my family house had been destroyed during the genocide. To make a living, I dug the fields for a farmer. Later, a fund for survivors was established, which provided me with a bit of support. I lost four brothers and sisters during the genocide, and one sister died of kidney failure right afterwards.

Before the genocide, I had never been intimate with a man, and yet now I have gotten to know many without my consent. Even after the genocide, in 2000, a neighbour came to my house, forced my door open and raped me. There was no use screaming, because no one lived close by. I became pregnant as a result of this rape, and the child died immediately upon birth. The doctors then pressured me to take an HIV test, and I discovered I am HIV positive.

I live in very bad conditions because I didn't go to school. I have no job and am too weak now to dig the fields. I get food from an organization that helps me to survive. I have had four children since the genocide, all from different fathers. The father of one of my children is a neighbour, and the others have jobs in the neighbourhood. I never see them. I only had sex with each of them once. Luckily, my oldest three children are not HIV positive, but my youngest child has not been tested yet. I wish I could give my children some more support, including buying them school materials and clothes. I am always sick, sometimes because of HIV and other times because of the beatings I endured during the genocide. I was hit on my knees and head with a club and I suffer from severe headaches now.

I don't think I can forgive the FAR soldiers or the *Interahamwe*. I don't want to hear about reconciliation. I accused them in the *gacaca* courts, including the one who raped me, those who participated in the killings in the church and those I saw at the roadblock, but now they are being released. *Gacaca* courts do not bring justice. I think the best punishment those men could get is the death penalty, because they killed others, too. We need justice. The *génocidaires* should not be released. I shared my testimony in order to help establish justice, and I hope it will do that.

MARIE LOUISE NIYOBUHUNGIRO

TESTIMONIAL: Kigali, 2018

EVEN THOUGH IT has been many years since I first gave my testimony, I am not wary of telling my story. While others might have problems sharing their stories inside Rwanda, I do not mind if everybody reads my testimony. What happened to me is not a lie; it is the truth. It happened in Rwanda and it happened in public. The whole world knows what happened here, including those who deny it.

I have six children now: one daughter and five sons, and we live together in Jari, an area outside of Kigali. My eldest is a twenty-one-year-old girl, and my youngest is a baby boy. Without the support of the government's FARG programme, Solace Ministries and the Mukomeze Foundation, I would have died long ago. FARG provided me with a house. Solace Ministries provided me with comfort. After many years, I started to love myself again and to take care of my children and myself. I opened my own bank account, and now I have money in the bank. Because of Mukomeze's support, my children can go to school, we have food to eat, and I am able to pay for our medical insurance.

My family situation is not without challenges. Eleven months ago, I was raped and became pregnant with my youngest son. I was in Kigali visiting my younger sister, and took a moto taxi on my way home. When we reached the bush, the driver took a different turn and forced himself on me. When I discovered that I was pregnant, I was shocked. During the first months of the pregnancy, I went to Solace Ministries to talk about the assault because I had lost all hope. Mama Lambert was the first person who tried to comfort me. She held me and told me, "It is okay; there is still hope."

At first, I thought about having an abortion; I did not want another baby born of rape. A friend of mine encouraged me to do it and even gave me some money so I could pay for the procedure. But I could not go through with it. I wasn't happy to give birth to my son, and I could not love him at first. But as time went by, my love for him grew. When I looked at him, I thought: "Why should I hate my baby? He is mine." That is when I started to love my child. I wanted him to have a unique and positive name, despite how he was conceived. Consolée, my eldest daughter, named him Miracle.

Another challenge I recently faced is when the father of my second-youngest son took him from me because he did not want to pay me child support. Instead, he prefers to give the money to his own mother to care for our child. This way, my son's father doesn't also have to pay for the child's health insurance. My son's father is a soldier, so he gets special medical insurance that allows him to cover his child free of charge. But because we are not married, our son's health insurance cannot be freely covered if he is living with me. So the father took the boy out of my care and registered him as his own child. He had no choice but to register me as the child's mother, so he cannot block me from visiting my son. But it would be better for my son to come back home to me. I am his mother. It hurts to be without him.

Nothing gives me more joy than being a mother. Many women of my age died during the genocide, so I am so happy that I am still alive and even have children. My children make me feel valued in life, and I am overjoyed when they call me "Mama." When I look at my children, I see my family: my brothers, sisters, uncles. When I see them, I see my future ahead; because of them, I have hope.

In general, my children are doing well. We do not have much, but we are okay. They go to school, eat and play with other children. I know that because my children go to school, life will be better in the future.

Even though my children have different fathers, their relationships with each other are good because we share ideas and we talk. When things get a little difficult, they tell me "Mama, never mind; tomorrow will be better." They always tell me that they pray for me, so that I will live long and attend their weddings.

I teach my children to pray. I teach them to honour and obey God, but I give them the freedom to choose what they believe. My daughter is Catholic while I am a born-again Christian. During the genocide, many people died in Catholic churches, so I do not like to go there. But when my children want to go there, I let them.

Although the area we live in is secure, I am not comfortable in our house because it is falling apart. The government gave us this house under the FARG program, so we stayed. But the roof is not steady: when it rains, water pours into the house. It also appears that the whole area is not suitable for living, because the houses were not properly constructed. For this reason, the government is now planning to relocate us.

Over the past ten years, I have done a lot to become financially self-sufficient. I have a plot of land where I cultivate cassava, manioc and beans. I have a cow that produces milk and manure to fertilize the land. I paid for a company to connect a water tank to my place, so that I could sell water to people in the neighbourhood during the dry season. I also built a small house next to mine for rent, but it is not easy to find tenants in this area because it is deteriorating. It is challenging to find work in this area, so I hope the government relocates us to another area where there are more possibilities.

Psychologically, things have changed considerably. Although my mental health is not perfect, I feel much better now and I am living a normal life. I used to sleep in the bush, and now I sleep in a house. But the trauma from the sexual violence continues to haunt me, especially since I was recently raped again. It is in my head every day. But I am hopeful that one day I will get past it. I am trying to cope by following Mama Lambert's advice: to keep to myself in prayer, to walk away from bad friends, and to stay with friends that give me comfort and motivate me to do good. I must fight for myself and keep away from things that may be harmful.

After all the rape I endured, there is nothing good I can see in men. Having different children from different fathers is like a curse that follows me. There is nothing good I have ever seen in a man. They impregnate me, I go to the hospital alone, I take care of myself, I buy food after giving birth by myself; I have never received any real support from a man.

Physically, for a long time I felt strong, despite my recurring headaches, backaches and heart problems. But lately this has changed. I went to the hospital and discovered that, in addition to HIV, I have high blood pressure and kidney problems. So nowadays, I feel weak most of the time. This is difficult because one day I am able to dig my field, but then I lose all my strength and the next day I cannot go back to work. When I am not feeling well, I stay in the house and I sing to keep my mind off these things. This is the way I am now living with the consequences of sexual violence.

Luckily, none of my first five children have HIV, and we are waiting for the results of my newborn's test. Because of my health insurance, the HIV medication is free of charge. So far, the medicines are working well. The only challenge is that they increase my appetite, and sometimes we do not have enough food.

I try to avoid talking to people in my neighbourhood. I keep to myself; I am not open to others. My neighbours do not help me. Even when I went to the hospital to give birth, no one came to visit me. People stigmatize me for being HIV positive. Because of this, I do not retrieve my medicines from the nearest hospitals, but go FAR from here to a place where people do not know me. I do not want to sit in the local hospitals on the same bench with people who know about my HIV. Some of them killed our family and just returned from prison. I would rather go very FAR away.

People in my neighbourhood treat me differently because I endured sexual violence and am now living with HIV. In 2000, I was very sick. I was in front of my house and all my bodily fluids ran down my legs and I could not control it. People passed by and said that I was facing my last minutes, and that I was about to die. They were relatives of the *génocidaires*. They stood by and clapped their hands, rejoicing that I was dying. There was nothing to do. It hurt my heart to be treated this way, but there was nothing I could do about it. The perpetrators and their families are not happy to see that we have survived.

I also feel stigmatized because I have children from different men, and I am still alone. This has been difficult. But I do not keep my story in my heart; if I did, it would continue to burn me. When I open up with people at Solace Ministries, it feels like I am free.

In the past, I mentioned that the *gacaca* courts did not bring me justice because the pain that the perpetrators inflicted on me cannot be forgiven. Today, I still feel the same way. Because of what they did, I do not feel like I can forgive them. They must pay for it in some other way, not merely punished as they have been. The government has forgiven them after they served their sentence, and I am not happy about that. I do not think that someone who committed murder can just be forgiven and return to society; he cannot bring back the people he killed. For me, justice would be served if the perpetrators would be imprisoned for good and had to compensate the survivors for what they did.

Some of the *gacaca* courts functioned fairly and imprisoned the perpetrators. But some did not do a good job, because they handed out light sentences to some people who are now out of prison. For example, there is a woman who was recently released from prison, and she says that the genocide never happened. How can that woman be free? And even though I spoke out at the *gacaca* proceeding against those who destroyed our cattle and house, and the court ordered them to pay us back, there are still perpetrators who have not done so. Some of them are still in prison, others are outside, but they are not compensating us for our loss.

Despite all the difficulties I faced, when I look back over the last 10 years, I feel so much pride because of my children. My hopes for the future are bright. I hope that my story will help others understand what happened in Rwanda, and I hope that it helps other survivors through the proceeds of this book. Although we lost so many people we loved, we need to continue to hold each other and stay together. We thank God so much for our brother Paul Kagame. He will fight for us and make sure genocide never happens again.

OLIVE MAKABUZA

BORN: 1969
TESTIMONIAL: Kigali, 2008

I NEVER KNEW of the word "genocide" before the day I saw the genocide with my own eyes. During the genocide in Rwanda, I endured so much and wondered why I existed. I hated the world and asked myself whether there was a god. If he really existed, how could he allow these atrocities to happen?

I spent my childhood in Gikongoro, my mother's birthplace. Our family owned cows and land there. My father was a teacher, but he had retired from teaching by the time the genocide began. My mother was a housewife, and she took care of my seven brothers and sisters and me. When I first went to school, I studied at private schools because the discrimination against Tutsi in public schools was unbearable. However, private school fees became very expensive, and I could not continue my secondary studies there. So I attended a public Catholic school in Kigali, where I lived with my older sister Dorothy, who was married to a Tutsi man. I studied in Kigali because the community in Gikongoro knew my family, and my ethnicity was always mentioned in my school file there. Including students' ethnicity in school files was a way for teachers to discriminate against Tutsi. In Kigali I met my fiancé, Xavier, who was our neighbour. We were engaged for two years before the genocide began.

When the president's plane crashed, I was living with Dorothy in Muhima, a neighbourhood in Kigali. Two days later, on the morning of April 8, we heard the screams of Tutsi who were being shot by *Interahamwe*. That same morning, the *Interahamwe* approached Dorothy's house, but we managed to

escape, taking different routes. I hid in Dorothy's outdoor toilet. From there I could see my neighbour's children gesturing to me to hide at their house. My neighbour was an old Hutu woman named Marcelline, who was friendly with Xavier's sister. So I fled to Marcelline's house, where Xavier also happened to be hiding. There I spent a week hiding with Xavier and two others, a Tutsi boy and woman who sought refuge with Marcelline.

After a week, a group of *Interahamwe* approached Marcelline's house. They were led by none other than Nkezabera, a man who owned the house that Xavier was renting before the genocide. The militia had searched every house in the quarter and finally arrived at the house we were hiding in. They ordered Marcelline to show them the cockroaches she was hiding. Marcelline said she didn't have any cockroaches in her house, but her son Aimable, who also lived there, told her to let the militia enter if she didn't want all of them, including her children, to be killed too. Aimable had been kind to us, but I knew he wanted us to leave his house. Marcelline finally relented and let the militia in. They found all four of us cowering in a room and ordered us outside.

Once we emerged from the house, the *Interahamwe* descended on Xavier and beat him all over his body with every weapon they had. They targeted Xavier because they thought he was an RPF spy who planned to help the RPF take over Kigali. They suspected him of this because he had volunteered with the RPF before the genocide. The *Interahamwe* slashed his head with machetes, bludgeoned him with clubs and sawed off his legs. While they were busy with Xavier, they seemed to have forgotten about Marcelline and me, so we inched away slowly until we were behind her house. From there, we could watch what was happening without being noticed. Xavier screamed in a very high-pitched voice while they were sawing off his legs, and I felt an indescribable hurt in my heart at that same moment.

Three hours later, a man in an *Interahamwe* truck who was removing bodies from the streets passed by and left Xavier lying where he was. I think the man left Xavier lying there because he was not yet dead. Later, a Red Cross truck commandeered by another *Interahamwe* passed by, and one of the men inside it said, while pointing at Xavier, that he was "not yet finished." Xavier replied very weakly that he had always hated humiliation. That same man got off the truck and hit Xavier on the head with an axe, which finally killed him. The Tutsi boy who was hiding at Marcelline's witnessed all of this and told me about it later.

I continued to hide in Marcelline's house. Two weeks after Xavier's death, another group of *Interahamwe*, which this time included Marcelline's son Aimable, returned to the house. They ordered Marcelline to release her cockroach. She refused, but they threatened her, saying they would kill her too if she did not cooperate. Marcelline was about to argue with them when I came forward and revealed myself. I didn't want Marcelline to be killed because of me.

The *Interahamwe* took me to a little house not FAR from Marcelline's place. They were all very dirty and looked like bandits. I didn't recognize any of them. When we got to the little house, one of them removed my clothes. When I was completely naked, he asked his mates who was going to be the first. A fight between them then ensued, because everyone wanted to be the first on me. In the end, one of the *Interahamwe*, who looked to me like a homeless man, pushed me on the floor and went on me. After he was finished, another one came. I remember at least ten of them on me, but I don't know the exact number of those who followed, because I fell unconscious after that.

Almost all of them looked homeless. Now, whenever I pass through the area where I was raped, I see men on the street looking at me in a particular way, and I ask myself if any of the men who raped me are among those staring at me. What saddens me most is that the men who raped me are walking freely in the streets today and have never been held accountable.

When I regained consciousness, the *Interahamwe* were discussing how to kill me. One of the men, named Cyimana, said that he would take me to his house and make me his sex slave, because I was still beautiful. Cyimana then took me to Marcelline's house and told her to take good care of me, because he would be coming to retrieve his "property" any time he wanted. When Marcelline saw me she didn't seem too pleased. I think she feared I would be killed in her house. However, out of compassion, she washed me with warm water, because I was still aching terribly. When I started to feel better, she went to the nearest roadblock, which was under the supervision of a well-known, rich Hutu man named Kamanayo, and begged Kamanayo to hide me in his compound, saying that I was distantly related to his Tutsi wife, who had died before the genocide. This wasn't really true; I just happened to be from the same province as his wife. Still, he accepted, and Marcelline took me to his compound when it got dark.

At Kamanayo's compound, I met an old Tutsi woman who had begun renting a house there after having been chased out of her own house by her Hutu husband. I got to know Kamanayo a little better while hiding in his compound. He was an old man who did not kill anyone during the genocide. No one was killed at the roadblock he was responsible for, either. While he was not cruel to me, he was not kind, either. I stayed in his compound for one month.

While I was hiding at Kamanayo's compound, I heard that Cyimana, the *Interahamwe* to whom I "belonged," got very angry when he didn't find me at Marcelline's house and spent days hunting for me. He didn't know where I was hiding. Kamanayo told me that Cyimana planned to kill me on the date all Tutsi in Rwanda were to be executed—the last day of the mourning period for President Habyarimana, three months after his death. I was scared, but soon my fears were allayed. The RPF arrived in Kigali the day before the Tutsi execution date. Very early in the morning, Kamanayo woke the old Tutsi woman and me and told us to flee, because the government had lost the war.

As we left Kamanayo's compound, we met a small group of *Interahamwe* in front of his house. I ran and took my own route. I could see *Interahamwe* all around me, killing Tutsi while I ran. When I stopped for a short break, I encountered a young man who asked me who I was fleeing from. When I told him that the *Interahamwe* were pursuing me, he comforted me and said that everything was under control. The young man took me to a hotel in Kigali, where a group of survivors had gathered, among them recent widows and orphans. The survivors were wounded all over their bodies, and some of them were still bleeding. I found out that the young man was with the RPF. At the hotel, RPF soldiers told us that they knew we had lost our loved ones, but that we had to be strong and live on. I stayed there for two weeks. The RPF soldiers then informed us that the genocide was over and said we should return to our houses.

When I left the hotel, I went to live in Xavier's old house. No one was inside the house anymore, but it contained a lot of furniture that had been stolen from Tutsi houses. The *Interahamwe* leader, Nkezabera, stored his loot there. As people slowly returned to their homes, I learned from neighbours that my older sister Dorothy had been killed with her family during the genocide. The neighbours didn't know how she had been killed, though. In August, I made a trip back to Gikongoro to find out what had happened to my family. There, I learned that my entire family had been killed.

After the genocide, I worked in a prison stockroom. On the bus to work one day, I met a young man from the north of Rwanda, a university student. He fell in love with me, but he kept pressing me about whether I had been raped during the genocide. I always denied that I was. He said that if my health was fine, we could live together. After two years of living together, I became pregnant with our first child. During my pregnancy, I became ill and went to the hospital, where I told the doctor I had been raped. He advised me to take an HIV test. I took the test, but I did not receive the results.

After I gave birth to my second child, I had another blood test. I did not receive the results of that test, either. Then I became very ill. While I was ill, my boyfriend abandoned me. I went to see the doctor, and only then did he reveal to me that I was HIV positive. The other doctors in the hospital were angry with my doctor for not giving me my results immediately. All hope abandoned me then as I realized that my life was going to be cut short.

After my boyfriend abandoned me, my children and I lived in very bad conditions. I heard about organizations that provided comfort and support and I started attending counselling sessions at one organization, which also provided me with antiretroviral medication and food. There I met women who faced the same problems I did. Whenever we shared our problems, I felt better. Today, I live with my two children. Thankfully, they are not HIV positive. My children make me very happy, but the thought that they will be alone when I am gone breaks my heart.

No one has ever asked for my forgiveness, and I do not forgive the *Interahamwe* who hurt me. Nkezabera, one of the *Interahamwe* who murdered Xavier, offered me 100,000 Rwandan francs so I would not testify against him in the *gacaca* court. I told him that no money in the world could replace the loss I still have in my heart. Nkezabera was eventually convicted at the *gacaca* court and sentenced to five years. However, he has since appealed the case, after bribing the panel of judges for a shorter sentence. Even if I felt like forgiving, it is not easy, because those *Interahamwe* continue to lie during their trials.

I have shared my testimony here so that the world may know what really happened in Rwanda. So much pain still lives inside of us, and the fact that most of us live with HIV makes things worse. I live in poor conditions, and I do not have money to pay for my children's school fees. I wonder what will happen to my children when I am dead. I hope people will reach out and help them. I pray that the truth about the genocide will one day be revealed. Genocide is a vicious cycle. I hope the world ensures that genocide never happens again, because I want a bright future for my children and I never want them to endure what I have.

OLIVE MAKABUZA

TESTIMONIAL: Kigali, 2018

WHEN I SHARED my testimony for *The Men Who Killed Me* in 2008, I wondered how I was going to survive with my two young children. But I thank God for Solace Ministries, especially Mama Lambert, and for the Mukomeze Foundation. Over the past decade, they held my hand, stood by me and kept me in good health. Now my children are grown up, and Mama Lambert has sowed a good seed in them. When my children go away for school, I give them a little pocket money. And they always save some of the money for the holidays when they return, so that they can give a little bit of it to the eldest woman who comes to pray with us in church. It shows the compassion they have in their hearts.

I live in Nyarugenge district, an area outside of Kigali, and I feel safe in this area among other genocide survivors. I received my house through the government's FARG programme. The house used to be in poor shape, but the government is currently renovating it by reinforcing the cement, and replacing the wooden windows and doors with metal ones. For the duration of the renovations, I moved to the small shed that I built next to my house for our cow, using sponsorship funds. Since the cow died, the shed has remained vacant.

Since the father of my children abandoned us, I have not been with a man, and I do not want to be with a man anymore. I live with my two children, although they are only home during holidays. My son is nineteen years old, and he is studying to be a veterinarian; my daughter is seventeen and still in high school, where she is studying all kinds of subjects, including physics, geography, history and economics.

My relationship with my children is good. When we are together, we take our time to sit and share ideas. They worry about my headaches. Sometimes I stay quiet and avoid telling them how I feel, because I do not want to scare them. A few years ago, when they were old enough, I sat them down and told them that I am HIV positive because this has seriously affected my health. At first, I was afraid of telling them, and it was not easy for them to comprehend. But I thank God that they learned to accept it, and that they know about my health situation now.

I did not tell my children how I contracted HIV. I do not have the strength to tell them that I was raped during the genocide, and they do not ask me about it either. They know I have a problem with my head, so they avoid asking me about things that will cause me more headaches. One day I was having a conversation with my son, and it seemed like he was going to ask me. He said: "Mama, we know some women were raped during the genocide." And then he suddenly stopped. I think they are scared of asking me directly, but they know it happened to me, too.

My children ask me a lot about the genocide. They ask me how many relatives we had, how they died, the reason they were killed, and who killed them. My son was so eager to know that he took an additional course at school about the history of Rwanda and the genocide. It hurts my heart to talk about it with them, but when they ask me, I gather all of my strength and tell them. But I also try to be careful about sharing too much about the genocide with my children because I do not want them to develop hatred and fear in their hearts. Children who grew up in Hutu families learned to hate the Tutsi at home; we were killed during the genocide because of the words that children once heard from their parents. I do not want my children to feel hostility toward the Hutu. One day, when I still had a cow, my children discovered that the cow keeper was a Hutu, and they asked me: "Mama, why do you let this man take care of the cow? Will he kill you?" So I tried to reassure them that, "No, not all Hutus killed, and he will not kill me."

Because of everything that I have endured, I teach my children that hatred is not good. The wedge driven between two ethnic groups has made me who I am today; I am sick because of division and hatred. So I tell my children not to separate themselves from others, but to live in harmony with them. I also tell them to take care of themselves and behave well, and to avoid going outside with people they do not know. I emphasize to them the importance of being educated; the key to succeed in life is education. Finally, I tell them to obey and respect God, and to love each other.

One day, a boy who attends the same church as us confronted me and asked why I shared my story in *The Men Who Killed Me*. He came to know about the book while he was abroad. He was born after the genocide to a family that killed ours. I explained to him that it is not easy to share these stories. This confrontation did not hurt me much, and at least by reading the book, the boy learned more about what happened during the genocide.

The greatest challenge I am currently facing is my poor health. I have chronic and painful headaches, and I have had these headaches since the genocide. The doctor believes that I have headaches because I think too much about the past. He has prescribed me medication and wants me to finish this treatment before he considers referring me to the hospital for a scan. I need his referral to be able to get the scan free of charge. If I had the money, I could go to the private hospital to get the scan to find out the cause of the headaches. But since I do not have the means, I need to wait until my doctor agrees to refer me to the hospital.

I have medical insurance and I only need to pay ten percent of the fee that is charged at the hospital. I receive HIV medication for free. But recently, I stopped receiving my previous HIV medication and am on new treatment. I am not sure why it is not provided anymore. Those tablets used to help me, and maybe this is why my headaches are becoming worse.

Despite the challenges with my physical health, my mental health has improved because now I try to avoid thinking about the past. But I still worry a lot about the future. A relative of mine died recently, and she left her child behind. That is my greatest worry: what will happen to my children when I am gone? Then I remember that Solace Ministries will be there to keep an eye on my children, and that brings me some comfort, but I still continue to worry.

Before I came to Solace Ministries, I used to always stay at home. I did not want to see or talk to anybody. I was born into a family of eight, and I am the only survivor. I found it difficult to share my stories and burdens, and I just learned to be alone with my problems. For a while I could not pray to God because of the role the churches played during the genocide. But after a while, I managed to find faith again, and now I love praying. I survived alone but I am still alive, so I know that the Lord has protected me. It was the feeling that I wanted to pray again that brought me to Solace Ministries. At Solace, people not only understand me because they too survived the genocide, but also because of the touching hearts they have and the gift of giving that they received from God. Now I have people at Solace with whom I can share my problems or who can console me when I am dealing with my trauma. I just call Agnes or Mama Lambert and they comfort me. I am hopeful now, because I have people to talk to when I am in need; I am no longer alone.

Gacaca has also helped us in in dealing with our past. Some *génocidaires* were put in prison and others were forgiven. *Gacaca* played a big role in revealing where the dead were left so that they could receive a proper burial, but I did not get a chance to know where my own relatives' bodies were left. Some people may still have a heavy heart, but *gacaca* helped me to forgive. After the genocide I could not even greet Hutu, but *gacaca* helped me to live in harmony with them again.

When I look around in my area, where many other genocide survivors continue to live in desperate situations, I realize that I have made tremendous progress. I see that some survivors are sick, and some suffer from mental illness because of their trauma. Others cannot make ends meet and are without children who can support them. In contrast, I realize that I have developed myself, and that my children and I spent the financial support we received wisely. It empowers me to see my children and how they have developed.

My children grew up without the help of an extended family; I did not have an uncle, father or sister to help raise my children. Rather, it is through the support of Mukomeze that I was able to raise them. I use the support for school fees, food, clothes and health insurance. Even my neighbours wonder, "Why is that lady going to the bank? Where does she get her money?" When they ask me, I tell them I go to the bank because of God.

I used to be a businesswoman, but since my health has deteriorated, I am no longer able to work. When the headaches come, I cannot do anything. Hopefully one day, when I am free from headaches, I can try to start running a small business again in a market stall, and when the children come home from school, they can help me with it. Or I could run a chicken farm with my children's help. I would prefer chicken farming to taking care of a cow, because the latter requires a great deal of energy and I have lost much of my strength. But as long as I have these headaches, it is difficult. When I realize that I cannot work because of my illness, I just lose hope. I have nothing to do. But then I look around me and I see that there are people who are thinking of me, and this really consoles me.

When I meet other genocide survivors of sexual violence, I try to show them that they are not alone. I tell them how I was before and how I am doing now. People used to commit suicide because they could not cope with their traumatic experiences. But I am still here. They see I still have the strength to walk around and live on, even after all of these years. And I am proud of myself because of that.

In the years to come, my children will be doing well and have families and homes of their own. They will be educated and will have good jobs. When God helps me, and I no longer have these headaches, then we might enjoy that good future together. All I know is that life will be better than it is now.

When I first shared my testimony for *The Men Who Killed Me*, I thought I was just going to explain what happened to me during the genocide, but that nothing would come of it. But the book turned out to be a blessing for us survivors. One day, I received a letter from a student in Canada thanking me and telling me how moved she was by my story and strength. It has comforted us that people outside of Rwanda have come to know about our history and have been thinking about us, and that we received proceeds from the book and additional support. Because of *The Men Who Killed Me*, my voice was heard all around the world, and with this updated edition of the book, my voice will be heard again. Talking to people who care makes us feel strong and warm again. I thank God for everyone abroad who is thinking about us, and those who come from FAR just to meet and talk to us.

I am most thankful for the fact that I am still alive, twenty-five years after the genocide. Just after the genocide, after I learned that I was HIV positive, I did not think that I would even live another ten years. With this frame of mind, I decided to sell my property for very little. But I am happy when I see my children and how things have turned out; I did not expect to witness my children grow up, and luckily neither one has contracted HIV. My children are the only family I have, and because of them, my life has changed for the better. Once my children finish school, I know they will take good care of me. That warms my heart and gives me hope for tomorrow.

JEANETTE UWIMANA

BORN: April 2, 1972
BIRTHPLACE: Nyarugenge quarter, Kigali

TESTIMONIAL: Kigali, 2008

BEFORE THE GENOCIDE, my father, my sister and I lived in Butare, but in 1978 we were forced to move to Kigali. My father was not safe in Butare; he could not spend more than a month without going to prison, because he was Tutsi. Since 1959, his identity card had been regularly checked for his ethnicity, especially upon his return from Burundi, where he met my mother. My mother, a businesswoman, had gone back to Burundi. She refused to stay in Rwanda because of the discrimination Tutsi faced. My father was lucky to find a good job at the National Bank in Kigali. People initially did not know that we were Tutsi, and we thought we would be safe there. But in 1990, when the RPF tried to invade Rwanda, my father was accused of being an RPF spy and was fired from the bank. He went to prison for two months.

I married Diogene on November 28, 1990. He was a friend of my cousin, and we had met for the first time at my cousin's house, while my father was still in prison. Very quickly, I became pregnant, so we decided to get married. I stopped attending secondary school because of my pregnancy, after having completed only two years. We found a house to rent in Nyarugenge quarter in Kigali. My husband, who was also Tutsi, owned a bar, and I was a merchant in the market, where I sold rice, sugar, fruit and powdered milk. We also had some land in Shyorongi, a village near Kigali that was my husband's birthplace. There we were building a house, which we planned to live in once it was finished. We grew potatoes, beans, bananas and cassava there, and we ate this produce ourselves or gave it to our parents. Sometimes we sold it to neighbours.

We had a very good life. Even though our neighbours were almost all Hutu, that didn't seem to be a problem. In the beginning our neighbours didn't know we were Tutsi, but when the multi-party system was introduced in Rwanda in the early 1990s, they found out that my husband belonged to the P.L. party, which was composed mostly of Tutsi. We had two beautiful children, a daughter and a son. In 1994, our daughter was three years old and our son only three months old.

On the evening of April 6, 1994, our daughter was staying at her grandparents' house. My brother-in-law was staying temporarily at our house, preparing for his exams. My husband and I didn't have a chance to listen to the radio, because our power had been cut off. The Presidential Guards were at our front door the next morning, though, and while we were still wondering about what was happening, they forced us to leave our house and to show them our identity cards, which specified our ethnicity. A large crowd of Tutsi and Hutu had gathered in the street, and the Presidential Guards told Tutsi to go to one side of the street and Hutu to another. I knew exactly what was about to follow for Tutsi, so I threw my identity card away. The *Interahamwe* shouted that they were killing the *inyenzi*—the cockroaches—and the guards went to see what was happening. We took that opportunity to return to our house, where we tried to come up with an escape strategy.

While we were still thinking through all the possibilities, the *Interahamwe* came to our house and took my husband with them, without explaining why.

He never came back. I don't know how he was killed or where the remains of his body are, but one of my neighbours told me afterwards that he must have been killed, because she saw one of the *Interahamwe* wearing my husband's jacket. About two hours later, at around ten-thirty in the morning, the militia returned. They accused my brother-in-law of being an RPF spy and took him with them. The *Interahamwe* came back yet again at around one in the afternoon. This time, they took me to a hall where Tutsi were being killed. They beat me with their guns until a policeman who was a friend of my husband's begged them for mercy in order to spare my life. This helped, and they told me to go back home. I did, since I didn't know where else I could go.

I felt very lonely, and I hated myself. I felt responsible for what had happened to my family. Right before the militia took my husband away, they told us that all our other relatives, including our daughter, had been killed. The wife of the leader of a militia group—a woman who had gone to school with my husband and who knew many people—had betrayed them to the *Interahamwe*. My baby son and I were still alive, but I felt that I should have died along with my husband, my daughter and my other relatives.

That same day, five *Interahamwe* came to my house and ordered me to show them all the guns I had. I told them that I did not have a gun, because I was not a soldier. One of them pushed me into the bedroom and said that I would be a good replacement for a gun. He threw me on the bed and tore off my clothes. He raped me while his mates pointed their guns at me. After he was finished, another one raped me, and then another, until all five had had their way with me. Eventually they left, saying that their "work" was calling them. Killing Tutsi was their "work." I hated myself and considered myself less than a human being. I thought that those who had died were in a better position than I.

My private parts were aching and bleeding profusely. Four days after the rapes, one of my neighbours, a Hutu female friend, found the courage to come into my house. All of my neighbours had seen or heard what had happened to me. She came regularly after that, comforted me, brought me some food, helped me to wash myself and the baby and gave the baby some milk. My neighbour urged me to escape, but I was afraid I would be killed no matter where I went, so I decided to stay in my house. I gave some money to this woman so that she could cook food for me at her own house and bring it to us.

Two weeks later, a large group of *Interahamwe* militia came into our area and commanded everyone to leave their houses. I had no identity card anymore, and I took my time putting my baby on my back. One of the *Interahamwe* entered the house and said if I gave him some money he might spare my life. I gave him all the money I had, and he left me in my sitting room.

Apparently this man's militia friends asked him why he had only demanded money from this rich woman. They told him that he should also rape me. Some hours later, he returned with other *Interahamwe*. They raped me in my sitting room, saying that they had not spared me for nothing.

This continued for two months, practically every day. The rapists were mostly Presidential Guards, but also *Interahamwe* militia and FAR soldiers. They were all very brutal; the *Interahamwe* most brutal of all. The *Interahamwe* would rape me wherever in the house they found me. Sometimes the rapists came alone, sometimes in a group. Often they came both in the mornings and in the evenings. They also told others about the possibility of raping me. They would cruelly ask where my husband was and threaten to kill me later. They called me a snake and said that it was the end for all snakes. I was regularly beaten. This whole time, a policeman kept assuring me that the RPF were getting closer. He also advised me to keep myself dirty, not to wash myself, so that I would not attract the rapists. Although this policeman was decent with me, two other policemen raped me.

During this period, I felt like I was no longer a human being, and I wanted to kill myself. But I couldn't do it, since I still had my son to care for. Eventually I no longer felt pain; instead, I felt like a ghost. I didn't really think about escaping, since I felt I would be killed either way. There was no one to help me, and I preferred to die in my own house. This nightmare ended the day the *Inkotanyi* arrived, July 4, 1994.

As the *Inkotanyi* were approaching, the *Interahamwe* tried to kill all the remaining Tutsi, and they forced me to flee Kigali with them. I remember seeing a girl who tried to escape. She was immediately stabbed to death, so I didn't try to follow her example. We marched northwest towards the DRC, the Democratic Republic of Congo. There was a lot of panic. When I arrived in Gisenyi, someone offered me a ride to Kibuye for five thousand Rwandan francs. I thought it would be safer in Kibuye for my baby and me, as I had heard from other survivors who had returned from Goma, in the DRC, that Hutu were killing Tutsi there. Congolese soldiers were also killing Tutsi in the DRC because the *Interahamwe* had told the Congolese that the Tutsi were rich. Those who tried to cross into the DRC had their belongings taken away by the Congolese. Every time Tutsi tried to cross the border, the Congolese soldiers asked them for money. If they didn't have any, or didn't hand over what they had, they were killed. I decided that I would rather die in my own country, so I paid the driver the five thousand francs to take me to Kibuye.

Upon my arrival in Kibuye, I tried to find a house to stay in. It was very difficult, because there were dead bodies everywhere, and they had started to rot and smelled terrible. I finally found a school in the centre of Kibuye that did not contain any rotting bodies. It was very hard, because I was sharing the room with the *Interahamwe* and I could not do anything about it. Although the *Interahamwe* were still killing people in Kibuye, they only killed those they were certain were Tutsi. They didn't know that I was Tutsi. During the period I stayed in the school, I had no time to think about myself, because my baby was sick and vomiting all the time. I didn't want him to die. I was able to give him a mixture of some herbs and milk I got from an old lady, and that helped.

In Kibuye, I met a woman I knew from the market where we both used to work, and we hatched a plan to escape. Since the *Interahamwe* militia were still killing Tutsi, we decided to leave Kibuye at night. Over two days, we marched all the way to Gitarama, where we met RPF soldiers on July 20, 1994. They took us to Kigali in their car.

Back in Kigali, I met a female friend who let me stay at her house. My baby was still very sick, and I gave him milk and bathed him. Like other survivors, I tried to locate any remaining relatives and went to the Red Cross to see if they knew anything about the whereabouts of my family. I looked at the pictures of people who were still alive, but I couldn't find any of my relatives among them. My previous house was now occupied by Hutu. Since I'd been renting that house before the genocide, I couldn't kick them out.

It was complete chaos after the genocide, with everybody taking what he or she could get. A Tutsi friend had taken my furniture and given it to his sister. She refused to return it to me. When I reported this to the police, a soldier went to the house of my friend's sister to investigate. She claimed I had lied about it, so I was not able to get the furniture back. I finally managed to rent a house in Kigali and I worked several jobs in order to earn a living.

Almost all of my family and in-laws had died during the genocide. Whenever I got sick, I had no one to support me. My father had escaped to Byumba, where the RPF were already in control. He died in 1994, though, soon after the genocide. Perhaps his death was caused by the beatings he had endured. I never got to see him again. I have only seen my mother once since the genocide.

In 1995, I married a cousin of my husband. We had three children together. I found out in 2005 that I am HIV positive. My youngest child was permanently ill, and we went to the hospital to test her for HIV. When she turned out to be HIV positive, I also got tested. I think I was infected with HIV during the many rapes I had to endure during the genocide. When I found out that I was HIV positive, I had my other children tested. The child I had had before the genocide turned out to be infected with HIV as well, probably because I had to breastfeed him after I was infected. In November 2005, my second husband got sick, and he died only three days later. He had asthma and was HIV positive, but at that time we didn't know he was also infected. I think I might have been the one who infected him.

I have managed to find jobs here and there, but it is really hard, because I don't have a lot of education. Currently I am selling charcoal. The house we were building in my husband's birthplace was destroyed during the genocide. I now live in a house in Kigali that was given to me as a gift by some relatives who currently live in Belgium. I experience a lot of trauma all year long, especially during the annual mourning period for the genocide in April of each year. My stomach, my head and my private parts ache a lot. Sometimes my private parts start bleeding without a reason. I live in constant fear, wondering who will take care of my children if I die.

I think I have forgiven the man who killed my daughter and my in-laws. Maybe it is because he asked for forgiveness, and his request seemed to be heartfelt. He told me that my daughter and my in-laws were beaten with a nail-studded club and then thrown in a ditch, where they spent two days in agony. Their bodies were covered with soil and later thrown in another ditch. The man who killed my first husband fled right after the genocide and is no longer in Rwanda. I don't know where he is now. I don't go to the *gacaca* courts anymore, because the people we are accusing are being released. I don't see the point in taking the risk of sharing my testimony there if it doesn't make any difference.

My life is hard. My children go to school, and I need to pay for their school fees and materials. I would like to get some support for them without being a beggar. One day I would like to have my own business where I can sell clothes. I tried to set this up once before, but I didn't have enough money to do it.

I shared my testimony hoping that this book will spread my message farther than I could ever do myself. The international community should help us to rebuild our hopes and dreams.

JEANETTE UWIMANA

TESTIMONIAL: Kigali, 2018

I AM HAPPY to share an update on my life since I shared my testimony for *The Men Who Killed Me* a decade ago. I feel that I have made a great deal of progress. In the past, life was harsh, and I did not have anyone with whom I could share my problems, but now things are different. Of all the things that happened over the past ten years, I am most proud of my children.

I have been raising my four children in Kigali. But in March 2017, my younger daughter passed away. She was only twelve years old. It has been very difficult; I believe she was poisoned. I took her to the hospital when she started bleeding from her nose, and she died there. I get overwhelmed speaking about her.

My other children are growing up quickly. Over the past ten years, my children were able to get an education and that is just amazing to me. My eldest son has finished high school, my second son is in his sixth year of high school, and my daughter is in her fourth year. My first-born is like a father at home; he pays the rent. He is going to university on a scholarship. Of all people, I am most proud of him. I always tell my children to love God and to love people. I encourage them to do well in school and to be clever, so that they can make important contributions to their country and to their family.

Unfortunately, my second son is struggling. He started to use drugs because I think he compares his life to others, who have a higher standard of living. Even though we work hard to improve our financial situation, he wants more. He will finish high school soon and I do not have the means to send him to university, while all of his friends will go. Sometimes I talk to him and try to show him how much progress we have made. When I see him struggling, it just hurts my heart.

As I mentioned in my previous testimony, my second husband died in 2005. Since then, my children and I continued to live together, and I have been caring for them on my own. For a brief period, I received some support from a man I met at church, but after he got into an accident, he could no longer help us.

We live in Remera, a quarter in Kigali, in a rented house. Our neighbourhood is not really safe; there are some robbers in the area. But luckily, I have good neighbours, and we live together in harmony. I generally do not like to be alone. I prefer to be among people, so it is great to be able to meet with my neighbours and share our stories. They comfort me. When my child died, I was devastated but I felt that I was not alone because people came to visit and console me. When I go to the hospital, my neighbours are the first people to see me and take care of me. Also, when my children go away to boarding school and I am alone at home, my neighbours are the ones to make sure that I am all right. When we do not have anything to eat at home, people always come and give us food. The people in my community love me, and I love them. The leaders of my church have even chosen me to be a leader for the women in our community when they themselves are not around. It makes me feel so good to know that there are people thinking about me. I am part of the community, and when I am sad, we pray together.

Over the past ten years, Solace Ministries has comforted me and I have received support from the Mukomeze Foundation. This invaluable comfort and support enabled me to study Restaurant Management for one year at a Christian school, and I received my diploma in 2010. While my daughter was still alive, Solace Ministries also provided her with financial support so she could go to school.

My education has helped me to improve our financial situation. I have learned many things such as making cakes and decorations. However, it is difficult to find steady employment in my field. So I often find other jobs to support my family, like doing laundry or sewing clothes for others. Of course, I would prefer to work in a restaurant, not only because this is my field, but also because in this line of work I can meet many people and make friends, so that I will not be alone. I used to work for a Kenyan man in his restaurant. He loved how hard I worked, and he even paid for my daughter's school fees. I still dream of running my own restaurant one day. I just need the capital to start my business. Sometimes I receive money for the work I do, but I use it to pay for my children's school fees and for rent, food and clothing.

For now, there is still a long road ahead of me. Sometimes I feel empowered, and sometimes I do not. To me, being empowered means that I feel like I am able to live and work well. Having a job empowers me.

Overall, I have been doing well psychologically, but from time to time, when something triggers me, I get flashbacks of the genocide and I feel so hurt. In those moments, I stop caring about life. One of these triggers was my daughter's death, but also my son's drug use. And my mind also goes back to the genocide when I see people fighting. During those moments, I tend to stay inside my house, close my eyes, and remember. I cry and pray; I prefer not to talk much under these circumstances.

When I am busy with other activities, I generally do not experience these flashbacks. Being busy keeps my mind from recalling difficult memories. I also have people around me who can give me advice, and that comforts me. I have support from my community, my neighbours and God. Most of my neighbours do not know the details of my trauma and the source of my flashbacks because I like to keep quiet. Only my friends with whom I pray know what happened to me. Luckily, reliving these traumas has not hurt my relationships.

Sharing my testimony for *The Men Who Killed Me* has been helpful, because the experience made me realize that I was not alone. It also gave me another family. My older son is the only one among my children who knows what happened to me, because he read the book. At first, my son struggled with the fact that I shared my testimony for the book. But I explained to him that this has allowed people around the world to know what happened in Rwanda, and after several discussions, he finally understood the importance of sharing our stories.

Although I was raped during the genocide, I now feel physically strong. For a while, I stopped taking my HIV medication because I had lost all hope. I began suffering from headaches, infections and stomach aches and finally, I was admitted to the hospital. My Solace Ministries family and community members visited me at the hospital and comforted me. They told me that I still have children to care for, so I should not give up.

Since my daughter passed away, my first-born is the only one among my children who is HIV positive, and it is hard for him to accept that he is living with HIV. Counselling began to restore his hope for the future. At school he also found a group of students who have HIV, and that has helped him to realize that he is not alone. Finding others in the same situation allowed him to start to feel free and to love himself.

Over the past decade, I also began to feel my sense of justice being restored, and the *gacaca* courts played an important role in this process. When the *génocidaires* come and ask for forgiveness, we forgive them, and those who do not seek forgiveness are punished. *Gacaca* helped us to accept the people who murdered our loved ones, and in their confessions, they disclosed to us where the dead were left. Sometimes I think of forgiving the ones who raped me, but they have not sought my forgiveness, so my heart will not allow me to forgive them. If they would ask me to forgive them, then I would; but otherwise, they should be punished. On the other hand, the *génocidaire* who killed my child had asked for forgiveness, so I forgave him.

Looking back, when I first arrived at Solace Ministries, I was devastated. Mama Lambert, the counsellor of Solace Ministries, comforted and counselled me, and I was very touched by her kindness.

I am also grateful for Mukomeze's support, and the pictures that my sponsors sent to me. I finally feel like God has a plan for me.

When I think of the future and where I will be in ten years, I think of my children. They will finish their studies and get good jobs, so we will be all right. I think we will be more financially stable. We rent our house now, but one day I will buy my own house because my children will support me. I will stay outside of the city so that I can grow crops and raise animals. Perhaps I could even open my own restaurant and serve milk from my own cows and my own chicken and fish.

What I wish for other survivors is to somehow be comforted. We know that we cannot forget what happened. Although we forgive and think about our futures, in our hearts we still remember our lost loved ones and all the horrors that we faced. We need to pray and to love each other, to come closer to one another, share our stories, and together form another family.

ADELA MUKAMUSONERA

BORN: 1966 (date and month unknown)
BIRTHPLACE: Nyakivala, southern Uganda (near the Rwandan border)
DIED: November 17, 2016

TESTIMONIAL: Kigali, 2008

I WANT TO share my testimonial with you for two reasons: I want the world to know what happened here in Rwanda and what we had to endure, and I want to heal myself by unburdening my heart. When more people learn the truth, I hope that their voices will add to the chorus of those ensuring such crimes never happen again.

In 1959, before I was born, my family left Rwanda for Uganda because of the discrimination that Tutsi faced. I was born in Uganda, but my family returned to Rwanda when I was just a child, because my father worked with Catholic priests from Belgium who wished to start a congregation here.

Despite the hardships that Tutsi experienced, we made the most of our lives in Rwanda. My family lived in Kigali. In 1987, I went to school to learn to be a seamstress. The school was located near a FAR soldiers' training camp, and that is how I met my first love. He used to come from the camp to visit me at school, and I got pregnant soon after we met. He rented a house for me to live in when he was away fighting. In 1990, when my son was only one, my dear soldier was killed in a battle with the *Inkotanyi* in the north of Rwanda.

After his death, I moved in with my older sister, who was a tradeswoman. I survived by selling milk. That is how I met my boyfriend; he owned a truck and delivered potatoes from Ruhengeri, in the northwest of Rwanda, to Kigali. I saw him every day when he came to my shop to drink milk, and we soon fell in love. Five months after meeting my boyfriend, I moved in with him. He was so good to me and loved me very much. He also loved my first son as if he was his own. In 1993, I gave birth to my second son.

Despite my bond with my boyfriend, his family never accepted me or approved of our relationship, because I was Tutsi. I remember his sisters would always say that one day all Tutsi would die. Where we lived, Tutsi were a minority. Our neighbours put up with me, but only reluctantly. I always felt that, given the opportunity, some of my neighbours would harm or kill me. But all those thoughts were banished when I remembered that my boyfriend was a Hutu, too. I thought he would be able to protect me.

My boyfriend knew, even before the death of President Habyarimana, that mass killing would begin. I suspect he knew of the impending genocide because his family had very good relations with the *Interahamwe*. For that reason, shortly before the genocide began, my boyfriend took my sons and me to the Butamwa quarter of Kigali. The very strange thing was that he was doing this to protect us from his own family. I was only twenty-eight years old at the time. I moved back to my parents' old house on Mount Kigali, and my boyfriend returned to Ruhengeri. He thought it would be safer if we remained separate. That way we would draw less attention to our family.

My mother and my grandmother lived at my parents' old house. My father lived nearby with his girlfriend. My mother didn't own a radio, so we only realized that things had deteriorated when barricades sprang up on every street. On April 7, the *Interahamwe* militia started killing Tutsi families, looting their possessions and burning down their houses. We decided to stay inside because it seemed more dangerous to leave the house.

A few days later, while breastfeeding my younger son, I saw a group of *Interahamwe* militia armed with machetes, swords, spears, batons and other weapons approaching our house from across the street. I also noticed that a barricade had been erected in front of our house. I decided to secure my baby to my back and flee. I hid in a nearby bush, but my baby started to cry, which alerted the militia to our whereabouts. The militia soon found us. When they saw me hiding in the bush, the militia laughed loudly and shouted a phrase that I will never forget: *Akanyu karashobotse*, meaning "your last day has come." I was pushed to the ground and gang-raped by three of them right there and then. Once they were finished with me, they gave me a bag of corn and ordered me out of the neighbourhood they were in charge of. I immediately fled.

After what seemed like weeks of hiding in bushes with my baby son, eating nothing but the occasional cassava and sweet potato I was lucky enough to scavenge, I met my mother, grandmother and older son not FAR from our house. They had also been hiding. Their lives had been spared temporarily after they handed over all their property, including their house and their fields, to the *Interahamwe*. My mother informed me that most of my uncle's family had died after being beaten; their bodies had been thrown in a ditch. As we were talking, we heard people approaching. My mother and my grandmother decided to flee to our house, taking my sons with them. I decided to go to my uncle's house to see if there were any survivors among my uncle's family and perhaps to hide there.

On my way to my uncle's house, I was caught by another group of *Interahamwe* militia. They detained me, and the leader of the group, a twenty-one-year-old named Damascene, ordered me to strip my clothes off so that he could "see what Tutsi sex looked like." I recognized Damascene from before the genocide. He lived in a house in my neighbourhood. He was a quiet person, and no one really knew him. As I started to undress, he hit me on the head with a stone and hit my back with a club. He grew impatient with me and started to tear off my clothes himself. He pushed me into a ditch and raped me in front of his friends, who were standing nearby. Many other Hutu, who were my neighbours, were also watching. I knew them all. They watched and laughed, as if Damascene was an artist painting his masterpiece.

While Damascene raped me, one of the *Interahamwe* decided to call my father and force him to see what was happening to me. When my father came, he begged the *Interahamwe* to kill him instead of raping me, but they wouldn't. He ran back to his house, screaming in agony. When Damascene finished raping me, he offered me to the two youngest males in the group, who were young enough to be my children. They were both ordered to rape me. While they did, I felt like I was already dead. I was crying the whole time.

Damascene was responsible for one of the many barricades erected by the *Interahamwe* to prevent Tutsi from escaping. While he was busy raping me, some people took advantage of his absence and fled with their belongings. Eventually, Damascene noticed people running with their bags. He pursued them, leaving me in the ditch. After Damascene and his group left, a Hutu thug called Bajyahe, who had been watching, told me to run also, and he gave me his jacket. I covered my naked body with it and ran back home.

At home, I found my mother, my grandmother and my two sons. They had not been harmed, but they feared I was already dead. I would soon learn that after I was raped by Damascene and his thugs, another group of *Interahamwe* went to my father's house and beat him severely. The *Interahamwe* did not kill him right away. Instead, they gave him his date of execution. This was how the *Interahamwe* dealt with older Tutsi.

My mother, grandmother, two sons and I stayed inside our house for three days. Eventually we ran out of food, so I ventured into our fields to find something to eat. To my horror, I encountered Damascene there. When he saw me, he pushed me into a shallow hole, threw banana leaves on top of me and set the leaves on fire. I was being burned alive. I used my arm to shield my face from the fire, and I now have a long scar on my arm as a result. I think Damascene tried to burn me alive because he had no other weapons at hand.

While the banana leaves were burning, I heard people shouting that the *Inkotanyi* had taken over the country. It was a wonderful stroke of luck. Damascene heard this also and started running. That is how I escaped. I threw the banana leaves off me and climbed out of the hole. I returned to my house and waited inside with my mother, grandmother and two sons while the *Inkotanyi* and FAR soldiers fought outside. After two days, we made up our minds to leave; we heard many gunshots, and they seemed to be getting closer. Amidst the chaos outside, we didn't realize that the *Inkotanyi* had won and could have protected us if we'd stayed. Instead, we fled with others, including the *Interahamwe*, to the Congo. My grandmother stayed behind because she was too old to make the journey.

With my baby strapped to my back, I walked to the Congo with my older son and my mother. We walked every day. At sunset, we would go to sleep. It took us a week to reach our destination. In the Congo, we found shelter at a refugee camp. It was only once we were settled that we realized we were surrounded by *Interahamwe* who had escaped the *Inkotanyi*. Even so, we were too exhausted to make the journey back right away. I knew that Tutsi girls were being raped at the refugee camp, but I generally felt safe. The *Interahamwe* didn't try to hurt us, since I was being "protected" by my former Hutu neighbours. My neighbours had killed people during the genocide, and I knew the only reason they were trying to protect me was to make themselves appear less guilty should I accuse them of their crimes at a later date.

After two months, my family decided to walk back to Rwanda. We didn't tell anyone at the camp we were leaving, for fear the *Interahamwe* would kill us. I knew they were afraid of Tutsi returning to Rwanda to accuse them of their crimes. My mother, my two sons and I made the journey back to Kigali together.

The *Inkotanyi* had control of the city. In Kigali we saw bones everywhere, but the bodies had already been buried. We returned to our old house to find that my grandmother was no longer there. My older sister, who had fled to the Congo with her Hutu husband, had returned alone and moved into that house. She told us my grandmother had passed away while we were in the Congo and the *Inkotanyi* had buried her body. For the first little while after our return, the *Inkotanyi* gave us food. When that food was gone, we started digging our fields again, and I farmed cassava, sweet potatoes, sorghum and beans.

Because of the rapes I endured, I suffered very serious trauma. My mother was also traumatized and she cried all the time. I started drinking, because I needed to forget about what the *Interahamwe* had done to me. I became an alcoholic and went mad, and was in and out of the psychiatric hospital. At the hospital, I was tested for HIV. That's how I found out I am HIV positive.

I continue to have problems in my private parts. I rarely have enough strength to eat and I have a permanent migraine. To this day, I am rejected by my Hutu neighbours, who all participated in the genocide. None of them come to my house, and they will not invite me to their houses. Only God has not rejected me.

I am alone in this world. My boyfriend was shot to death in June 1994 by the *Interahamwe* while he was transporting potatoes for Hutu in Kigali. It is strange to think that the Hutu continued their daily lives during that time as if nothing out of the ordinary was happening. My boyfriend was killed because of his relationship with me. I learned about his death after the genocide, when the man who killed him told me. I knew this man from before; we did not live FAR from each other. When he told me about my boyfriend's death, he acted as if someone else had done the killing and he had just been watching. Anyway, he is now in prison. My father died from the beatings he endured during the genocide. He died when I was still in the Congo, and my older sister told me the *Inkotanyi* soldiers had buried him too.

I don't have any extended family. Recently, I returned to Ruhengeri to visit my boyfriend's mother, but she refused to let me enter her house, saying that her son is dead and I should have died as well.

In 2007, I went to the *gacaca* courts to accuse Damascene of what he had done to me. He was convicted but released after less than one year. Considering what he did to me, one year is not enough. I think he should be in prison for his whole life. After his release, Damascene came to my house and demanded forgiveness. I think it's because he learned about unity and reconciliation when he was in jail. The government had already forgiven him by releasing him, he said, and now it was my turn to do the same. He asked me if I would forgive him in exchange for a cow. That really upset me. This man who reduced my life to nothing thinks he can make amends by giving me a cow? How can a human life be exchanged for a cow?

Damascene and his wife are now my neighbours. They are getting richer every day, while my situation remains the same. One time, Damascene passed by my house and saw that my mother was ill in bed. He gave her three hundred Rwandan francs and told her to go to the hospital. He put the money in my mother's hands, but she threw it back in his face. She did not want to take money from him. That is humiliation. It made me so angry! I might have forgiven him before, but I can't forgive a man who thinks forgiveness can be bought. Why should I forgive him? I don't want to be corrupted for forgiveness' sake. I can forgive, but not in exchange for money or a cow. I just want sincerity.

ADELA'S SON GILBERT DUSHIMIMANA

TESTIMONIAL: Kigali, 2018

MY MOTHER WAS brave to tell her story. She said she had nothing to be ashamed of and nothing to hide because people knew her story. Once I was old enough, my mother explained to me what happened to her during the genocide. It was hard to hear. I will never forget it. But I am glad that she told me about it in person. It showed me that she did not only want to tell other people, but that she also wanted me to know about her experiences. Also, when she told me about the trouble she faced, it made me think about God's plan for her to survive, because she was in such a bad situation.

We faced many struggles in life growing up without a father. It was hard for my mother to take care of my brother and me all by herself, without a paying job. When my mother died in 2016 the situation became worse. My older brother had already left the house to work and live in Uganda, where he got married. When my mother died, I was seventeen and I continued to live with my grandmother, who is now eighty years old. I try to support the both of us. Although I do not have a permanent job, I sometimes get temporary work. I learned filmmaking, so sometimes my friends ask me to make films or take photos. It is very difficult to find assignments, but when I find them it really supports me. Although I like filmmaking, my wish is to continue my studies in university. Unfortunately, I do not have the means to do this.

I always think about my mother, especially in November, the month that she died. HIV, secondary health issues related to the sexual violence that she suffered during the genocide, and her recent heart problems became too much for her. She had done so much to support me in growing up well. The most valuable lessons that my mother taught us were to keep learning in life and to tell the truth anywhere you are. That is what I will tell my future children: to be truthful, just like their grandmother.

When I think about my best memories with my mother I think of all the time I spent with her because she liked to take care of me. I was always with my mother. She was very beautiful and loved people. She also loved to pray and tell us the word of God. My mother always told me to go to church with her and to pray. And I continue to do it even after she passed away.

When people look at me, they see my mother. When I was young, people would say I look like a girl because I resembled her so much. Now they also say I have her characteristics; it is the kindness we share.

My mother dreamt that her children would grow up well and become strong men. Although it has been very difficult for us since she passed away, we are striving to become what our mother wished us to be. And I believe that one day, we will fulfill her wish.

MARIE CLAIRE UWERA

BORN: August 16, 1970
BIRTHPLACE: Gacurabwenge, Gitarama

TESTIMONIAL: Kigali, 2008

BEFORE THE GENOCIDE, I lived in Taba commune, Gitarama Prefecture, which is in central Rwanda. I felt at home there. In my free time I liked to sew. I lived with my husband and our two sons, not FAR from my parents and my seven brothers. My husband ran a bakery, and I was a tailor.

There were only three Tutsi families in our neighbourhood; the rest were Hutu. But we seemed to have a normal relationship with our neighbours. I knew that in 1973, when I was only three, some Hutu had burned our house and stoned my mother. This event followed Habyarimana's *coup d'etat*, which overthrew the sitting president and resulted in many Tutsi being killed. When my father rushed my mother to the nearest hospital, the staff refused to treat the open wounds on her arm because she was a Tutsi, and my father had to heal her himself with traditional medicine.

My mother used to own a little shop in Taba commune, where she sold things like body lotion, soap and bread. On the morning of April 7, 1994, I stopped by her shop to buy something and saw that the surrounding shops were still closed. I asked my mother why the shops were closed, and she told me that our president had died the previous night. Upon hearing this, I felt very afraid, and I convinced my mother that we should return home together. My brothers were happy about the news; they said that if the president was dead, the time for peace had come. But my father did not share their opinion. He said that the time for the killing of Tutsi had come—and he was right.

Some days later, my mother and I ran into a rich man, one of our Hutu neighbours, who asked us where we were going. We were going to our shop, we said. He laughed out loud, then said, "*Akanyu karashobotse*," meaning "your last day has come." We were very afraid. Not knowing what to do, we went to a nearby shop, where we sat down for a moment. Hutu who passed by asked us what we were doing there, and we told them we were afraid of the *Interahamwe*. They responded by saying that if we were scared of the militia now, we should wait until we actually met them. That frightened us even more.

In our area, the killings began on April 21, 1994. My father was a judge, and he was the first one to be killed. A group of *Interahamwe* came to our house and tried to destroy it with my father and brothers still inside. When my father went outside, they killed him immediately by striking him on the head with an iron pole. They left his body lying there. They covered it with eucalyptus leaves afterward, because it started to rot and stink. My father was the first Tutsi killed in our community because he was an intellectual and we were a wealthy family. Our neighbours thought we were cooperating with the *Inkotanyi*, and they were jealous that my brothers had gone to school, which was not usual in those days for Tutsi.

After the attack on my father the rest of our family—among them my husband, our two young sons, my mother, and some of my brothers and nieces—fled. At the time, we were not sure who was trying to kill who, and we just followed other people. We finally arrived at a little nearby commercial centre, with shops selling manufactured goods, hoping that we could survive there. The *bourgmestre* of Taba, a man called Jean Paul Akayesu, came to the centre to ask us why we were there, and we told him that the *Interahamwe* were hunting us. Akayesu rejected us and told us to leave the place unless we wanted him to call the *Interahamwe*. Since we didn't know where else to go, we stayed. We were afraid, and had nothing to eat or drink except some coffee beans that we had found.

One day, some FAR soldiers arrived and took my husband to a police station. They beat him severely on his back. I would find out later that he was able to bribe one of the guards at the police station to let him go, but I didn't see him again until after the genocide. On another occasion, I remember a Tutsi girl of about fourteen years old who was taken from the commercial centre by an *Interahamwe*. I recognized him as one of my neighbours. The girl told us that she was raped by more than ten *Interahamwe* in one day. Every time she returned after being raped, they came looking for her in order to rape her again. After she returned from being raped a third time, there was blood streaming down her legs from her private parts. At this point she could not walk any longer, and she had to use her hands to drag herself. She cried a lot and did not say anything. As we were all waiting for death to come, we were not able to care for her, or anyone else, for that matter.

On Tuesday, May 3, 1994, the *Interahamwe* detained my mother and forced her to leave the commercial centre. I still remember this date so very well, since the nearby market was open, and the market only opened on Tuesdays. I decided to follow the *Interahamwe* with my two sons. We arrived at a big hole. There, my mother's clothes were ripped off and she was raped by *Interahamwe* who were not even twenty years old. Then one *Interahamwe* took a long sword and stuck it into my mother's belly. They also hit her with a club, and she fell in the hole. She was killed while she was still naked.

I did not feel anything except fear. My older son cried. I begged them to kill me, too. Though they beat me, they said they had no reason to kill me; they were not in a rush, since they could kill me anytime they wanted. Instead, they killed my older son, who was four years old, because, as a boy, he would have been able to fight them after growing up. He was thrown into the same hole as my mother. After the killing of my child, someone shouted that there were some cockroaches, and the *Interahamwe* left us. I sat there for hours and hours, not feeling anything. I wondered whether I was still a human being.

When I finally returned to the commercial centre with my surviving baby son, I saw that all Tutsi there had been killed. After three hours, I fled to a little forest nearby, where I hid with my son in a bush for about a week without food or water. My son cried a lot. I constantly hit him to stop him from crying and make him sleep again, so that we would not be discovered. But the *Interahamwe* found me with the aid of their dogs. One of them asked me if my child was a boy or a girl. I told him that my boy was a girl, and he said that he was going to make me his "wife," and that my "daughter" would replace me when I did not satisfy him. He took the two of us to his house, where he ordered me to cook some beef for him. I saw that the cows for the beef were from my house; someone else had slaughtered them and given them to the *Interahamwe*.

I knew this *Interahamwe* militiaman. He was called Yubu. Before the genocide, he had told me many times that he loved me, and I had always rejected him. Now it was his time to take revenge on me. He told me that he was going to do to me whatever he wanted. I never truly understood the meaning of those words until the day he inflicted his savage desires upon me. He abused me in every kind of position: from behind, in front and even with his fingers. The very first day he raped me, I begged him to kill me, but he said that I still had a lot to endure. I lived that hell on earth every day for about three weeks. Even though I was not locked in the house, I was afraid to go out, because other *Interahamwe* militia might kill or rape me. Yubu hardly spoke to me, and he did not want me to do any household chores, as he was afraid I would poison him. I stayed in the house doing nothing; I was too afraid to do anything.

One of my brothers somehow found out that I was there and came to see me. He told me how I could escape from that evil when Yubu was not around. But on his way back to his hiding place, an *Interahamwe* who was a former neighbour saw my brother and killed him instantly with a sword. I found out the next day that my brother had been killed, because I overheard people passing by the house who said so.

I felt so sullied and so dirty. Around June 16, 1994, which I remember because I was counting the days since my mother had died, I managed to escape with my son through a window at the back of the house. I didn't want to use the front door, in case people saw me and pursued me. I have a scar just above my eye that I got when I was fleeing Yubu's house. I finally decided to escape because I was afraid of being killed by Yubu, and what he did to me made me feel like I was being killed already.

I spent the night in a hole in the ground. The next day, I went to see a Hutu woman who was my friend. She refused to let me into her house, because I was a Tutsi and it would get her into trouble. But one of the woman's nieces saw me and took me to the outdoor toilets behind the woman's house, where I spent the night. The next morning, the woman's brother and his mates found me. They ordered me to get out of the toilet and threatened to call the *Interahamwe* if I didn't cooperate. So I went to a big sugarcane plantation near Nyabarongo River and hid there. While I was there, I ate sugarcane. My son was very hungry, and he had lost a lot of weight. I tried to feed him sugarcane by chewing it for him first.

After about a week of hiding there, a Hutu man with a gun found me. He took me to his house and raped me every day, sometimes four times a day, for about two weeks, until the RPF took over the country. I could not escape, since I did not have any other hiding place, and I could not refuse, because he would call the *Interahamwe*. During this period he made many cruel remarks. He would taunt me and ask me how I was going to survive with such a young child, and say that all my Tutsi "brothers" were dead. Like Yubu, this Hutu man did not want me to do any household chores, because he was afraid that I would poison him. I was hurting so very much. I asked God to let me die.

When the RPF arrived in that area on July 4, 1994, the Hutu man came to the house with a group of *Interahamwe* militia to kill me, but the RPF saved me by shooting them. The RPF came and took my son and me with them, gave us clothes and shoes and brought us to a safe place near the Nyabarongo River, where many survivors from neighbouring areas had assembled. There I reunited with my husband.

I never told my husband what had happened to me. I feared his reaction to the rapes, and I had no other relatives I could turn to. Even though he asked me a few times whether I had been raped, I always denied it. I lied to him and said that I was hurting because of the many beatings I had had to endure during the genocide.

We had three more children after the genocide. In 2000 I started feeling very ill, so I got tested for HIV and discovered that I am HIV positive. My son who survived the genocide with me was not infected, but two of the three children I bore afterwards also tested HIV positive. While my oldest son seems healthy, he has difficulties sleeping. Sometimes he falls out of his bed and starts running around. He does not perform well in school. I don't know why he's like this, but maybe it has to do with the gunshots he always heard during the genocide and the fact that I used to slap him in order to make him quiet. One of the most painful things for me is to see my children suffer for something they didn't do.

In 2002, my husband died as a result of the severe beatings he endured while imprisoned during the genocide. His passing left me in deep poverty. The house I lived in before the genocide was destroyed. I don't own my own house, and sometimes I don't have enough money for the rent. I don't have the ability to work, but I must feed and take care of my four children. I have psychological problems because my neighbours and my community don't know who I really am. Still, I don't mind if they find out when this testimonial is published. I want the world to know what really happened here in Rwanda in 1994. I would have died had I not received support from other survivors.

After the genocide I found my mother's body, with the sword still in her belly, in the hole where I last saw her. My son's body was also in that hole. I recognized his body because of the jacket he wore that day. Their bodies have now been reburied, as have the bodies of my father and my brothers who died during the genocide. The men who raped me are all dead. The ones who killed my family are being released, and I don't know what to do. The man who killed one of my brothers is still free, even though I accused him before the *gacaca*. He is a rich person; maybe that is why he is free. Living with the perpetrators of the genocide is a serious challenge for all of us who survived. Those atrocities must never happen again. Only God can bring us justice. I hope that God will also bring me hope for the future.

MARIE CLAIRE UWERA

TESTIMONIAL: Kigali, 2018

I USED TO have no hope. Sometimes, I wondered whether I would live to see another day. But now I am happy; I never thought I would reach the age I am today. And Solace Ministries and my sponsors helped me get here. Over the past decade, they provided me with the means to pay for shelter, clothes and my children's school fees, and supported me in making my daily ends meet. When I got very sick, they came to visit me at the hospital. I am grateful for the support and the comfort that I continue to receive.

As you know, my husband passed away in 2002. It was difficult at the time, but I have learned to accept it. I will always remember how much he loved me. He did not beat me, he did not curse at me. Now I am left with my four sons, who give me so much joy, and we live peacefully together. I am taking care of my boys by myself, and they are growing up quickly. They love me so much and I am proud of them. The support I received allowed them to pursue their education. They all study well and get high marks at school. My two older sons have both finished high school, the third is in in his fourth year of high school, and the youngest is in his second year.

We have overcome many challenges as a family. Only a few years ago, I struggled with my two younger sons because they resented me. They turned out to be HIV positive and blamed me for it, but I could not bring myself to tell them the truth about how I had contracted HIV. I reached out to a sister of the Catholic church, and she helped me to tell them what happened to me during the genocide. When they heard my story, they felt sorry and realized I was not to blame. After that, they started to love me again, and we have not had another conflict. Despite living with HIV, they are in good health.

My second son Patrick was conceived when I was raped during the genocide. At first, I found it very difficult to love him, and I did not have the heart to tell him the whole story. But our neighbours knew, and they would just say to him: "Ask your mother who is your father." Then he would come to ask me about his father, but I could not say anything. It was Mama Lambert from Solace Ministries who provided me counselling and support, until I could accept him. Later, she helped to explain our story to him, and counselled him as well. Since then, our love for each other has grown. Once my husband died, all of my children were left without a father, so Patrick is not alone.

We live in a rented house in Gatenga, an area in Kigali. The houses in Kigali are very expensive, but I managed to find a house that is decent and still affordable. Our house is very good compared with the previous one, which only had one bedroom for all of us. Our house is bigger; it has two bedrooms and a sitting room with chairs. I hope to one day buy my own house.

I am on good terms with my neighbours. Nowadays, we no longer have problems related to ethnicity. We live in harmony together; my neighbours come to visit me, and I visit them. During *umuganda*—one day a month when all Rwandans perform community work—I work alongside them. In the area where I lived before, my neighbours stigmatized me because I have HIV; whenever I got very sick, people would isolate and hurt me. So I decided to move in 2015, and in my current neighbourhood, things are different. My neighbours come from different regions of the country, and they do not try to interfere with my life. We greet each other and go our own way. When I go to the hospital, I find others who have the same problem as me. All they know about me is that I am HIV positive—nothing else. How I contracted HIV is something I only tell people at Solace Ministries.

I do not feel stigmatized being a survivor of sexual violence. Here in Kigali, people do not know my history, so they cannot think negatively about me. Even during the commemoration period each year, when I return to my village where the sexual violence took place, people respect me. I meet the *génocidaires* and I even greet them, because I have been able to forgive.

In that sense, our society has changed considerably over the past decade. *Gacaca* played a major role in reconciliation. When *génocidaires* wanted to ask for forgiveness, they had to come clean about what they did. This way, we knew that they really killed our loved ones. The *génocidaires* testified about where they left the dead—whether they threw them in the river or in a pit, for example—and that helped us to find the remains of our loved ones and bury them properly.

Although I do not know all the men who raped me, and some of them are dead, had they asked for forgiveness, I would be able to forgive them. But they never did. I forgave from the bottom of my heart the *génocidaires* who killed family members and asked for forgiveness, because if I could not do it, nothing would have changed. That is why I think it is important to forgive, because otherwise it would just hurt my heart. It was very difficult for me, so it is God's miracle. Our government helped us to be strong and to think about our future in order to be able to forgive.

I was happy to learn that Akayesu, the mayor from Taba, the community where I am from, was convicted before the International Criminal Tribunal for Rwanda, and that his was the first ever conviction of genocidal sexual violence. It was a formal acknowledgement of what happened to me. I also think it is important that our government leaders helped us to get justice by punishing the *génocidaires* in Rwanda. It shows that our leaders are with us, and that genocide will never happen again.

I am also doing much better in terms of my mental health. When I first shared my testimony in 2008 for *The Men Who Killed Me*, I was still very traumatized. It was hard to deal with the fact that I was raped and conceived a child as a result—a child that I did not wish to have. But through counselling, I regained my strength. When I go home, and I find my children eating, dancing, singing and telling stories, I am simply grateful.

Despite my progress, I have been struggling with my physical health. The HIV medication is working well, but I have also contracted many secondary infections. At times I felt too sick to work, and I have often been hospitalized. A few years ago, the doctors discovered that I had cancer. Luckily, they were able to remove the cancer through treatment. I also had ulcers and continue to struggle with chronic bronchitis and constant coughing. I believe that God will take my life when the time is right.

I feel that I am well on my way to becoming economically independent. After receiving counselling, support and comfort at Solace Ministries, I decided to take classes so that I could attain a better standard of living. I did not want my children to walk around in borrowed clothes; I wanted to make sure that we would always be well dressed. I decided to complete a tailoring program, so that I could continue working as a seamstress, like I did before the genocide. Now I sew clothes not only for my children, but also my clients. Even my neighbours, who do not have much money themselves, support my business by coming to me whenever they need to repair clothes.

For my business, I rent a shop with some other seamstresses in Kimironko. We share the location, but not our profits. While we wait for clients to arrive, I make handicrafts that I put up for sale. I like to keep myself occupied. I do not have time to sit; I only have time to work. The clients choose which one of us will help them, and I do my best to provide good quality work so that clients will return to me and become regular customers. Even when I am at home, I try to occupy myself by sewing clothes and making handicrafts. I use all of my income to support my children. I just need more regular customers to make my business more profitable, and I am not giving up.

Over the past decade, I have come a long way and now I feel empowered. When I wake up in the morning, I want to find activities to do. I want to live and strive everyday for a better tomorrow, for my children and me. Although I feel sick, I have to continue to work hard and educate myself.

My happiest moments in the past years were at Solace Ministries' special events with the members of Mukomeze, my other family. One time, my sponsors sent me Vlisco fabric, and I used it to make a dress. These original Dutch wax prints with bright colours are very popular in Africa, but because they are very expensive, I cannot afford them myself. I will never forget how happy I was to receive this gift, and I feel proud to wear my dress.

In the future, I hope to have my own house and land, and continue to live peacefully. I would love to see my children buy land for themselves as well, and I hope to be able to continue to take care of them so that they can finish their education and get jobs. I want them to do well, to help those in need in the community, and to contribute to the development of our country. The lesson I would like to pass on to my children is to love others the way they love themselves, and to nurture peace within the community. I have restored my hope to live long and to have a bright future, just like my children. Even if I become physically weak, I believe my children will help me. I believe that in the future, we will be even happier than we are today.

In *The Men Who Killed Me* our stories showed the suffering we faced during the genocide and in the years that followed; now we can show how our lives have changed for the better. We have found the will to live again and we are doing well. While we are sick, we have medication. I feel blessed to have had the opportunity to share my testimony because other survivors of sexual violence can read it and find out that they are not alone, and that there are others like them who continue to live. I hope that survivors know that being comforted will help us to live longer. I hope survivors continue to have hope for a better life and find a way to forgive those who did us wrong. We have good leaders, who have helped us to attain peace and security, and have brought us justice. So, let us live in peace together.

PASCASIE MUKASAKINDI

BORN: July 25, 1959
BIRTHPLACE: Karambo, Gikongoro

TESTIMONIAL: Kigali, 2008

TO THIS DAY, when I think back to the genocide of 1994, a feeling of coldness comes over me and I start to shiver. I remember the freezing house where the *Interahamwe* enslaved me in nothing but my undergarments. But I still wish to share my testimonial with you to help let the world know what happened during the genocide and bring justice to those who suffered. I wish to have a better life. Without people who care about our plight, we will die.

My family has had a long history of suffering. My father used to tell me about the history of Tutsi oppression in Rwanda. In 1959, seven of my uncles and aunts were killed by Hutu, and their bodies were thrown in the Rukarara River, a large river in Gikongoro Prefecture. In 1963, some Hutu neighbours tried to kill my father, a Tutsi, but his Hutu father-in-law hid him on his banana plantation. In 1973, following the *coup d'etat* by Habyarimana, we were forced to give a few cows to some Hutu neighbours so that they would not kill us.

In 1990, discrimination against Tutsi got much worse as news spread about former Tutsi refugees who wished to return to the country from Uganda. That year, I was living in Nyanza, in the south of Rwanda, with my husband and my child. Tutsi traders and teachers were killed, and others were jailed. Traders and teachers were among the first to be killed, since the traders were considered rich and the teachers were considered intellectual. Despite these killings, I wasn't afraid myself, since I felt there was no reason to kill me.

Before the genocide in 1994, I was a trader in secondhand clothes, and my husband was a truck driver transporting food all over the country. My husband and I came from the same area and we got married in 1984. We decided to live in Nyanza because my husband's job was there. Where we lived, Tutsi and Hutu shared everything. My mother was Hutu, but my grandmother was Tutsi. I was considered Tutsi since my father was Tutsi. Ethnicity didn't seem to matter to the ordinary Rwandan; it seemed to matter only to the people who wielded power.

A week before the genocide began, I was in Gikongoro, in southern Rwanda, visiting my parents. I saw Hutu forming groups here and there and buying strange weapons. On April 7, 1994, while I was still in Gikongoro, we heard that the president had died in a plane crash. Soon after, we heard Tutsi screaming as their houses were burned by *Interahamwe* militia on the orders of the prefect of Gikongoro and the police. On April 12, 1994, the prefect asked the policemen of that area why they had not yet started to "work" when in other places the police and militia had already finished. As soon as I heard this, I went to a man called Marcel, who was a friend of my parents. My father had given him a cow, which is a sign of great friendship in Rwanda. Marcel was a Hutu and a demobilized FAR soldier, and his wife was a Tutsi, so I went to see if he would hide me. He agreed, and I stayed in their home for two weeks, until the day the *Interahamwe* came to burn Marcel's house because all his in-laws had sought protection with him. During those two weeks I felt very frightened. I stayed in a room with all of the in-laws, and we couldn't do anything. I was waiting for death to come. I didn't know what was happening with my husband and our four-year-old child, who were still in Nyanza.

While the *Interahamwe* were placing dry tree branches around Marcel's house in order to burn it, Marcel told us to run out the back door. Some of his in-laws were killed during our escape. While fleeing, I encountered a group of about fifty *Interahamwe* militia. They detained me near the bushes next to the Gasebeya River and stole everything I had: my bag, my shoes and my watch. I also had a bottle full of milk, and they threw that milk on me, saying that Tutsi were like cats because we all liked milk. A few men tore my dress off, and one *Interahamwe*, named Charles, told me that he wanted to kill me so I could be the hundredth person on his death toll. I was paralyzed with fear. I was so scared I could not think, and I saw death right in front of my eyes.

That group of *Interahamwe* took me to some bushes to kill me. Just as they were about to do so, a man approached and proposed to buy me from them. I think he wanted to rescue me. He offered them twenty bottles of beer and two hundred Rwandan francs, but the *Interahamwe* said if the man wanted to make me his wife, they would first have to rape me. In the end, they refused to sell me, and they pushed me to the ground, injuring my chest. Afterward, the men raped me, one by one. Even the youngest ones in the group raped me, and they looked like they were no older than thirteen. Almost fifty men raped me in one day. I was too numb to feel anything. I had been abandoned by the Rwandan authorities who were supposed to protect me. After they were done raping me, they shoved a nailed club into my vagina, threw me into a thorny bush and left me in that state. I removed the club very slowly and dragged myself to a nearby river, because I thought the water from the river would help heal me. There, I slept. By this time I thought that my family must have been killed already, and I was waiting for death to come to me also.

After I awoke, I slowly dragged myself to a bush, where I hid for three days. Then I went to the home of an old friend of our family, a Hutu named Charlotte, who gave me a piece of cloth before ordering me to leave her house. She was afraid for her own security, because I was a Tutsi. My family was on a list of Tutsi to be killed as a priority, because we were considered RPF spies. This frightened Charlotte even more. From there, I went to a mountain called Nshyundo, where many Tutsi had found refuge in bushes. I stayed there for a week, until the *Interahamwe* came and burned the whole mountain. Many Tutsi perished in that fire, including my aunts and five of my cousins.

I escaped down the burning mountain to the Mwogo River. Crossing it would lead me back to my home in Nyanza. Before the bridge that spanned the river were two roadblocks, though, and around one hundred *Interahamwe* and FAR soldiers. They were staying in that area in houses that had belonged to a moderate Hutu, Minister of Agriculture Frederic Nzamurambaho, who had been killed earlier in the genocide. The *Interahamwe* spotted and captured me. They placed some banana leaves on the ground and ordered me to lie down. Before raping me, they ordered me to perform all kinds of gymnastics, including handstands, which was difficult because I was very weak. They tortured me in so many cruel ways, forcing me to take their penises in my mouth and shoving their penises up my nose. Their sperm fell from my nose onto my body and into my mouth. I wanted to vomit. I felt so stupid, and I could do nothing. They insulted and humiliated me. They told me that I was ugly and dirty and that I stank. No one was there to help me. After they finished, they took me to one of the abandoned houses they were camped in. I could not escape, because they would lock all the doors when they left to do their "work." I was the only woman in the house, and for two weeks many *Interahamwe* raped me every day, using me as their personal sex slave.

During those two weeks I wanted to die. Instead, I remained in that situation. I was wearing only some ragged underwear. I was really dirty and smelled awful. Since I was there during the cold season, I was always extremely cold. Talking about it makes me shiver all over again.

After two weeks, the *Interahamwe* heard that the RPF were getting closer. They beat me with nailed clubs until one of them said that I was dead and told his peers to leave me there. The RPF arrived a few hours later and took me to an RPF camp in Nyanza. There, they gave me all kinds of treatment. First they washed my entire body, which was very dirty. Then they treated my private parts, which felt destroyed. They gave me food and medicine, including penicillin. Slowly, I started to recover.

The *Interahamwe* militia and FAR soldiers who raped me did not think that I was a human being. My parents, my brothers and my sisters were killed during the genocide, and I don't know what happened to my husband and my only child. I don't know how any of my loved ones died, because we all fled in different directions, and the perpetrators have not admitted how my family members were killed. There has been a resurgence of genocidal ideology in Gikongoro, so people are reluctant to admit the crimes they committed.

I hate all men, and I do not want to hear about them. I feel the *Interahamwe* militia and FAR soldiers killed what I would have become. I am HIV positive. I am not able to work, because I am very weak and constantly ill. I suffer from headaches, chest aches, backaches and pains in my vagina, and I have sinus problems as a result of the men who raped me in my nose. I live alone and have no one to help me, but I am surviving with the help of different organizations, which provide material and spiritual support. I find comfort and love through the support of those organizations and from seeing other widows who have the same problems. It helps me feel less lonely.

Some of the *Interahamwe* militiamen who raped me were imprisoned, but they are now being released. This is not justice. *Gacaca* courts were supposed to bring justice and reconciliation, but they are bringing more tears than smiles. The men who killed me should be better trained on how to treat survivors after they return to society. Soon, I will accuse some of the perpetrators myself in *gacaca* court. I am afraid of testifying against them, but I will not allow my fear to get in the way. Despite all that has happened to me, I can forgive those who ask for forgiveness from the bottom of their hearts.

PASCASIE MUKASAKINDI

TESTIMONIAL: Kigali, 2018

THE FIRST BOOK, *The Men Who Killed Me*, told the world about the genocide and the sexual violence that took place in Rwanda. Yet, in many countries, people do not believe that genocide happened in our country, and there are people who do not believe that women were raped during the genocide. This book gives value to Rwandan survivors and what we have endured. I am lucky that I shared my testimony for *The Men Who Killed Me*; my voice and my words are documented. It touched my heart when I received letters from people around the world who had read my testimony, and expressed love and compassion. These people do not know me, but they still wonder who I am and how I am doing. It makes me feel that my suffering touched somebody's heart. I came to learn that what happened to me can help others. I hope that my strength and courage can be an inspiration to other survivors of sexual violence. Perhaps they can draw lessons from what I have been through. That brings me hope for tomorrow.

I am living proof that things can change for the better. And this is also what I want to show the readers of this book; I am not the person I used to be. I am glad that there is worldwide recognition of what happened to us, and that *The Men Who Killed Me* played a role in accomplishing this. I hope the world will also see how FAR we have come. It has touched my heart that people who are not Rwandans have shown me love and compassion after reading my testimony—something that Rwandans did not show me then.

After what happened during the genocide, I felt like I could never love another man. Otherwise, I would have remarried and had children. But I am not living alone. Since the government gave me land and a house through

the FARG program, authorities asked me in 2012 to take in two orphans for a short while. The two teenage siblings came to live with me, and we all had to make some difficult adjustments. I have come to love them as a parent. They continue to live with me and are all grown up; both have completed university.

Although I love the children, I cannot look into their hearts and know whether they love me, too. It is normal for children to sometimes misbehave toward their mother. But some of the things they do make me feel that they do not love me. One day I came home from the market, and I found that they had built a small house beside my house. I discovered that they had stolen my land documents and gone behind my back to the Land Board to register the land under their names, too. I am not sure whether they returned the authentic documents to me. It hurts me, but there is nothing I can do about it, other than to seek legal advice. I would like to propose to the children that they move into the small house they built and leave me in my own house, so that I can be free again. I am still considering going to the Land Board to dispute their claim of ownership. The children know that I am HIV positive; I think they wish that I would die, so that they can take all of my property. They seem to think that I am a fool. They only pretend to love me. Their love for me is not the same as the love I have for them; it is not the love they could have for a parent.

I am happy with my house, and I do not want to move to a different place. I am pleased with the area, as only genocide survivors live here with the assistance of the government FARG program. It is a safe area and I am on good terms with my neighbours. Everybody just minds their own business; they wake up in the morning, work at their businesses or dig their fields. I spend time by myself at home, and also welcome and visit fellow Solace members who live close by. Together, we discuss the problems we face.

Overall, I am doing fine, but I still cannot forget what happened to me during the genocide. The trauma continues. Sometimes when I am alone, I think about all that I have suffered. I see it all playing in my mind like a movie. I do not think we will ever forget what happened; it will always come back. This is the life we must accept to live. We cannot forget; we just pretend not to remember.

Sometimes it comes when I am at home alone or at night. Then I try to think of some small verses from the bible, and I try to sing and pray in order to keep me from losing myself in re-traumatizing thoughts. And I just try to remember that I am strong. But sometimes I cannot even sing. When these thoughts become overwhelming, I try to visit Solace Ministries to seek comfort from Mama Lambert. But the pain... I do not think I will ever forget what happened.

In 2009 I was diagnosed with cancer. After the genocide, I used to feel sick every day. When the RPF soldiers rescued me, I was continuously bleeding from my private parts. They took me to the hospital where I received all kinds of treatments, but the bleeding continued and it was very painful. I was constantly using pads or cloths to absorb the blood. When I passed people on the street, they would say: "What is that smell?" At the hospital, the doctors found that my uterus was damaged because many different men raped me. I went home and prayed to God for healing, and one night when I was sleeping in my bed, I had a vision. I saw someone standing with his hands in the air, and he told me: "You are healed." After that vision, I went back to the hospital, and the doctors discovered that the bleeding had stopped and my uterus was healed. The same thing happened in 2013, when I had a stomach ulcer. At first, it was hard and growing bigger, but after I prayed and asked the Lord to heal me, it healed without any operation.

In addition to the cancer and ulcer, my back continues to ache, and I have a chronic cough and constant headaches. But I am used to living with pain. And when I remember the coldness of the house where I was kept nearly naked during the genocide, I still get shivers; just the thought of it makes me sick and sends me to bed.

To give my life meaning, I have operated several businesses over the years. I had a restaurant, but I had to give it up when the landlord became jealous and evicted me so that another person could rent it instead. Then I relocated my restaurant, but the space I was renting was sold and destroyed to build new houses. So I decided to run a business that does not require me to rent space. Now I go to customers—either in their homes or big stores—and I ask them what produce they need. Then I go to the market and buy the produce they order, and deliver it to them. I have different customers and they all order different items, like tomatoes, carrots, onions and bananas. I would advise any young woman who wants to do business to use her strength and her mind, and to always be reliable and accountable to encourage returning customers.

Because of my business mind, people within the community respect me. They see that I am always running some business, so they think I make a lot of money and they always try to borrow from me. They do not look down on me because of my history; they just think I am a strong woman and that I have everything in abundance.

Nevertheless, at times I do feel stigmatized for being a survivor of genocidal sexual violence. There are people who know me and my history. I feel ashamed whenever I meet these people, particularly those who are connected to the men who harmed me in the past. Through their words, they make it clear to me what they think of me. They blame me for the fact that these men are in prison. I just tell them that everyone needs to account for what they did. But I do not say much to them and I stay quiet; during those encounters I feel ashamed and afraid, so I try to avoid them. I am afraid that the bad things that happened to me in the past will happen again. In those moments I feel ashamed of my history, and I fear that those people might open up old wounds and hurt me again.

This is the reason I do not want this second edition of the book to be published inside Rwanda: the stigma and the way people look upon me. Still, it is better than it used to be; there is less stigma against survivors in Rwandan society now than there was before.

The government continues to work on forgiveness and reconciliation. But despite the progress after all of these years, I do not believe in the justice system. *Gacaca* was the appropriate way for the government to deal with the genocide, but *gacaca* did not bring me justice. If it were up to me, I would have never chosen to bring the *génocidaires* before *gacaca* because their crimes were too severe. By the laws of our country, it is forbidden to kill others, so I cannot take revenge on the killers. But if it were up to me, I would do the same to those who killed my loved ones. Ultimately, I did testify against the people who raped me, and the government imprisoned them according to the law. But if the government then decides to forgive them, there is nothing I can do about it. I must forgive them too, even though it is not from my heart. I still think that I could forgive those who ask sincerely for forgiveness. The problem is that they did not come to seek forgiveness.

During the genocide most of our property was destroyed and stolen, but at first, I decided not to seek redress. I only went to court in 2012, when someone took my father's land. But since that person had a lot of money and many lawyers, I was unable to pursue the case without a lawyer representing me. So I just accepted my loss.

Despite all of the challenges that I face, I still feel empowered; I am strong, and I have hope for the future. In the years to come, if God continues to give me life and strength, I wish to have a new house and my own car. I do not have my driver's license yet, but I will get it as soon as I have the means. I have come a long way, and I will achieve all of my dreams. I want to show the people who harmed me that they were wrong about me; I want to show them everything I am capable of accomplishing. I want to challenge them.

I am grateful to those who have supported us. I am most thankful to Jean Gakwandi from Solace Ministries, because he has devoted his life to support widows and orphans. He comforted me and showed me that life can go on. I am also proud of my president Paul Kagame; he stopped the genocide. If it were not for him, I would not have met *Muzehe* Gakwandi, and the members of Mukomeze. I know why I am still alive. It is because of Solace Ministries and Mukomeze. They went out and told the world about us: our stories and our needs. They came and supported me when there was nothing left of me, and helped me step-by-step to where I am now. Every night before I go to bed, I pray. And when I wake up during the night, I pray again. I get a pen and write down the names of the people who were good to me, and then I thank them in my prayers. I ask God to bless them. The reason why I am still alive today is because of these people. I bless them because there are still people in need. I pray that God may give us more people who can support others.

MARIE MUKABATSINDA

BORN: October 22, 1956
BIRTHPLACE: Ruhashya, southern Rwanda

TESTIMONIAL: Kigali, 2008

BEFORE THE GENOCIDE started, I had never experienced the discrimination or difficulties the Tutsi did. When I was in school, Tutsi children were forced to stand up and identify themselves so that the Hutu children could beat them up after class. Many Tutsi were forced to flee the country because of discrimination. But I did well in school. After my studies, I found a good job as a typist in the office of the *bourgmestre*. Not long after I started working there, I met my husband. His sister had married a friend of mine, and we met at her house. My husband was an animal caretaker for the ISAR, a government institute of agricultural research, and he was from Mugusa, another commune in Butare Prefecture. I quit my job at the office so we could live together in Mugusa. We were very happy together and had four children. When the genocide began, I was pregnant with my fifth child.

In the middle of April, I heard that Tutsi from neighbouring areas were fleeing the country for Burundi. The killings had not started yet in Butare, but shortly afterwards, President Sindikubwabo, the new president, came to Butare himself to ask the Hutu of Butare what they were waiting for and tell them to start their "work." The Hutu president didn't need to repeat himself, because local Hutu immediately took all the weapons they could find and started hunting Tutsi. Even though I was Hutu, I was in the same situation as Tutsi because my husband was Tutsi. Our house was torched by the *Interahamwe* just as other Tutsi houses were.

The local authorities ordered us to go to the ISAR, where my husband worked, in order to "protect" us. In hindsight, I can see they really wanted to kill us without spending time searching for us in our homes. Everyone, Tutsi

and Hutu, was ordered to go. But as we made the journey there, someone stationed on a hill near the ISAR shouted for Hutu to return home, because only Tutsi were wanted at the ISAR. When we arrived at the institute, I lost sight of the rest of my family, except for the little boy I was carrying in my arms. Because there were so many people there, my husband and my three other children disappeared from my sight.

Some hours later, many *Interahamwe* came to the ISAR and started killing Tutsi. I saw babies crying for their mothers who were already dead, and women who were bleeding to death and asking for water to drink. I heard very traumatizing screams, and I could not stay any longer waiting for my hour to come. I ran, with my baby in my arms, and hid in some bushes in the ISAR compound. I stayed in those bushes for two days, but on the third, my son started crying from hunger. An *Interahamwe* found us, slapped my son and beat me on the shoulder with a nailed club. I fell to the ground, and the man left me, probably because he thought I was dead. Because I was hiding, people assumed I was Tutsi. A little while later, a man who used to work with my husband passed by, and I asked him for some milk. He laughed at me and told me that there was no milk left in the country.

After those three days of hiding from the *Interahamwe*, I left the ISAR during the dark of night. I spent the next two weeks in Mugusa, begging for food at the houses of people I knew. They wouldn't let me spend the night in their homes. I slept in the bushes, and during the day I begged for food for my baby. I felt that the rest of my family was probably already dead. When I had the opportunity, I would check among the bodies lying in the streets to see if I could find them.

One month later, the local authorities announced that the killing was over and anyone who was still hiding should return to normal life. Many Tutsi and a few Hutu emerged from bushes and from among the corpses. At the time, we didn't realize that genocide had occurred. We thought that the killings of 1959 or 1973 had merely repeated themselves, but not that these killings were meant to wipe out an entire race. In fact, the "normal life" the authorities were talking about was a return to the ISAR, where they could attempt again to kill us easily, by surprise.

At the ISAR, *Interahamwe* and FAR soldiers killed the remaining Tutsi men and raped all the women and girls. They worked as a team: the FAR soldiers would shoot Tutsi, and those who weren't dead would be finished off with machetes by the *Interahamwe*. They did this in front of everyone. I fled with my baby boy, and I was lucky not to be shot. I managed to run from the ISAR to the house of my sister-in-law, who was married to a Hutu. She was happy to see me, but she could only hide me for one week, because her husband was worried about having a Tutsi baby in his house. After I left their house, I wandered from bush to bush, feeding my son and myself with wild fruit. But I could not evade the *Interahamwe*.

The first *Interahamwe* I encountered approached me with a spear and told me he could either rape me or kill me. He raped me. Afterward he left me there. I went to another bush nearby, where I spent a week. While hiding there, I encountered another *Interahamwe*. He asked me how I was doing and then asked whether I could point to other bushes where Tutsi were hiding. I refused and said I was the only one hiding there. He replied that he didn't have time to negotiate with me, that I should just let him sleep with me. He said that if I refused, he would call other *Interahamwe* to kill me. He raped me, as well.

Two days after the second rape, I met another *Interahamwe*. I begged him to show me the way to Ruhashya, where I was born. I thought perhaps the *Interahamwe* there wouldn't kill me, since they knew I was Hutu. That *Interahamwe* said he would show me the way to Ruhashya only after raping me. After he raped me, he walked part of the way to Ruhashya with me. I didn't tell any of the men who raped me that I was Hutu, because I didn't think they would believe me. I was four months pregnant by that time, but they didn't care. My two-year-old son saw all that happened to his mother. Fortunately, none of the *Interahamwe* tried to hurt my son.

I arrived in Ruhashya after walking all night long carrying my little boy. My parents' old house had been destroyed, so I moved from relative to relative. My relatives stayed safe during the genocide because they were Hutu. They would welcome my son and me into their houses, but after a few days they would be afraid of the consequences of sheltering Tutsi and would tell me to go elsewhere. In Ruhashya, I discovered that my fourteen-year-old son had also survived. He had fled from the ISAR to Ruhashya to try to find me.

At the beginning of July, the *Inkotanyi* came and took us to Save, a sector in Butare. There, they had established a camp for survivors. The *Inkotanyi* fed us properly and clothed us. I stayed in this camp for a month. After that, I occupied the houses of people who had fled the country, moving from house to house with my two sons. Eventually, I returned to Mugusa. Because my house had been destroyed, I lived in the house of a neighbour who was an *Interahamwe* and had fled the country. That way, I could continue to take care of my fields. In September 1994, I gave birth to my youngest son. The government eventually built houses for survivors in Mugusa, not FAR from where I used to live, so I left the house of the *Interahamwe*.

After the genocide, I was always sick and was losing weight, so I decided to be tested for HIV. I found out that I was HIV positive. That was not at all a surprise after the rapes I had suffered. I believe my husband and my two other children were killed in the ISAR, though I have never seen their bodies. Now I live with my youngest child. My oldest child lives in Gisenyi with his cousin, and he is learning to drive. My second child lives at boarding school. I have felt increasingly weak in recent years, and I don't know how I manage to live. When I work in my fields, I only work for an hour at most, but I have managed to survive on what I farm.

I want you to know that the horrors people inflicted during the genocide are more than any human being can endure. For a long time after, I despised myself for what had happened to me. I hated everything that surrounded me, because it reminded me of what I had lost. I used to think that I would rather be dead than living with HIV, but I have received comfort from a charity that also provides me with antiretroviral treatment and food. I know now that I can continue to live with HIV. Sometimes I even forget that I am HIV positive. I no longer hate who I am, and I feel my love for myself grow.

MARIE MUKABATSINDA

TESTIMONIAL: Kigali, 2018

I THINK IT is important to share our stories and the progress that we have made over the past decade. There may be other survivors of sexual violence who have yet to speak out, and perhaps reading my story will encourage them to open up and share their own stories, so that they can be free again.

Before I shared my testimony a decade ago, I had no hope for the future. All I could think of was, "How am I going to live?" I did not want to say anything about what happened to me; my story was mine, and I did not see a need to share it. But when I finally found the courage to share my story, it went out into the world, and that helped restore my hope. By speaking with counsellors, I began to deal with my trauma. I also connected with other genocide survivors of sexual violence. Until then, I thought that I was alone, but when I heard that others suffered the same problems that I faced, it touched my heart. We exchanged phone numbers and continue to share how we are doing. I started loving myself again, and I regained my desire to live. When I look at my own pictures in the book, I remember where I was a decade ago, and realize how FAR I have come.

The happiest moment in the past ten years was when I was chosen for a sponsorship. It made me realize that there were people that cared about me. Because of this support, I have basic necessities. Now my children can go to school, and we have a home. I was able to fix my roof when it started leaking during heavy storms. I also bought some cows, and for a period I sold food staples like salt and rice to my neighbours at a shop stall near the market. Because of the support I received, we did not go hungry; I could always go to the store and buy food. I love to eat Irish potatoes and beans; we Rwandans like beans. Another thing I like to eat is meat, but it is difficult for villagers to afford it, so we only eat meat on special occasions like Christmas.

As you know, I lost my husband during the genocide and I have not lived with another man since. After what happened to me during the genocide, I could not bring myself to become too close to men. That is why I never re-married. As I mentioned, I have three sons. One is married and lives close by with his family, and the other two are still students at university. I used to take care of two orphans, my niece and nephew, but after I became gravely ill, I could no longer care for them. Now other family members take care of them.

Nowadays, I live with two of my young grandchildren: one is seven years old, and the other is eleven, and my third grandchild lives with my son and daughter-in law close by. I am very happy living with my grandchildren. It was difficult to live alone after my two younger sons left for university, and I was glad when my eldest asked me to look after his children. They tell me stories and help me around the house by fetching water and cleaning with me.

The house we live in is my own, and I am happy with it. Although it has cracks, I will repair it one day. The area where we live is quite secure. Some of our neighbours participate in the neighbourhood patrol—or *irondo*—to keep us safe, and each household in the neighbourhood pays them to be on watch at night. Because of them, we can sleep peacefully.

I live in harmony with my neighbours. When I was admitted to the hospital last year, they came to dig my fields and clean my house. We live happily together. Although I am a survivor of sexual violence, I do not experience any stigma or isolation because most of my neighbours do not know what happened to me. The children of the neighbourhood always come to my house and call me their grandmother. That makes me feel good. Within the community I feel loved and respected. When people need assistance, I do my best to help them; it is God's love that directs me. There is a man in our community who gives me a litre of milk every evening, and he does not ask for anything in return. I do not know why people love me, but it makes me happy.

I think that part of what has allowed us Rwandans to live together again is *gacaca*. After the genocide, I returned to the area where I grew up, and I became a judge at the *gacaca* courts. I advised people to reconcile: for the killers to tell the truth about what they had done, and for the survivors to forgive the killers. *Gacaca* was good because it brought us reconciliation, and now people are uniting again. Hutu and Tutsi families are starting to share cows and inter-marry, just like it was before the genocide. Everything changed because of *gacaca*.

Over the past ten years, my health has been my greatest challenge. I am HIV positive, and in the beginning, I did not take my medication because I had no hope left. But the doctors took good care of me: they talked to me, asked about my life, and gave me reasons to live, despite my HIV infection. After I started taking my medication, I began to regain my strength.

But last year I became very ill again, and it turns out that I have cancer in my uterus. The first time I received chemotherapy in February 2018, I got very sick; I saw death right in front of me. But now I am better. When I receive intravenous chemotherapy, I feel so dizzy sometimes that I need to vomit. I have lost my hair and nails, but luckily my hair is growing back now. I am still supposed to go to the hospital every month to receive treatment, so the cancer has not been eradicated. Every month I tell them how I feel, and if I am feeling bad, I receive treatment. This month the doctors postponed my treatment because they want to check whether my kidneys and lungs still function properly.

My health insurance helps cover my medical expenses but there is still a small contribution I need to pay. The extent to which your expenses are covered depends on your socio-economic status, which the government assesses before placing you into a specific category. The government provides full health insurance coverage to the poorest Rwandans or the most dependent, like orphans—they are in the first category. I am in the second category and that means that the government partially covers my expenses; I still need to contribute a little. Being in the second category is a confirmation of my increasing financial security over the past years.

Despite my recent health issues, psychologically I am feeling much better now than I did a decade ago. Before I could not think about myself, and I did not know the value of my life, but now I can think about my tomorrow. I have regained my dignity, and I feel human again. I can love again.

I usually no longer need trauma support, but whenever I do need it, I turn to Solace Ministries and Avega. At Solace Ministries, Mama Lambert leads the counselling sessions, and I love the way she supports me. She comforts me and shows me love, even from a distance. Usually, I do not attend the counselling sessions at Solace Ministries in Kigali because I live FAR away. But when I have a problem at home, FAR from Mama Lambert's office in Kigali, I call her and she comforts me over the phone. That shows how much love she has. Solace Ministries also has a branch in Rusatira, in the South of Rwanda, closer to where I live. Before I got sick and had to go to the hospital so frequently, I attended their community meetings there and we discussed our lives together.

In the Rusatira community, with the support of Solace Ministries and the Mukomeze Foundation, I joined a few women to set up an agricultural co-operative. The agronomist of the area helped us to get started, and together we grow pineapples and fruit trees. Staff from Solace taught us how to use terraces and fertilize the land. They also told us that we should think of our cooperative as more than a place where we work together. They encouraged us to nurture love among us; if someone is not available to work, we should visit her at home. The focus of our cooperative is not only to work the fields together, but also to help each other and love one another. When I was physically strong, I could work together with the other women. But since I fell sick, I stopped participating in the physically-demanding activities; now I like to go there to share ideas and offer support.

I used to be able to work the lands, but now that I am growing old, I do not have the strength to dig anymore. I plan to start selling different foods near the market again, like I did before. This would not require much energy, and I could still earn a little income. In the past, when I had my own shop stall, I had many customers. People from the villages would come directly to me. I sold popular items like rice, sugar and salt. I used to buy crops at a low price during the harvest season, and store them at my house until the end of the season when the demand grew. Then prices increased and I would sell my products at the market.

I feel that I have a bright future because my children are grown; they are finishing their studies and will be strong men. I think I have taught them well. I showed them love, and I taught them to love people and to love to work. I encourage them to be social within their community, to be self-reliant and avoid depending on other people. And I instilled in them a sense of dignity. In a few years' time, I will be older and weaker, so my children are my hope. They will be able to help me.

IMMACULÉE MAKUMI

BORN: 1949 (date and month unknown)
BIRTHPLACE: Kibirira, Gisenyi
DIED: November 16, 2010

TESTIMONIAL: Kigali, 2008

I AM GRATEFUL to be able to share my story, because it releases a huge weight from my heart.

Life is hard. I have lived in dreadful conditions since the end of the genocide. My son died during the genocide, and I have no one else to take care of me. In 2003, I took an HIV test because I was experiencing physical problems. That year there was an increase in the number of people who discovered they were HIV positive; they had been infected during the genocide and were beginning to experience the physical symptoms of AIDS. I am HIV positive because of the rapes I survived. I also suffer from asthma and have serious problems with my stomach. I take antiretroviral medication, but it is not easy, because I need to eat nutritious food that I can't afford to buy. I am not accepted in my community, because no one understands how an old woman like me got infected with HIV. I don't know why people are so cruel to me.

My father had two wives, which was quite common in the area we lived in. My own mother had two children, my brother and me, and my stepmother had three children, two boys and a girl. From the time I was born, we lived in Kibirira sector in Gisenyi, in the northwest of the country. Hutu and Tutsi there generally got along well with one another, though the Tutsi were richer. Naturally, Hutu were not happy with that, and they often stole Tutsi possessions. In 1959, when I was ten, our Hutu neighbours set our house on fire. My parents decided to keep me safe by taking me to my older stepsister's home. She had married a Hutu, and she and her husband hid me on their banana plantation.

My husband was a Hutu and also from Gisenyi. We had been distant neighbours, and our parents were friends. In fact, our grandmothers were sisters, so technically we were second cousins. We met in 1966 and got married a year later. We moved to Kigali because my husband found a job there. For me, there was little difference between our old home and our new home, because Hutu were FAR in the majority in both communities. I had some friends and relatives in Kigali, though. My husband's family rejected our marriage because I was Tutsi, but my family accepted it, especially since my husband's family had given my family an impressive marriage gift, which included beer and farming materials. The marriage gift is a Rwandan tradition, and is paid by the husband's family whether or not they approve of the marriage.

In the first five years of our marriage I gave birth to three daughters. It was really difficult to survive. We were very poor, because neither of us could get a good job. My husband had never gone to school, and I was forced to stop attending primary school after my parents' house was burned down in 1959. At first, I had a small shop where I sold beer, and my husband worked at a company that produced digging materials to work the fields. My husband always told his co-workers to go to my shop to buy beer, but they would never pay me; they would pay my husband instead. I never saw any of that money, and I think my husband spent it on a Hutu woman he was having an affair with. Sometimes she came to our house, and I felt very sad that my daughters would see this. Because he spent all the money on this other woman, I was forced to close my shop.

In 1975, my husband ordered me to leave our house because I was Tutsi and his family had rejected him because of me. I decided to go to my parents' house in Gisenyi, and I was lucky to hitch a ride there with a truck driver. Because I thought I would have to walk all the way to Gisenyi, I had decided not to take my three children with me and had left them with their father. The day after I left the house, he brought home the Hutu woman. I was pregnant at that time with our fourth child, and, when I gave birth at my parents' house, my husband did not come to see his son.

Two years later, in 1977, my husband came to visit me. I didn't want to see him, but my mother pressured me to, as he was still my husband and perhaps wanted me back. Although we spent the night together, he left again the following day and went back to the Hutu woman. I was pregnant again, however, and later gave birth to our fifth child, a son. When that child was only three months old, he died.

There is a Rwandan tradition that a woman must go back to her husband if their child dies. So I went back to my husband, but, when I arrived at his house, I found out that he was in prison because he had stolen mattresses and furniture from the hotel where he worked. I begged the Hutu woman to let me have my daughters, but she refused, so I decided to return to Gisenyi.

In 1980, I gave birth to a sixth child, a daughter. She was not from my husband but from another man who had always liked me. We never married. I spent some months at his house, but I returned to my parents' house when I discovered that other people accused the man of being a thief. To punish him, some locals cut his leg off. We sometimes still meet in the streets and greet one another, but that's all.

In 1990, in retaliation for the RPF invasion from Uganda, our house in Gisenyi was set on fire by Hutu. My mother perished in that fire, and I had to live for two months in a church. In 1991, the UN World Food Programme built me a new house where the old one used to be, and I lived there with my children.

That same year, I was out walking with a young Hutu cousin of mine and some other Tutsi friends from Kigali. While my cousin was returning to his home afterwards, the police savagely beat and killed him. It was said that my cousin was killed because he was seen walking with a Tutsi woman. But the police accused me of the crime and also of being an *Inkotanyi* spy. They arrested me, threw me in jail and beat me the whole night. For the next week, I endured horrible conditions, living in a tiny room that was alternately a torture room, bedroom and bathroom. They would make me sit on the floor and would beat my legs and then stand on them. They also shaved my head and beat my head with the handle of a saw. Whenever they saw a dog, the police forced me to call it by my father's name.

I spent the next year in different prisons, moving from the police station in Gisenyi to the prison in Gisenyi and then to the prison in Ruhengeri. I don't know why they made me change cells; maybe just to torture me, as I could hardly walk between places. I was imprisoned for a crime that I did not commit. Because of my imprisonment, my son had to stay with my brother in Kigali, and my daughter with friends in Gisenyi.

When I was finally released from the prison in Ruhengeri in 1992, I walked back to Gisenyi and stayed there for two days. But my house had been set on fire again; apparently some Hutu did not want me there anymore. I collected my daughter, and together we went to Kigali to pick up my son. My relatives in Kigali didn't really want to help me; instead, they gave me money and told me to look for a place of my own. That really saddened me. Luckily, I was able to find a place to live in Kigali. My children had to quit their studies, though, because we did not have any money for that. In 1993, my husband came to my house and told me he had left his wife for me. I got pregnant again, and we had another daughter in 1993. He never left his wife for me, however.

When the president's plane crashed in 1994, my son told me I should leave Kigali, and that is how I started my very long journey to survival. With my three children, I went first to my husband's house in Kigali. But his wife was not happy at all to see us, and she threatened him, saying that it was either her or my "bastards" and me who would live in that house. He initially agreed to take us in, but two weeks later told us to leave the house. I decided we should continue walking, without any specific destination, and we eventually arrived at a refugee camp in Gitarama. This was a camp of about two hundred people, set up by Tutsi. We stayed there for about three weeks.

One morning, as I was walking to the toilets in the refugee camp, two Hutu men abducted me. Those two men took me to a tiny forest nearby and ordered me to take my clothes off so that they could see what a Tutsi woman looked like. One of them raped me immediately in that forest, and while it was happening I could hear other people screaming and the sounds of guns going off all around us. The other man raped me after the first one was finished. After about an hour, I returned to the camp. My children asked me many questions about my long absence, and I assured them that I was alright. But I was terribly afraid and in a lot of pain. I didn't want to talk to anyone about what had happened. Instead, I found a certain comfort in being silent. I was afraid of all men and I still am, although to a lesser degree now.

In my absence, FAR soldiers had shot up the camp, and all the Tutsi had fled. Only my children were still waiting there for me. We decided to leave as well and walked to a camp nearby called Rushashi, near Gitarama, where about twenty Tutsi had gathered. Towards the end of the genocide, the *Inkotanyi* found us there and told us it was safe to return home. For the first three days, we stayed at the house of a Hutu woman who had also been at the camp, but then she told us to go home; she was afraid for our lives since her sons were *Interahamwe*. We left for Kigali.

Since the genocide, my oldest daughter has come to hate me. I was not there to take care of her during the genocide, and she cannot deal with the fact that her mother was raped. When I told her that I was HIV positive, she told me to kill myself so that I would not be a burden to her. My two youngest children even had to come to the hospital to protect me from my daughter.

I have forgiven the *Interahamwe*, because if I do not, I am the one who suffers. There is a curse on them, and one day they will pay for what they have done to me. My neighbours don't want me to testify at the *gacaca* courts, because most of the perpetrators will be leaving the prison any day now. I live in a neighbourhood with many *génocidaires* and I am afraid for my safety.

I have not received any kind of compensation since the genocide. I want the court to review my case of wrongful imprisonment, which I have shared with many people. The judiciary should review that case, but they still have not done so, and I don't know where to begin. I sometimes still meet my ex-husband in the streets, but we never talk. I could sue him for polygamy; he is legally still my husband, since we never divorced. I wouldn't be afraid for my life if I did decide to sue him. I want him to take care of our children. Some of them live in bad conditions, and I want my children to get their fair share of their inheritance when I die.

IMMACULÉE'S DAUGHTER CLAUDINE NYIRABAKOBWA

TESTIMONIAL: Kigali, 2018

MY MOTHER NEVER told me about her story of rape. But after she passed away, I read *The Men Who Killed Me*, and came to know what she had to face during the genocide. Only after she died did I take the time to read the book and see what it was about. I was very hurt because I had no idea about the terrible situation that she had endured.

I did not discuss this with anyone, including my older sisters, but I know that my mother had told them about her story. My mother used to share her experiences in the genocide with my sisters because they were older than me. After my sisters moved out of our house, I continued to live with my mother in Kanombe, a quarter in Kigali. My mother would regularly call my sisters and they would stop by the house to visit us.

My mother died in 2010. She had contracted HIV when she was raped during the genocide; this led to the cancer and tuberculosis that caused her death. After her passing, my sisters stopped visiting me, and our family fell apart. My father, who was never involved in my life, died before my mother. I remained on my own in the house where my mother and I had lived together, and that was not easy.

Although my life became more difficult, I was also lucky: despite the horrors my mother had endured, she was always a hardworking woman. Her dream was to improve her children's situation. This is why she acquired two houses from proceeds she received from *The Men Who Killed Me*. Her plan was to give me one and to live in the other house herself. Shortly after my mother died, I moved to the smaller house and rented out the bigger one. This way, I was able to pay for my school fees and become a teacher. In 2011, I even started caring for a seven-year-old orphaned girl, and she stayed with me for five years. My mother always wanted me to finish all my studies and do well in life. She wished that I would never experience what she had. She would always tell me to find what is best for me and to never give up on my dreams.

In 2016, I married my husband and I moved into his home. He has a job, and I take care of our two children. Our son is fourteen months old, and I gave birth to our daughter just one week ago. Now that I am a mother myself, I value my mother even more. As a mother, you experience immense difficulties; giving birth and raising children is not easy. I value my mother because she endured so much pain, almost entirely on her own. My mother used to tell me to spend as much time as possible with my children and to teach them to obey rules, love one another and pray.

When I think about my mother, I get very emotional. I have so many fond memories of her, but I find it difficult to recount them because her death is still too painful for me. What I remember most about my mother is that she was hardworking, and she was so lovely to others. She often visited people and everybody loved her. I resemble her in her kindness.

My mother never had a paying job, so she would use whatever support she received to take care of us. After she shared her story for *The Men Who Killed Me*, my mother received some of the book proceeds that helped to make ends meet. We even used the proceeds of the book to buy my mother's coffin. I hope that the second edition of the book will be as successful as the first, and that our mother's legacy will continue to support us.

FAUSTIN KAYIHURA

BORN: August 1980 (day unknown)
BIRTHPLACE: Muyira sector, Butare

TESTIMONIAL: Kigali, 2008

I DON'T KNOW of any other men who experienced sexual violence during the genocide, but I know they wouldn't talk about it if they had. It was a very difficult experience, and not all men are brave enough to talk about it. It is considered shameful to be raped by a woman. I first spoke about it only in 2007. I don't want Hutu to hear about this, because I don't want to give them the satisfaction. They may ridicule me. I can only share this with other survivors of the genocide.

Before the genocide, we lived in Muyira commune in Butare. We were a happy family of eight—my parents, my four brothers, my sister and me. In 1994 I was only thirteen years old and the youngest of the family. I liked to play soccer. My parents were farmers. We owned cattle and a large expanse of agricultural land, where we grew beans, cassava and peanuts. Although we were not very rich, we were not poor. Our soil was very fertile, and we didn't need to think about buying food at the markets, because we had everything we wanted from our fields. We even had enough to sell at the market.

We had decent relations with our Hutu neighbours. We would invite them to our parties and ask them to help us when we needed it, and they would do the same. Nevertheless, numerous Tutsi had left school because the conditions were horrible. We were continually frustrated, and the teachers would sometimes make us stand so they could humiliate us before the other students. The Hutu children would laugh at us and mock us. Being Hutu seemed to give a person license to be proud and to humiliate everyone who was different, including Tutsi or Twa. There were few Tutsi in primary school, and none in secondary school. We weren't given the opportunity. Our ethnicity was written down in the school files. Because places in schools were given to Hutu children, and Tutsi children were discouraged from studying, many of us abandoned school. Only Hutu were encouraged to go to school. Before the genocide, there were also some killings of the most intelligent Tutsi. I didn't know any of those people personally, but they were well-known Tutsi, such as teachers and important merchants.

By April 6, 1994, killings had already started in Kigali. We only heard about this on April 15, when many Tutsi who were fleeing and passing by our region told us. The genocide started later in our region, because the prefect was Tutsi, and he was able to delay the killings, until he was killed himself. I wasn't with my family at the time the genocide started, because I was watching over our grazing cows. When I returned to our house, I found it empty, and I decided to flee to a Tutsi friend of my father's, who lived near a Catholic church. From his house I could see that our house was on fire. I learned later that, while I was watching the cows, my family and other Tutsi from the region had fled to a commercial centre with shops not FAR from our house, where they spent two days in hiding. The *conseiller*, the head person of the sector, told my family to stay at the centre so that they would not be killed. He actually wanted them to stay so that they could be easily killed, all together. When the Presidential Guards came to Butare, my family overheard them asking the *Interahamwe* why the militia had not started their "work" yet. Soon after, the prefect was killed, and then killings started to happen in Butare.

I spent two days at the house of my father's friend. On the second day, when I saw two buses full of *Interahamwe* coming our way, I decided to leave. While running from the house, I heard people say that many Tutsi from our area, including my family, were still in the commercial centre. The people who told me that were fleeing from the commercial centre; the *Interahamwe* there had stolen their cows and chased these people away.

I decided to hide under some nearby bushes. Some Tutsi were killed close to me, but the *Interahamwe* did not see me. At night, as soon as the *Interahamwe* militia weren't looking, I would change my hiding place, hoping this would prevent them from finding me. After about a week, a Hutu woman found me and took me to her house.

The woman locked me in her house. I was only thirteen, and the horrors I experienced in her house were more than I could endure. She forced me to have sex with her. She raped me three times a day for three days. She made me lie on the floor, and because I did not have any experience with sex, she instructed me on how to do it. She would stroke my penis up and down with her hands first. Because I was still young, I had a hard penis fairly quickly, and then she would force my penis into her vagina. Sometimes she forced me to go on top of her, and sometimes she went on top of me. She was much stronger than I was, and since I was afraid, I did everything she told me to do. She also threatened me, saying that she would call the *Interahamwe* if I did not cooperate and that they would surely kill me. I don't know why she did this to a young boy like me, but she didn't have a husband, and it seemed she saw me as her husband. It was pure cruelty, especially considering my young age.

It seems unbelievable, but it is true. I don't have the words to describe what I was living in those days, but I know that I don't wish it for anyone else, not even my worst enemy. I cried and screamed the entire time. I felt empty. I did not feel anything: no pain, no fear, nothing. I don't recall her saying much to me, but my senses were no longer working. I remember hearing cries and people yelling outside. Somehow I was still alive, and I was thankful for that. During the evening of the fourth day, I told her I had to use the outdoor toilet, and found the courage to escape.

I didn't know where I was going. I only wanted to go far, FAR away, to someplace where I would never see that woman again. I hiked up a nearby mountain called Nyamure. As it turned out, my family and others from the commercial centre had been gathered there for some days, since the *Interahamwe* militia had attacked the commercial centre two days after my family arrived there. I was reunited with my family the day I arrived on the mountain, and we were very happy to see each other again. Because I had thought they were dead, it was a miracle to see my family alive again. We shared what had happened to us, but I didn't tell them about the rapes. They told me that after they left the commercial centre they went back home to bury an old woman. She was the first who had been killed in our region, and my family had heard others say she was hacked to death, so they wanted to give her a decent burial. However, some *Interahamwe* neighbours told them not to do so, because they wanted to feed her to the dogs. My family got frightened and fled to Nyamure mountain.

On the same day that my family and I were reunited, we were attacked by the *Interahamwe*. There were many Tutsi on the mountain—from Gikongoro, Nyanza, Butare and Gitarama—and to protect ourselves we threw stones at any Hutu who tried to climb up. Because of this, the *Interahamwe* could not climb the mountain and fight us, but they shouted that although they hadn't been lucky this time, they would be the next time. I stayed three days on that mountain, and we survived three attacks from the *Interahamwe* each day. On a Sunday night, when it was raining, I fled with some Tutsi from Gikongoro who knew the way to Burundi. The decision to leave felt suicidal, because the mountain had been safe up until then. But the situation we were in was never good, so I decided to follow this large group of Tutsi. Because it was late at night and I couldn't make out who was who, I found out only the next morning that my second brother was in this group, too. The rest of my family had stayed on the mountain.

The day after I left with the others to escape to Burundi, the *Interahamwe*, with fresh support from the police and FAR soldiers, attacked the mountain. The Tutsi who remained behind were no longer able to fight them, as the attackers had brought guns and grenades. The *Interahamwe* killed whomever they could lay their hands on. Those who were not killed immediately, but were severely wounded and unable to move, were finished off later with machetes. My family and others died during this attack. After the genocide I found their remains still on the mountain.

With the group of people who knew the way to Burundi, I fled towards the Kanyaru River, which forms the border between Rwanda and Burundi. For almost our entire journey, we were followed by *Interahamwe* militia. At some point we ran into a roadblock manned by *Interahamwe*. In our panic, one part of the group ran in the direction of the main road, and the other towards the sorghum fields. Only the latter group, of which I was a part, survived. We ran for about six hours. Eventually, the *Interahamwe* abandoned their pursuit of us. After we reached the sorghum fields, we walked through rice fields in the water and long grass, so the *Interahamwe*'s dogs were no longer able to track us.

When we arrived at the Kanyaru River, a Hutu man saw us. While pretending to help us find a boat to cross the river, he went looking for *Interahamwe* to kill us. Many of the Tutsi tried to get across the river by tying women's clothes together and forming a cord, but it was still very difficult to cross. There were many Tutsi corpses floating down the river, and that made it almost impossible to reach the other side.

Some people committed suicide by throwing themselves in the river the moment a group of *Interahamwe* arrived. They preferred to drown rather than be chopped to pieces by the *Interahamwe*. I didn't know how to swim either, but some of us were able to ask for help from some Burundian soldiers positioned on the other shore. The soldiers tied a cord around a tree on the Burundian side of the river, then crossed the river and tied the cord around a tree on the Rwandan side. I managed to save myself by holding onto this cord while crossing the river. I was so grateful to God for allowing me to make it across safely. My second brother survived in the same manner. Hundreds of Tutsi had left Nyamure mountain; only forty-seven of us survived.

The local authorities in Burundi took us to a Catholic church where about a thousand Rwandans had sought refuge. We stayed there for about a month and were given some food. At the end of that month, a white woman arrived with some big trucks. She wanted to take us to a camp called Bunyari, near the border with Tanzania. I think she wanted to kill us, though, because that camp was full of *Interahamwe*. We all refused, and she got very angry. She kept pressuring us to go with her. Instead, we left the church and went to the main camp in Burundi, called Kiyonza, which had been set up by Tutsi survivors. We stayed there for a week, until the end of the genocide in Rwanda in late June. After that the *Inkotanyi* arrived and helped take us back to Rwanda.

Before returning to my birthplace of Muyira, I stayed for over a month in a refugee camp in Bugesera, because Muyira was not yet under the control of the RPF. When I was finally able to walk back home, I met my former neighbours again. Some of them must have participated in the killings, but I wasn't afraid.

Of my eight family members, the only one who survived the genocide was the brother who had crossed the river with me. He did not join me in Bugesera after we left Burundi, but instead joined the RPF in Ruhengeri, because he wanted to do something good for his fellow Tutsi and his country. After all that had happened, he no longer felt safe and comfortable in his birthplace.

After I returned, I learned that one of my other brothers had died on the first day of my family's stay at the commercial centre. Apparently, he had gone back to our house to collect our cows, and a little while later, the wife of another one of my brothers and her two daughters saw him writhing on the ground. A militiaman pointed out the body to them because he knew they were related. The militiaman killed my sister-in-law, but her two daughters managed to escape, and they were the ones who told me all this later.

After the genocide, I tried to continue my secondary school education. It was very difficult because I constantly saw visions of the woman who had raped me. I know she died, but I don't know how. In my fifth year of secondary school, I decided to stop going. I was living in a boarding school and felt very lonely. I was thinking more about our house and about how to cultivate the land to have something to eat. I am now cultivating the land, and I live in a house that I built all by myself.

I hated myself for a long time. I hated my life and wanted it to end. I am so thankful that I have now found people who care for me. They rescued me. They helped me to rebuild my house after the roof was destroyed by heavy rainfall. I also met women who showed an interest in me, who listened to me and wanted to know me. For some time, I hated all women and did not want to see them, but I am now healing. Now I have seen the other side of women and human beings in general, the good side that I had not known since 1994.

What I hear in *gacaca* court is unbearable, though. For example, in one of the trials, I heard that my aunt's arm was chopped off and that she was forced to eat it. After she did this, they killed her. Although I still testify, I find it harder and harder to do so. The perpetrators plead guilty and get released quickly, and they start killing again. Personally, I have not received any threats or intimidation. Not yet; it might just be a matter of time. Even though the government is pushing us to testify for unity and reconciliation purposes, it is very difficult for us, the survivors of the genocide.

I would like to study again, but I am afraid I may not be able to do so, because it has been such a long time since I was at school. I would also like to start my own business, maybe a shop where I could sell things like clothes, soap and body lotion. My house is still not strong enough and could fall apart any time heavy rain falls. I wish that someone could help me with this. I live all alone, which I find very difficult. Maybe someday I will get married, but I want to live in better conditions first.

FAUSTIN KAYIHURA

TESTIMONIAL: Kigali, 2018

OVER THE PAST decade, my life changed in ways that I could not have predicted. After I began to see the good in women again, I decided to get married. My wife grew up in the same area as me; we used to be neighbours and friends. It was at one of the meetings at Solace Ministries that we started to develop feelings for each other. We were both living alone at the time, as we had lost most of our relatives in the genocide. As survivors, we had a similar history and we understood each other well; we shared death. So we decided to continue our lives together. We fell in love, and when I asked her to marry me, she happily agreed. I love my wife's kindness and her caring heart. She is so beautiful. We do not have conflicts at home; we respect each other deeply.

After I shared my testimonial in 2008, I started studying again for a while, but had to quit because it became too difficult to work my land at the same time. My big wish was for us to raise a large family, just like my father had done. After losing so many loved ones in the genocide, I was also afraid of remaining alone in the world. My wife felt the same way, and now we have five children. Not having children would have hurt us even more than our experiences during the genocide. It feels so good to have a big family. Nothing makes me happier than coming home and hearing my children call us "Mama" and "Papa".

We are all doing well, except that my wife has a kidney problem. Also, she still suffers from frequent headaches because of the beatings that she endured during the genocide. But we have medical insurance, and I believe we will be fine. Although we would receive better treatment at a private hospital, we can go to the public hospital and get medication whenever one of us is sick.

My parents always told us to make sure that we have enough food because life is difficult when you have nothing to eat. When I was growing up, we had milk from our cows and we had beans and cassava. I have tried my best to be a hardworking man so that we have enough to eat, and so FAR I have been successful.

Years ago, when I first started receiving financial support, I did not spend it very well. At the time, I was still traumatized and did not even have hope for a tomorrow. I only managed to keep myself fed. But now, with the support of the government, Solace Ministries and Mukomeze, I have been more thoughtful about how I invest the money, and come up with new ideas about how to make good use of the support in order to have a strong, bright future. At home, we have food and everything else that we need. We bought land, and sometimes I pay my neighbours to work on our land. We have two cows. We have electricity in the house. And I still have many plans.

Although the house we live in now is our own, I do not like it. I would like to build small market stalls or "boutiques" on our plot of land that can be used for business. Since our land is next to the road, it is a good place for business. I am thinking of selling rice and salt because these are the things that we lack in our area. My wife could run the businesses and I could do some other work.

I would also like to build a nicer house for us, in the same area where we live now. Our area is nice and secure, and I feel that we can continue to get along with our neighbours. I am happy that I can help my neighbours by giving them food, despite the crimes they committed against us in 1994. And our children play together. Sometimes they come to our home and we eat together. Ten years ago, I would never meet and discuss anything with my neighbours. Now, I can ask them to work for me on my land, and I feel very happy if they agree. Whenever I have a problem, they help me, and I also help them when they are in need. When we have a party, we share everything.

Despite all the progress that our country has made over the years, genocide survivors of sexual violence definitely continue to experience stigma. Sometimes we are re-traumatized. We do not live side-by-side with people who murdered our loved ones and tried to kill us because we love them or because they love us. It is because of our children; we need to make sure that our children can live happily together. We try to ensure that the genocide does not have a lasting impact on our children. Of course, we do not know what is truly in the hearts of those who committed crimes; maybe they did not change that much after all. As survivors, we must share our own testimonials so as to protect our future and the future of our children. There is no need to hide our stories, because it is the truth; the *génocidaires* did what they did and people should know about it.

I am glad that *The Men Who Killed Me* was published. This way, people who read the book learn more about what happened to us during the genocide. By telling our stories, we found people who supported us. I also came to realize that I am not the only man who experienced sexual violence. Other genocide survivors have read my story and had similar experiences, and when we started sharing what we endured, we became friends. Despite all the positive developments that followed the book, here in Rwanda, I also felt the sting of stigma: some Rwandans abroad read the book, and when they returned home they questioned whether this really happened to me. Children in the neighbourhood who come to our house also read the book and ask about it. Although I tell them the truth, I would still prefer it if only people outside Rwanda read the book, because it is difficult for me to talk about this with our neighbours.

Although many people know about my story now, I do not wish to tell my children yet; they are still young and they play together with the children of the *génocidaires*. I worry that when I tell my children, they might start hating their neighbours. I will try to tell them my story, or a part of it, when they are older.

Although I have not shared my story with my children, I do not hide from them the realities of Rwanda's history. During the genocide commemoration period from April until June, I always take my oldest children with me to the memorial site. They hear testimonials from genocide survivors there, and they become curious and wish to know more about the genocide. They hear the names of our murdered family members, and they always ask me about it: "Those people who killed our family members, where are they?" But I cannot explain the whole story yet, so I just tell them that a genocide took place in Rwanda and people killed us. I tell them that we are at the memorial site to remember our loved ones. That is enough of an explanation for now.

As they grow older, my children are becoming more curious. They always like to ask my wife and me about our parents. They see other children who still have their grandparents, and wonder about their own grandparents. It is very upsetting, and I find it harder and harder to respond. Those people who killed during the genocide have been released from prison, and sometimes they pass by our house and say, "Oh we are sorry, we ask for forgiveness for killing your mother and your brother." When my children hear this they ask, "Are you the one who killed my grandmother and my uncle?" As much as I try to protect my children from the legacy of the genocide, they are affected by its aftermath. It is very hard; the *génocidaires* still have their families, and their children can visit their aunties and uncles. But my children are at home, with no other family to visit. And it hurts to remember how big our family used to be. But there is nothing we can say. The grief remains in our hearts.

When my children ask about their family, my wife and I tell them that they still have family members from outside Rwanda: *Abazungu*. We tell them that they love us, and sometimes send us money and pictures. I always tell them, "Do you see other families who have aunties and uncles from around the world? We must be very special." Then they ask me, "But why do they not come to visit us?" So I show them pictures of their aunties and uncles, and when they are surprised that they are *Abazungu*, I joke with them that we share the same mother. I tell them they will visit us soon. The children are very happy to hear this, and they tell all the neighbours that they have aunties and uncles from around the world and that they are coming soon. It makes me smile just talking about this. I am so very touched by the love we receive from our extended family. It is very comforting to have people from abroad think about us, visit us, and ask us how we are doing.

Sometimes, the neighbours come to our house and ask for forgiveness, seeking to reconcile with us. We feel that, in a way, we cannot blame them for what they did; instead, we blame the government at the time that encouraged them to execute the genocide. Of course, we must forgive, because we cannot simply live with bushes; we must live with people. But it is very difficult for us survivors. I remember during one commemoration a man stood up and said: "I killed your older brother," and he asked for forgiveness and also showed us the area where he murdered him. He also said that he took all of our cows. Before we found this out, I had worked with this man. Hearing the *génocidaires'* testimonials is re-traumatizing survivors; some go to the hospital to get counselling. Survivors find the commemoration periods extremely difficult, but there is nothing we can do other than forgive.

Over the past decade, I have noticed real changes in my mental health. Over the years, I have grown close with other survivors; we share our stories and we find that we are one family. We find changes in ourselves, and it feels good when we are together. It helps to be open with others and for others to be open with you. It feels good when you have money, and you even have enough to give it to someone else in need.

When I feel triggered or re-traumatized, other genocide survivors, including Mama Lambert, help me. Most of them knew my father, and they always tell me to be strong like him. Nowadays, I rarely feel triggered. I am usually the one who counsels others. My wife is more traumatized than me. I always support her by telling her that she should not worry and that I am with her. Even though it is very hard, I tell her that we had better focus on today and be happy.

Although my mental health has generally stabilized, I had a very traumatizing experience in 2014. That year, I spent a few months in prison. Some of my cousins wanted to take my land. I had worked very hard and our family was doing well. They were jealous and I got into a serious fight with them. In the end, I was released from jail because I explained the whole story in court, and I could not be blamed for the fight. But the experience in prison was very hard. It was good that I had had counselling beforehand, because otherwise I think I would have died in prison. I was there together with *génocidaires*. Those prisoners said that Tutsi are now starting to imprison other Tutsi; that now we have conflicts among ourselves. They also believed that I was in prison to find out more about them. But because they were taught by the government not to say or do bad things, they did not hurt me. I just kept quiet and showed them that I had no problem with them. I knew they would not hurt me since I had my Solace and Mukomeze family members supporting me. The other prisoners even knew me by my nickname *Girinka*, meaning "the one who has cows." When they saw me in prison they said, "The one who has cows has come." Luckily, I was moved to another part of the prison so that I was no longer locked up with those *génocidaires*.

I can also say that over the past ten years, I have made progress in restoring a sense of justice in my heart. When I look back on *gacaca*, I can say it was very good because it brought us reconciliation and harmony. Now we share food and our children go to the same schools. It was very difficult to go to the *gacaca* courts and to hear all the things the killers had done to our loved ones. But because of *gacaca*, the killers were imprisoned and released only after serving their sentences. Perpetrators confessed what they had done and promised not to repeat their crimes. Through the *gacaca* process, we could find out who was guilty and innocent, and those who were wrongfully imprisoned were released. The most important thing is that we must forgive. Without *gacaca*, I do not know what would have come of Rwanda.

As for the woman who raped me during the genocide, all I know is that she died during the liberation war. So I could not accuse her in the *gacaca* court. Although she raped me, I feel that I was still blessed because she gave me food and a place to hide, which may have ultimately saved me. I wanted to find her, because I wanted to thank her. Despite the sexual violence she committed against me, I survived the genocide because of her.

When I think of my children and their future, I want to advise them to live happily with others, no matter their background. The reason I am still alive today is because of the way my father used to live; he lived together with Hutu in harmony. Wherever I go, people tell me that they knew my father and that they loved him.

I am happy to know that I inspired other men to talk openly about their own experiences of sexual violence. I know one man who started to speak with Mama Lambert about the sexual violence he suffered during the genocide because he had found out about my testimonial. I am glad that I have been able to tell the truth in order to give value to what happened to me, and that people respect me for that. It is a blessing to have a family within Solace Ministries and Mukomeze, where there is room to openly discuss what I endured; I think of them as my parents. I would like to advise other genocide survivors to face their past, to love each other, and to work hard. Only then can we have a bright future.

FRANÇOISE MUKESHIMANA

BORN: 1968 (date and month unknown)
BIRTHPLACE: Bugesera
DIED: June 2014

TESTIMONIAL: Kigali, 2008

EVERY TIME THE annual mourning period for the genocide approaches in April, I feel a terrible pain in my head and in my womb. I go to the toilet every five minutes and I feel really horrible inside. When people counsel me, I feel the pain disappearing, little by little. I have been comforted by meeting new people, some of whom have become my sisters, brothers and children. Yet I do not feel like living in my community. I just want to live alone, on my own, and have nothing to do with other people—especially Hutu.

My family is originally from Gikongoro, in the south of Rwanda. My father told me that in 1959 my grandparents were forced by the colonial regime to move to Bugesera, just south of the capital, Kigali. The regime wanted to expel Tutsi from nicer areas like Gikongoro. In 1973, Hutu killed my grandparents. That was the year of the *coup d'etat*, and many Tutsi were killed. My grandparents were not spared, because everyone in Bugesera knew they were Tutsi.

My mother died when I was still very young. My father was a farmer, and I grew up with six brothers and sisters. I spent my childhood helping my father farm, because he could not afford to continue sending me to school. He could only afford to send my older brother to university, because he was the cleverest of the children. The community I lived in was mixed, with mostly Tutsi and some Hutu. While Hutu were the minority, we got along easily with them, because quite a few Hutu men married Tutsi women.

That all changed in 1990. Between 1990 and 1992, the *Interahamwe* killed Tutsi boys from Bugesera after the boys were accused of hiding suspected RPF spies. Many of the boys didn't even know that the term cockroaches referred to people. Tutsi boys who were not killed were forced to flee the country in order to escape death. I remember that my older brother returned from university sometime in late 1993 and told our father that Hutu would soon be killing Tutsi. He said that the best thing to do was flee to Burundi until the crisis was over. My brother went to university in Butare, and his Tutsi classmates had joined the RPF, so he had a strong sense that something bad was about to happen.

My father wasn't sure how much of that was true, so he decided to stay in Bugesera. He just didn't believe mass killing would occur. Instead, we left our house periodically and hid in bushes close to our home. At the time, Tutsi houses were being burned by Hutu, and we didn't want to risk being burned in our own house. From June 1993 until the beginning of the genocide, we stayed in the bushes and returned to our house only to pick up food.

I remember that, when the genocide began in 1994, a bus full of FAR soldiers in uniform arrived in our neighbourhood, and one of the soldiers asked people why they had not started killing Tutsi and slaughtering our cows. No one said anything, so the bus continued on its way. Nearby, three young Tutsi men were walking along the street. When the bus got close to them, the boys ran, and a soldier ordered an *Interahamwe* to kill them. The *Interahamwe* ran after the boys and killed one of them with a machete. That boy was the first person to be killed in Bugesera during the genocide, and many more followed his fate.

One of the first things the *Interahamwe* militia did during the genocide was to remove all the boats from the Akanyaru River, which led to Burundi, preventing any means for escape. After the death of that young man, our family started to hide in bushes that were farther from our house. The *Interahamwe* were hunting Tutsi with dogs by then, and they found our hiding place in the bushes three days later. That is when they killed my brother-in-law and five of my brothers and sisters. I don't know how they were killed, but when I fled from the bushes where I was hiding, I saw their bodies lying on the street.

My remaining brother, my father and I managed to escape, and we went to the home of a Hutu man in Bugesera to whom my father had given a cow. The man showed us to a hiding place outside his house, on his banana plantation. But the next day he told the *Interahamwe* where we were hiding, so they came and captured us. They forced us to go to their favourite bar in Bugesera, all the while saying it no longer mattered that our father had given most of them cows, because we were Tutsi snakes.

They ordered my brother to dig his own grave outside the bar. When he was in the middle of doing that, they ordered him to lie down in the grave to see if it would fit him. My father couldn't bear to see what was happening, and he begged to be killed by the *Interahamwe* or to be let go. They let him go.

My father went to a roadblock and asked the *Interahamwe* there to kill him. The *Interahamwe* said he was a snake, and with their machetes they cut him on the neck and legs. My father, who was a tall man, was forced to go down on his knees. That was the *Interahamwe*'s way of cutting him down. My father died at that roadblock. We could see all of this, because the roadblock was not FAR from where we were.

Back at the grave, the *Interahamwe* hit my brother with a huge club and told him to look at his sister for the last time. As he looked at me, he begged them to kill me first, because he feared that I would die of pain. Instead, they continued to bash him, until he died looking into my eyes.

The *Interahamwe* then proceeded to discuss how they would kill me. One of them argued that it would be a great mistake if they killed me without humiliating me first. He said that they should strip me naked and do to me all that they wanted, in order to tell others that they had been thorough in carrying out their "work." I was nothing but an instrument of gratification for them. The men ordered me to undress, and I could do nothing but obey. After that, they asked me if I still refused to have sex with them. Tears burned my eyes, and I started weeping. They laughed at me, saying that there was no one left to hear my cries and no one to stand with me. They ordered me to lie down, and a man I had refused to date before the genocide raped me first. Before he raped me, he said I now had no choice but to accept him. After he was finished, another raped me, and another and another, until I did not have the courage to keep count.

These men were so sadistic that they tried to cut my vagina into two parts with a sword in order to share me. I still have the deep scars on my pelvis today. I was bleeding so profusely that the next man about to rape me did not do it, saying that I was disgusting. All of this happened during the daytime, in front of the bar. Many *Interahamwe* were watching, dancing and laughing at me. The whole time, I felt nothing. I thought I was going to die. An old man passed by when they were about to kill me and quoted a Rwandan saying: "If you drink of a cow's milk, you cannot kill it." He added that if they killed me after raping me, my blood would always remain on their hands. Rather, they should leave me there and let me die by other hands.

Despite my wound, I managed to put some of my clothes back on and flee to the area under a bridge not too FAR away. I stayed there because it was a good hiding place. I knew that some traditional herbs growing among the bushes would help my wound to heal, so I left my spot under the bridge every night to find herbs to rub onto my wound. I ate nothing the entire time. Because I ate and drank nothing, whenever I went to sleep I thought I would not wake up again. I was always surprised when my eyes opened.

After three weeks, I heard some people walking on the bridge say that the RPF had rescued them. I decided to walk out into the light of the day, something that I had almost forgotten about doing. I saw two children on the bridge, and they saw me. They were frightened by my appearance and started to run away, but I gestured to them and they came back. They helped take me to a camp that the RPF had established. When I met the RPF in the camp, I was not recognizable. I was very dirty, with blood all over my body and my clothing in rags.

The RPF took all survivors to a camp called Kamabuye in Bugesera, about a twenty-minute walk away. There I met an older Hutu man whose Tutsi wife had been killed during the genocide. We stayed in the camp for three months. I left the camp with that man, and we went to Muyira commune in Butare. He proposed to me there. I agreed to marry him, but the marriage was not a happy one because his children, who were my age, still lived with him and they hated me.

When I first got pregnant and found out that I was HIV positive, I told my husband what had happened to me during the genocide. He comforted me and was supportive throughout the pregnancy. If not for the fact that I didn't get along with his children, I would have stayed with him. But they used to tell me I didn't have any right to live in their mother's house. After twelve years of marriage, his children continued to drive me crazy, so I left my husband after the birth of our third child.

My two oldest children were not infected with HIV. I'm not sure about the youngest, because he has not been tested. I live with all three of my children, and my ex-husband and I are still on good terms. Even now, he comes to see me and comfort me.

When I first separated from my husband, I didn't have a place to live. A Hutu man offered me accommodation in a room outside his house, in exchange for my help in cultivating his land. I cultivate for him once a week.

I don't like this man, and the fact that he is a Hutu doesn't make it any better. But I must work for him, because I need a place to live. The farm work has been really challenging because of my HIV status. I am constantly ill and weak. Cultivating is really hard. If I want to survive, though, I must ignore my condition and work. Fortunately, since I started taking my antiretroviral medication, my health is improving.

I have not forgiven the *Interahamwe*. Those who wronged me did not face justice, and I cannot go to the *gacaca* courts as long as they are still free, because I am afraid the *Interahamwe* will kill me. Those who have been in prison since the genocide are being released and are shopping at the same market as we do. They should be sent back to prison and stay there for the rest of their lives or, better, be killed as they killed our people.

Knowing that there is someone who cares enough to listen to my experiences really comforts me. Now that I am talking about my experience with other survivors of the genocide, I know that I will feel better.

FRANÇOISE'S SON MUSAFIRI NIYOMUGABO

TESTIMONIAL: Kigali, 2018

My mother passed away four years ago in 2014, when I was sixteen. I was not yet born in 1994, but I continue to endure the legacy of her experiences during the genocide. My mother died of AIDS-related illnesses after contracting HIV during the genocide, and now I am responsible for our family. I am doing what my mother would have done, and what she would have wanted me to do. My brother also faces the consequences of our mother's past: he was infected with HIV during childbirth, and he is now fighting for his life. I am left struggling for the whole family. Describing my mother and my life is not easy.

I live in Muyira, in the countryside, in a small house that I rent. My eighty-year-old father and younger sister and brother live in another house close by. Our mother was forty-six years old when she passed away. She had a severely swollen stomach and there was nothing that could be done for it. I miss her so much. People tell me that I have the same character as my mother, and that I look like her. They say I have her smile. She is always with me in spirit.

We live in very difficult circumstances. Our father is very old and sick. Like my mother, he is living with HIV, but he contracted the virus prior to the genocide. He cannot do anything on his own, so I must care for him. While she was alive, my mother was the one who was strong enough to dig the fields so that we had cassava, beans and peanuts to eat. Now this task has also fallen to me, and there is no one else to get this done. Besides digging the fields and caring for my father and siblings, I also try to find part-time work so that I can earn some income. But my strength is limited, and what I do to support my family is just not enough.

After my mother's passing, I had to drop out of school to find ways to support all of us. At the time, I had only finished my fourth year in primary school. My sister also had to stop going to school when she reached her sixth year in primary school. We simply do not have the money to support her education. As I said, my younger brother is living with HIV, and he is very sick. Since we live in hard conditions and do not have medical insurance, he is not getting proper treatment and we cannot afford to take him to the hospital.

My mother did so much for me. She taught me to be a good person and to value people. She taught me not to be wasteful. When my mother was still alive, she regularly visited Solace Ministries, and she always told us that in this place we had a family. She told us that whatever happens, we would always find love at Solace Ministries. She used to say, "Solace Ministries is my family. Please remember to follow my footsteps there." One day my mother brought me there, and she said, "Let me show you my family." Since then, I have continued to visit Solace Ministries, and I always feel comforted by seeing and speaking with other genocide survivors.

My mother had a good plan for us for the future. She always thought about what would be best for her children. She never wasted the little money she earned. She spent it on us, to build us a better future. I remember that even on the day she died, she bought a piece of land to build a house for us. We still have the land; it is on the main road, near our house.

Living in our difficult circumstances now, I do not see a future for us. I struggle just to make ends meet. When I was younger, I used to envision a promising future ahead of me. I had a dream of buying a motorbike so that I could make a living by transporting people. I even acquired the license to ride it. But now, with my mother gone, everything seems to have changed.

One day, my mother showed me the book, *The Men Who Killed Me*, and I saw her picture in it. Because I am the first-born in our family, my mother would always tell me everything. But she did not tell me much about the book, except that she had been raped and that is how she got HIV. She said that she shared her story for my siblings and me. Learning about what had happened to my mother was very difficult. I was hurt. I felt that there was nothing I could say to her. But I hope that her story will help to build a better future for my family, and for all of us in Rwanda.

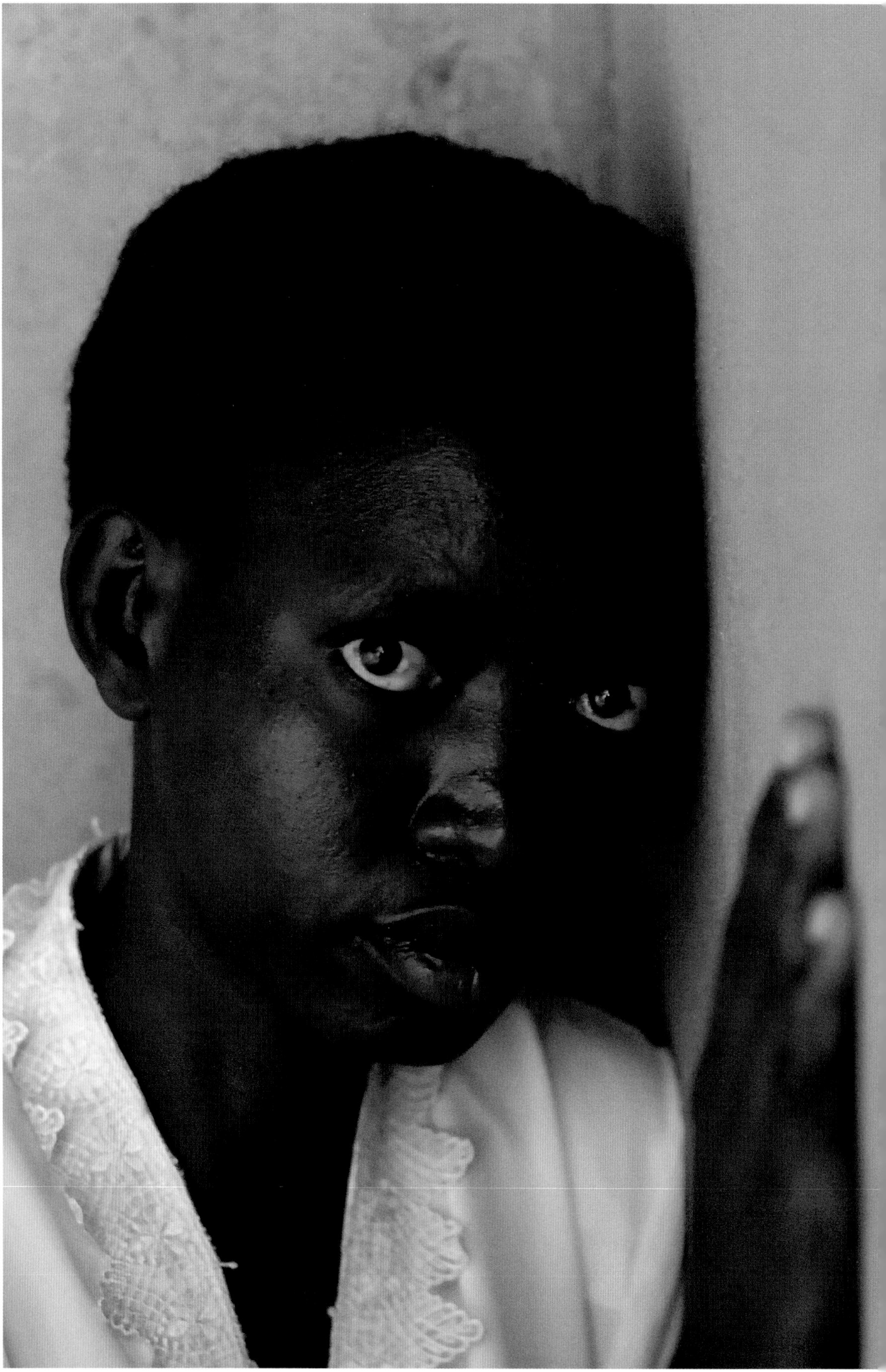

GLORIOSE MUSHIMIYIMANA

BORN: July 8, 1975
BIRTHPLACE: Gitarama

TESTIMONIAL: Kigali, 2008

IT WOULD BE a lie if I said that I can forgive the *Interahamwe*. I will never testify at the *gacaca* courts, because my sister was beaten on her way home from the *gacaca* court where she appeared as a witness. She had testified against our former neighbours and accused them of destroying our house and taking our possessions. Survivors of the genocide are living in terrible conditions, and those who make the mistake of testifying have been beaten or stoned. Even though we report the violence to the authorities, there is no change. The perpetrators should receive the punishment they deserve.

When I was growing up in Muhanga, Gitarama Prefecture, in central Rwanda, I lived in great harmony in a community full of Tutsi. We didn't have any Hutu neighbours. However, my primary school teacher was the *bourgmestre*'s wife and a Hutu. She was awfully cruel to Tutsi children. Nothing I could do would please her. She would beat us Tutsi without reason, call us snakes and ask us what Tutsi were doing among human beings. One day, she beat me until my dress was torn, just because I arrived at school a little late. I felt a lot of anger towards her and wanted to hit her back, but I also hated myself, because nothing I could do would make my teacher happy. In those days, I liked to sew clothes and do handicrafts.

In 1983, when I was eight years old, I had stomach problems caused by the poverty we were living in. My mother took me to the hospital at Kabgayi, about three hours away from our house. People there stared at my mother, whispering to each other that she must be King Musinga's granddaughter. My mother was very tall and beautiful, just like members of the king's family, but she was not related to him. Since she resembled the Tutsi king, though, others did not want to talk to us.

When I was growing up, my mother was always ill. Her legs were swollen, and she needed expensive medical treatment. Because my father couldn't afford my school fees in addition to my mother's treatment, I didn't have the chance to go to secondary school. That made me very sad, because I had always wanted to become a doctor or a teacher. My mother died in 1988. I was only thirteen.

A year later, I was surprised to hear that my father was going to marry a Hutu woman. It was so soon after my mother had died. This woman didn't love us, and she treated us badly. She gave my older sister, my older brother and me so many household chores to do that I was again prevented from going to school. After only one year, the woman left my father, taking all his possessions with her.

In 1990, a multi-party system was introduced in Rwanda. Many Hutu joined political parties and started stockpiling all kinds of weapons, especially machetes. Starting that year, we could not walk safely in the streets, and many of my friends also stopped going to school. In the bars and on the streets you could hear Hutu making speeches in which they proclaimed that the last hour of the Tutsi was very near. We were afraid that something bad was being planned. Back then, we had a Belgian priest named Michel, and, by the end of 1993, he was warning my father about a possible genocide. In the coming months, Hutu started burning houses and taking Tutsi possessions. In April 1994, we heard that the president had gone to Tanzania. There were whispers in the community that he had gone there to recruit more soldiers to help kill Tutsi in Rwanda.

Fearing for our lives, we fled our home on April 4. Our priest, Michel, drove my sister, my father and me to a stadium in Gitarama, near Kabgayi. Michel had planned only to rescue old women and children using his car, but my father happened to be nearby, so he took the last space in Michel's vehicle.

My brother walked to the stadium with my cousin. Along the way, the *Interahamwe* found them. They slit my brother's neck with machetes and beat him with a nailed club. My cousin fled to the stadium, and he told me later how my brother had been killed. Michel dropped us off at the stadium and drove away without realizing that the *Interahamwe* were actually killing people in there, even before the president's plane had crashed. They started killing the men first. They stabbed my father with knives and beat him with a nailed

club. I witnessed the *Interahamwe* beat him on the head with the club and then leave him on the streets for the dogs and vultures to eat.

On the day the president died, April 6, we heard screams, babies crying, and the *Interahamwe* shouting that they would kill all Tutsi, without sparing women, babies or the unborn. My older sister, my aunts, my cousins and I either hid in the toilets in the stadium or pretended to be dead by lying under corpses. Women and girls were being raped outside the stadium, including one of my aunts and three of my cousins. They were all killed afterwards. The *Interahamwe* would return to the stadium to brag about their crimes after committing them. None of my aunts survived their stay in the stadium in the end. I felt so afraid; my mind was no longer working.

Two days later, a new group of *Interahamwe* militia came to the stadium. They continued to separate the men from the women, so that the men could be killed and the women could be beaten. Some of the women died from the beatings, and others were severely wounded. I remember a little girl named Sandrine, who begged the *Interahamwe* to stop killing us. They responded by saying that the God who would have saved us was frightened and left the country when the president died.

I saw girls and women disappear day by day. We all knew that they were killed after being raped. We knew because the *Interahamwe* said they were looking for other women and girls to rape and kill. My sister and I were spared because we were still too young. After a few days, there were only girls and young women among us. One night a priest from Kabgayi came to the stadium and took my sister, my cousins, some other children and me to a classroom located in a priests' compound. There we hoped to be safe. The priest had friends among the *Interahamwe*, and he had bribed them with beer for our security. He went a second time, to collect the remaining children at the stadium, but that time his car was stopped, and he had to leave those children behind.

We were fed at the priests' compound, but there wasn't enough food for all of us. Four days after we arrived, the *Interahamwe* came to search the compound. The militia weren't singling out the priests; they were searching everybody's houses. They saw that some pieces of the ceiling were missing and they realized that young men were hiding there. The militia summoned the men to come down. When they did, the *Interahamwe* hacked off their legs and arms and then plunged swords into their chests. The priests had all fled and hidden by then, because their lives were at risk for protecting us.

Later that evening, the *Interahamwe* returned to pick up young girls to rape, even girls no more than thirteen years old, because they had killed all the older girls and women earlier that day. One *Interahamwe* approached me and asked me to choose between life and death. I couldn't answer him, so he tore my clothes off and ordered me to lie down. When I refused, one of the other militiamen hit me on the back with a nailed club. I fell and was bleeding heavily. This disgusted the *Interahamwe* who had wanted to rape me, so he left me there.

More *Interahamwe* returned to the compound the next day. After ripping our clothes to pieces, they took seven girls, including my older sister and me, to a small classroom in the compound. There were six of them, and they spent three hours raping us, without taking a break of even five minutes. After all six had finished raping us, they left, saying that their "work" was calling. We all lay where we were because we were so weak. I felt a lot of anger and wanted to die.

When the *Interahamwe* returned later that night, we were still in the classroom, lying down. They spent the rest of the night raping us, and from that day on, being raped by six different men a day became our routine. The *Interahamwe* hardly spoke to us, except when they ordered us to come to them in order to be raped. We had to go through these horrors for one week. We were too weak to escape that place; we could barely get up on our feet. Hunger killed several of the girls who were in that room. Only four of us survived.

Some soldiers came into the classroom on June 2. They didn't look like the *Interahamwe* we were used to seeing. They were very kind and gentle, and we eventually realized that they were the *Inkotanyi*. They brought us clothes to wear, because we were still naked, and fed us little by little. The *Inkotanyi* carried those of us who could not walk and took us to a Catholic church where local people were bringing water to the wounded. Sadly, five of the people who drank that water died immediately, because it was purposely contaminated by Hutu. The *Inkotanyi* moved us to Bugesera, where we remained until the end of the genocide.

I survived, as did my older sister, but the rest of my immediate family perished in the genocide. My sister and I returned together to Gitarama, but we found that nothing was left. We no longer had a house or a plantation. I went to Kigali to live with my surviving cousin, but it was difficult for me there, because he used to visit me at night and rape me. He threatened me whenever I was about to tell his wife about the abuse, so I chose to leave his home. I wandered all around Nyamirambo, a quarter in Kigali, spending the night under bridges or anywhere else. During that time, I would beg for food or do odd jobs, like washing clothes, for money. I hated myself. I felt worthless as a human being, since people just did whatever they wanted to do with me.

One day in 1999, I was sitting by the road when a stranger approached me. I had seen him walking the streets before. He asked me what I was doing on the streets, and he offered to let me spend the night at his house so that I could have at least one night of decent sleep. I accepted his offer, as I had no better opportunities. When we arrived at his house, though, he locked the door and said I had no alternative but to have sex with him. He raped me that night. The next day, telling him I had to use the outdoor toilet, I escaped.

I became pregnant from that rape, and I found an abandoned house in which to spend my days and nights. People feared me because they thought I was insane. I looked dirty, wore torn clothes and was living in an abandoned house surrounded by bushes. I didn't really care what they thought, since I felt I no longer needed human contact. Eventually I went to the hospital, where I gave birth to a boy named Mugisha in 2000. Someone I didn't know paid my hospital fees.

When Mugisha was born, I didn't like him at first. But I learned to love him. I haven't seen his father since he raped me. After Mugisha was born, a Tutsi man named Damien, a survivor whose leg had been cut off during the genocide, felt compassion for me and let me live in his outdoor kitchen. With him, I had a boy named Oscar in 2003.

I didn't love Damien, but I felt that unless I slept with him he would evict me from his kitchen. One day, when Damien was away, his sister came to the house and was very cruel to me. She didn't like the fact that I was living in Damien's kitchen and had had his child, so she started beating me. I left the place. Although Damien was not really interested in finding me, he tried to locate me because of his son. We are no longer in contact, but he still tries to support his son as well as he can. Because he is a survivor of the genocide, he is not a wealthy man.

I am HIV positive as a consequence of the rapes I endured during the genocide, or perhaps those I experienced after the genocide was over; I don't know. I am receiving treatment, and luckily my two children are HIV negative. The community in which I live has rejected me because I am HIV positive. They suspect the nature of my condition, because I am always sick and going to the hospital. I don't know where else to go. I can't expect any help from my neighbours, as I have no friends or relatives among them. I suffer from headaches and back pain as a result of what happened to me during the genocide. Since my parents died, I no longer feel happiness.

My church has provided me with some rent for the house I live in and school fees for my children. I hope that one day I may have a house of my own, where I could live with my surviving sister and another cousin. My sister lives with a friend now, and I am required to live in a house with friends, too, some of whom are also survivors of the genocide, because the church pays the rent for all of us.

I hope that my testimony will be proof of what happened in Rwanda. Some people deny this part of our history, but it is a reality they must face. I hope that some of those who read this testimony will help genocide survivors, because we urgently need help.

GLORIOSE MUSHIMIYIMANA

TESTIMONIAL: Kigali, 2018

RIGHT AFTER THE genocide, people who saw me walking on the streets used to tell me that I was crazy. But I was not crazy; the life I was living was merely the result of the genocide. I had no one to take care of me. My most difficult moments were when I could not offer my children anything to eat. Those were the times when I felt that I had lost everything. But I am so thankful to God for my new family at Solace Ministries, where the staff counselled me, regularly visited me, gave me food to eat, and checked to make sure I was taking my HIV medication. If it was not for Solace Ministries, I would not be alive today.

Since 2008, my life has changed considerably. With the support I received from non-governmental organizations, I was able to rent a nicer home. Previously, I was living in a house without windows and doors. I have a small business and a bank account. I am so proud that I am able to go to the bank to collect my money. With the money I earn, I can buy food to eat, milk to drink, and clothes to dress my children properly. Like other parents, I can afford to send my children to school, and pay for their school materials and uniforms.

Over the past decade, my health has stabilized, and I feel strong. In 2008, I only weighed seventeen kilograms. At the hospital, the doctors used to change my medication every day because my body was not responding well to it. I had rashes all over my skin. Now, I weigh fifty-seven kilograms and I can take my HIV medication without any problem. I only recently experienced some problems with my eyesight; I need glasses, but they are very expensive. Over all, we are doing well. No one mistakes me for a crazy person anymore.

As you know, my older son Mugisha was born in 2000 after a stranger raped me. At first, I had no love for him. He was a constant reminder of what had happened to me. I did not want to look at him or breastfeed him. But as time went on, my love for him started to grow. Going to church really helped me. Preachers reassured me that what I experienced was not my fault, and I slowly began to feel better about myself. Now, I love my son very much. We sit together and share ideas. He is my best friend.

Although my son and I are very close, I have not yet told him that he was conceived by rape. He is still young, and I worry that it would traumatize him. I worry that he might quit school and start taking drugs or doing other harmful things. When he asks me about his father, I just tell him that he is not around. Maybe I will tell him one day when he is older.

My happiest moments are when I am with my two beautiful children. Mugisha is eighteen and in his fifth year of high school, and Oscar is thirteen and in his first year of high school. Like other Rwandan children, they both go to a boarding school. My children are smart, and they receive high marks in school. When the boys are at home during the holidays, Mugisha teaches Oscar math. My children are different: Mugisha likes to study and wants to become a doctor, and Oscar loves football and wants to become a great football player. He is already on the Rwandan football team for his age group. My children get along very well together, and they bring me so much joy. As a mother, there are no happier moments than to be with your children.

In 2013, I married Damien, Oscar's father, as I wanted to give Oscar a good future. Even though we struggled in the beginning of our relationship, as genocide survivors we felt we needed to stick together and take care of each other. We had both lost so many of our relatives in the genocide. Our feelings for one another grew over time. Like me, Damien was HIV-positive; luckily, neither Oscar nor Mugisha have HIV. The Lord must have protected my boys, especially Oscar, because I breastfed him for twenty months.

Damien had two children with another woman, a boy and a girl. When we got married, Damien asked me to live with him in his house, which was given to him by the government's Genocide Survivors Assistance Fund. The house has two rooms and one sitting room. But since we did not earn enough money, we decided to rent out that house. With the little rent money and the sponsorship we received through Mukomeze, we were able to take care of our family.

Now we live in Kimironko, a quarter in Kigali, in a small house that the government provided us and other people who have nowhere else to live. Our house used to be a kitchen, and we share this space with another family. Although it is small, it is not a problem for me. The house is in good condition. When the children are home during the holidays, they sleep in the sitting room and the bedroom. We live in a nice neighbourhood, and I get along well with my neighbours; we often share food. Some of my neighbours are survivors like me. We share the same history.

My world changed since I began sharing my life with Damien. We were raising a family together—something I never would have imagined for myself a few years ago. But just a few months ago, on July 18, 2018, Damien went to work as he would on any other day, and never came home. He was a community nurse, volunteering to take care of people in our community. That day he was handing out free mosquito nets to protect people from malaria. I waited for several days for him to return, and then I went to inform the community leaders, who helped me search for my husband. But we could not find him. Two weeks later, on August 1, his body was found on the shores of Lake Muhazi, about two to three hours from where we live. I heard on the radio that a man's body had been found at the lake, and when I went to the hospital to identify the body, I realized that it was indeed my Damien. We buried him shortly after that. I still do not know how he died. No marks were found on his body, and the police are still investigating the cause of his death. I realized later that he might have committed suicide; at home, we found a short goodbye note from Damien, saying that I would never see him again, that he loved me and that I should always take good care of the children. We are all still confused about what happened, and we are all devastated.

For the children, their father's death is incomprehensible. Oscar finds it hard to believe that his father is no longer here. He stopped speaking almost entirely, and no longer laughs. He loved his father very much. He still loves playing football, but you can clearly see the changes in him. The other day, he told me: "I will play professional football and make a lot of money so that my father would have been wealthy and proud." Mugisha is also very hurt. Although Damien was not his biological father, he always treated Mugisha as his own son. Damien's death has also been very hard on his two other children. Although his daughter does not live with us, I continue to take care of them. I take time to talk to all the children and I try to explain to them that we need to accept their father's death. But all I can say is that when a child loses a parent, something big changes in them.

Damien's death also continues to be incomprehensible to me. Even now, I still cannot believe that he is no longer with us, that I will never see him again. He was everything to me.

To make matters worse, Damien's relatives continuously come to my house demanding that I give them the entitlements to Damien's land. They never accepted me as Damien's wife. But this land is legally mine, and they do not have the right to take it away from us. The government is supporting me in this, and I keep praying that things will calm down soon.

So, now I am alone with my children again. But I thank God because, despite everything that I have been through, God has never forsaken me. And I have Solace Ministries and Mukomeze to rely on as well; they are my family. I pray for my children. Taking care of them alone is not easy. There are times when they listen to me, and times when they do not. But they can have a good life and future ahead of them. I need to raise them well and teach them to be humble and to pray. I always encourage my children to do well in their studies. Getting a good education is the best way that they can take care of themselves, in case I die too. And I always tell them to love each other.

With everything that has happened in my life, I am never completely fine. I try not to think about the genocide, but it is not easy and I end up thinking about it a lot. Sometimes I cannot sleep at night. Then I pray and hope that my thoughts will go away. I often get severe headaches and I try to alleviate them by taking pills. In those situations, I feel like no one is beside me and I prefer to be alone. But I try to stay among other people so that I feel better. I visit my pastor, who lives close by. Sometimes he even visits me at home and we pray together with the children. When I am very down, I go to see Mama Lambert, the counsellor at Solace Ministries. I tell her what is on my mind and she comforts me. I always feel better after speaking with her. Nowadays, I do not spend a lot of time visiting friends because I need to find ways to earn a better income. Only then will I be able to take care of my family. You see, now I am both a mother and a father to my children.

I have a business selling charcoal. A friend of mine who lives in my area has a veranda facing the road. I rent her veranda to sell my charcoal. I put ten sacks of charcoal on her veranda and people who pass by can buy it. I work there every day from the early morning to late in the evening. I cannot say that I am completely financially independent, but it makes me feel good to be busy working. It is hard to compete with others who can buy and sell one hundred sacks of charcoal a day. If I made more money, I could expand my business and become more independent. But nowadays people use gas more frequently, and this is not good for my business. I think I might need to sell fruit instead. Some years ago, I worked as a cleaner for a company, but the company was taken over and I lost my job. I also worked as a seamstress for a while and even had my own sewing machine, but that did not work out either.

I always try to find work running small businesses, but when I get sick the business stops, and we lose our only source of income. It would be wonderful if I could find a permanent job.

I think there is still some stigma towards genocide survivors of sexual violence, although this has decreased over time. Before the genocide, we used to have parents, we used to have families, and we could speak openly to each other. But now, some of the people I meet on the street know my story or did bad things to me, and I cannot be free and open with them. I am afraid they might speak badly to me, so I prefer to stay inside my house; usually I have very little to say to them anyway. But as I said, things have been improving in the past ten years, and there is less stigma in society. People living with HIV can go to the hospital for treatment without being humiliated. Before, people would point at you and shout, "Eh, she has HIV!" The government told Rwandans not to point and make bad remarks. Now, I go to the hospital just like other people. I get into the queue to collect my HIV medication and no one points at me. There is no problem. This is a major change in our lives.

I also noticed that people's minds have changed about certain things. In the past, verbal abuse took place openly in public; nowadays, you might only see it in private settings. But the government is doing a lot to stop stigma; it is a process, step by step. People need to be educated. One important thing the government introduced is the community meetings. People meet regularly to talk about societal issues. Anyone can attend the meetings—men, women, rich and poor—and we discuss what is happening at home, in the community and in the country. Together we try to solve problems. For example, when a woman informs us that she is finding it difficult to start her own business, one of us teaches her how to do it. Or if we learn that a woman is married and there is domestic violence in the family, we visit the family and try to resolve the issues that cause the fighting. The meetings are also helpful in tackling stigma and biases in society. In the meetings we often discuss behaviours that we should avoid, such as talking badly about others. Although I cannot stand in public and talk about the sexual violence I experienced during the genocide, if someone started pointing at me and hurling insults at me, I can go to the leaders of the community and report that person. They can be taken to court, where they will need to explain themselves. This kind of behaviour is not accepted in society.

I also found that my own views have changed over the past decade. In the past, I did not have faith in the *gacaca* courts, and I was not able to forgive the perpetrators. Today, I think the *gacaca* courts were helpful, and that the proceedings were conducted in the right way; many people were convicted and sent to prison. They also had to pay compensation to the survivors. *Génocidaires* who asked for forgiveness were forgiven. After observing and better understanding what *gacaca* was capable of achieving, I began to change my views. I have even sincerely forgiven those who committed the atrocities. The bible says that if you do not forgive, you will not be forgiven, and I agree with that. My capacity to forgive came very slowly, through much prayer. And although I can forgive, I can never go back to my hometown. I do not wish to be confronted by those who hurt me and the people that I loved.

My advice for other genocide survivors of sexual violence would be to learn to accept what happened to us. I would also suggest that it is better to avoid sitting around all day long doing nothing. If you do, the trauma related to the genocide comes back to you. You constantly think about all of the things that happened. Instead, I would advise survivors to engage in some small business, perhaps at the market in the company of other women. And we need to work hard. Being together and working with others keeps you busy, and it makes you feel you are doing something meaningful with your life.

I see a good future ahead for my children and me. If God keeps me alive, and if my children finish their studies and find a job, our lives will be good. Despite all that has happened to me, I will stand firm. I feel strong. I am a responsible woman and I will continue on the right track. I want to be a good example for others.

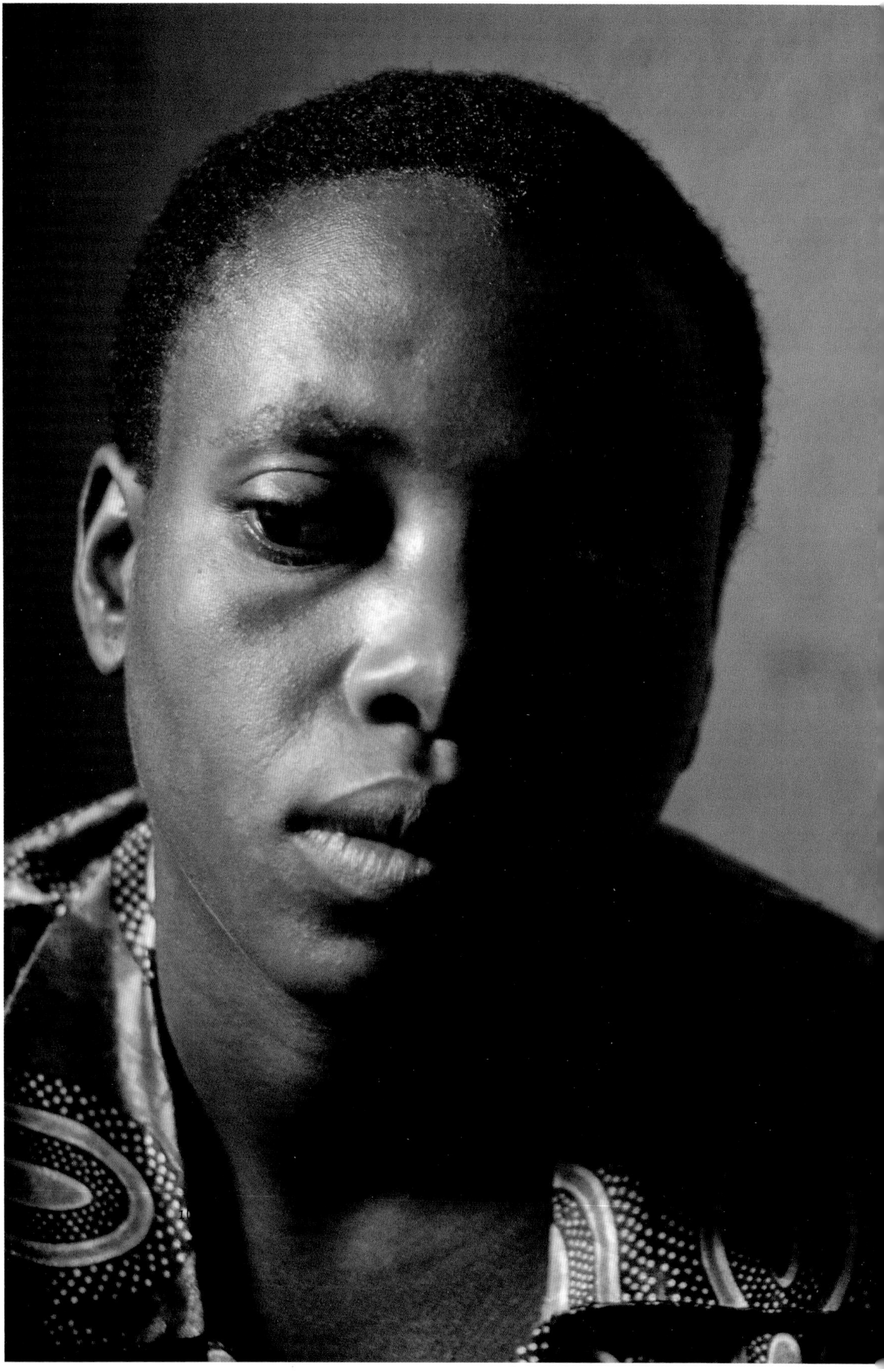

HYACINTHA NIRERE

BORN: August 1981 (day unknown)
BIRTHPLACE: Rusatira, near Butare

TESTIMONIAL: Kigali, 2008

I WAS ONLY twelve years old when I was brutally raped during the genocide, at different times by different men. Because of the events that occurred in those months, I never got the chance to live my life as I had wished. So many of those dear to me were killed during the genocide. Only my mother, cousin, one brother and two sisters survived. I never had an opportunity to choose my destiny. I became a woman without even having a chance to be a girl. I did not know anything about sex; my parents never explained anything to me. I was not prepared to become a mother and take care of a baby. I have never loved my daughter, who was born out of rape, and even though I try my hardest to love her, there is still a long way for me to go. I often wonder why God planned this life for me.

When I meet the *génocidaires* on the streets, they do not seem happy to see me. Sometimes they do not allow my cattle to cross their fields. They do not say anything to me, and when I ask them about my families' possessions, they refuse to tell me anything.

I was born sixth in a family of nine children. Our female cousin also lived with us in Rusatira, in the south of Rwanda not FAR from Butare. We were all very happy and very close to our parents. Before the genocide, my mother was a housewife and my father was a policeman in Rusatira. My father got this job through an uncle who already worked as an accountant at the police station. My uncle was hired because he had good handwriting. Ultimately, the *bourgmestre* was not happy with having a Tutsi in an official institution and he told the inspector of police that my father was too old to be a policeman.

The *bourgmestre* forced my father to quit his job in 1991. From that moment, my father was obliged to farm the fields in order to earn an income.

On another occasion, one of my brothers was jailed for three months for listening to Radio Muhabura, a station controlled by the RPF. Radio Muhabura promoted unity and reconciliation for all Rwandans—Hutu, Tutsi and Twa—and my brother secretly wished to join the RPF in Uganda. He was caught, together with three other young people, by the *conseiller* of the sector. They were listening to the radio in a sorghum field, where they thought nobody could see or hear them. I think the crime my brother committed was not listening to the radio, but being a Tutsi.

Even though we got along with our Hutu neighbours, we could sense, especially since the RPF invasion from Uganda in 1990, that there was no trust between us. For example, Hutu stopped their conversations whenever a Tutsi passed by. In schools, Hutu and Tutsi were made to identify themselves. The Hutu majority would then ridicule the Tutsi minority.

We didn't know what was happening in the rest of the country until April 14, 1994, the day the local authorities invited the Hutu, civilians and soldiers alike, to some special meetings. We knew these meetings were special since Hutu were screaming "Hutu power" and only Hutu were allowed to attend. Our Hutu neighbours told us our end was nearing.

The next day, we saw many trucks full of Hutu soldiers going to the neighbouring hill, which was almost exclusively inhabited by Tutsi. We were quite sure that these soldiers weren't going there to offer security; they went there to kill Tutsi. We also witnessed Tutsi from Gikongoro coming en masse to our area, and at that moment we saw the reality in front of our eyes. The genocide had started in Gikongoro on April 7, and now Tutsi were passing through Rusatira in order to reach Burundi to save their lives. Massacres were happening across the country, and Tutsi were definitely the ones who were being killed.

On April 15, my father left the house after our Hutu neighbour instructed him to go to a nearby roadblock to fight the invading RPF. The neighbour was following orders received from the *bourgmestre* and another high official of the sector during the special meeting the day before. These instructions were a lie told to kill Tutsi. Until then, no Tutsi had been killed at a roadblock; my father was one of the first. On his way there, he met a group of *Interahamwe* militia, who abducted him and beat him to death with a nailed club near our house.

After my father was killed, some of our Hutu neighbours warned us to leave immediately if we did not want our lives to end in a few hours. We all took different paths. I followed my oldest sister, who was nineteen at the time. We met one of her Hutu classmates and another young Hutu on the road, and they said they would hide us in their house. Even though my sister's classmate was a Hutu, he had also been her friend for a long time; we trusted him. When we got there, it appeared that the house they were living in had been taken over from someone else. I later realized that they had killed the Tutsi owners and kept the house for themselves.

Whenever my sister and I wanted to leave the house and go somewhere, they refused, saying it was too dangerous for us to do so. One night, the young man came into my bedroom and ordered me to take off my clothes unless I wanted him to take me to the killers. I said I would rather die than do what he wanted. He replied that he didn't even know why he was arguing with me. He jumped on me, took off my clothes himself and raped me. My sister was living the same horrors in the next room with her classmate.

The young Hutu man raped me all night long, except when he was tired and took a break. I felt a lot of fear and thought I would be killed soon. After the first attack, the young man raped me again on the second day, twice. The two men went out killing Tutsi during the day and raped my sister and me during the night. We were forced to choose between being raped or killed, and they locked our room so we could not escape. There was nothing we could do in that room; we just felt so much fear. I was bleeding from my private parts and aching everywhere. I could not join my legs together, because it hurt too much.

After two days, while the two men were out killing, my sister and I managed to escape from the house. Since the house was near the street, we were able to ask passersby to tell the man who had married our aunt, a well-known Hutu, to come and rescue us. He did come and take us away from that house, and he and my aunt sheltered us in their home. We were there for a week. Unfortunately, the *Interahamwe* somehow found out that there were two cockroaches hiding in my aunt's home. We managed to escape before they arrived.

My sister and I went in different directions. On my way, I met a group of FAR soldiers. Some of them pointed at me, saying I was Tutsi, and one of them, named Emmanuel, asked me if I was. I said no, but he inspected my eyes, my ribs and the palms of my hands. Based on his inspection, he concluded I was a Tutsi and ordered me to follow him. I joined a group of five girls who were following the soldiers. They looked so subdued. We were all between twelve and twenty years of age. We arrived at a little forest, where there was a camp controlled by the French. It was in Zone Turquoise, in Gikongoro.

For about three months, this FAR soldier came anytime he wanted and raped me. He would take me from one of the tents in the camp to a nearby forest, outside the camp, where no one could see us. When the young Hutu man raped me for the first time in that house, I screamed and shouted, but when I was raped in the forest, I did not say a word. I had accepted what was happening to me and realized that I didn't have a chance to escape.

About three hundred women and girls were at the camp. The soldiers just picked whoever among us they wanted to rape. The French knew what was happening and did nothing to prevent it. The rapes sometimes took place right in front of their eyes. In fact, the French were also raping Tutsi women. They would come and pick a girl and take her to some place to rape her. Sometimes the girl would only return after several days. Rather than protecting Tutsi, the French were helping the Hutu, and towards the end of the genocide, the Zone Turquoise was used by many Hutu as an escape route from Rwanda to the DRC.

Emmanuel was not the only soldier who raped me. Another soldier raped me multiple times in his house outside the camp. He was nicknamed Rukokoma. When the FAR soldiers learned that the RPF were approaching, they moved the camp to another area within the Zone Turquoise. That is when Rukokoma found me. For the four days we stayed at this second location, Rukokoma forced me to be his "wife."

As the *Inkotanyi* were approaching, the FAR soldiers burned their uniforms and started wearing normal clothes so they would look like civilians. One day I was able to go to a nearby Red Cross post, where they provided me with some biscuits, food, blankets, oil for cooking and medicines. I told the doctor what was really happening in the little forest. That same night, the *Inkotanyi* attacked the place and took all the FAR soldiers away with them. Some of the FAR soldiers were re-educated and later joined the RPF. The girls and women were taken to a secure place.

For me, the genocide did not end after the *Inkotanyi* rescued us from the camp. For about two years, Rukokoma, who pretended to be a civilian not involved in the genocide, forced me to stay in the "marriage." We remained in Gikongoro until I was six months pregnant with his child. At this point, he fled to the DRC, since he had become more and more afraid I would tell the RPF about his true identity. I don't know where he is now. In January 1997, I gave birth to a girl, but I hated her, because she was a constant reminder of what had happened to me. I didn't breastfeed her because of that, though the doctors pressured me to forget about the past and to feed her.

In 2003, I found out who killed my father. The man's name is Hussen. Before appearing in *gacaca* court, he wrote a letter from prison confessing to the murder and to other crimes. He asked for forgiveness only to avoid a longer sentence in *gacaca*. Our government had installed a policy that encouraged *génocidaires* to confess to the crimes they committed, in order to achieve justice and reconciliation among Rwandans. This would help genocide survivors learn what had happened to their loved ones and where their bodies lay, so that they could receive a proper reburial. It would also ease the enormous caseload for the courts, which needed to process the cases of around 800,000 *génocidaires*. A confessing *génocidaire* would, in return, receive a reduced sentence. However, Hussen managed to flee when he was temporarily released before appearing in *gacaca*, and I don't know where he is today.

Because I wasn't able to go to school, I am now forced to cultivate the land, even though I am weak because of my HIV status. I eat some of the food that I grow myself and sell the rest at a nearby market. Even though I am frail, I have to farm in order to survive and to take care of my daughter and my sick mother, who live with me. It is my biggest wish that someone can help me farm the fields, so that I can have a better life.

A few years ago, I was desperate and lonely, but after meeting with other survivors, I felt comforted and helped. An organization provided me with food and antiretroviral treatments. I received counselling and was able to consult a doctor. When I first found out that I was HIV positive, in 2000, I refused to take the antiretroviral treatment, because I wanted to die. I am happy now that I have taken the treatment, since it is better for my health. Other rape survivors who were on antiretroviral treatment comforted me and inspired me to take the medicine. If it weren't for the treatment, I would probably not have been able to cultivate the land any longer.

I have not forgiven those who killed my family, those who raped me or even those who took our possessions. I go to the *gacaca* courts, but I am more and more frightened to give my testimony when I see what happens to other survivors when they do so. They are intimidated or, even worse, killed. I wonder why I should give my testimony, because the *Interahamwe* are being released. It seems that our testimonies in *gacaca* courts are more formalities than truly helpful.

The international community abandoned us in 1994. If the international community is still denying the realities and atrocities of the genocide, then they are still killing us. Maybe our testimonies will help them open their eyes. Maybe. We are still hurting, and we wish someone would notice.

HYACINTHA NIRERE

TESTIMONIAL: Kigali, 2018

THERE IS A big difference between who I am today and who I was ten years ago, when I was first interviewed for *The Men Who Killed Me*. This updated edition of the book is important to me because it shows how my life has progressed over the past decade, and where I am headed now.

Today I feel empowered. I am now earning an income, and this has helped me to plan for the future. I am so grateful for the Mukomeze Foundation and Solace Ministries. I am where I am today because of them. The genocide left me with nothing and no one, but these organizations took me in at my lowest point of depression and held my hand all the way until I could stand on my own. They helped me a great deal, along with many other survivors of sexual violence. I am also very grateful for my husband, who I married in 2008. My husband does what no one else can do. He takes care of me, listens to me and gives me his time, love and warmth. I am also proud of myself, because I try my very best and work hard. If you visit my home, you can see with your own eyes all that I have achieved, despite everything I lost because of the genocide.

My husband and I live in a small village in the countryside, and together we take care of our two children: my twenty-one-year-old daughter and his twenty-two-year-old son, from another relationship. We are farmers. My husband and I work together on our land, but sometimes we also pay others to work our fields. We grow crops, especially cassava, which we sell at the market, and we also have cattle. I also have my own small business to make extra money. Over the past six years, I have been buying bananas, from which I make juice to sell. Financially, we are doing well. We have a roof above our heads and food to eat, and when we need to go to the hospital, we can afford it.

It has not been easy to get to this point in our family. My daughter was born from the sexual violence I continued to endure in the aftermath of the genocide, when I was enslaved by a *génocidaire*. For a very long time, I could not love her because she was a constant reminder of my horrifying experiences of the genocide. But this has changed so much over the years. It has been a lengthy process, and three years ago I noticed that my feelings towards my daughter were evolving.

It was through the counselling that I received from Mama Lambert at Solace Ministries that I realized that I was not to blame for what had happened to me. In the counselling sessions, I sat with other survivors who also had children born from genocidal rape. We shared our stories and supported each other. We came to understand that the blame fell on the rapists rather than on us. Some survivors had contracted HIV but did not get pregnant, and after the genocide, they were no longer able to conceive children because of the severe sexual violence that they had suffered. When I heard these stories, I felt happy to have a child, even if she was the result of a terrible experience. And I started to wonder why I was mistreating my daughter, after all the abuse I had experienced myself. This was not fair to her; she deserved to be loved, just like every other child. Despite everything, my daughter has always been very wise. Her name means "a gift" and I started to see her that way; she is indeed my gift from God. I felt that I should cherish this beautiful gift. Today my daughter is doing very well in school, and she has a good future ahead of her. I love my daughter very much.

I love taking care of my children. I cherish my role as a parent, and I strive to teach my children about important values in life. When the children are not in school, we are usually together in the morning while they do their homework. After lunch we play cards, and in the evening we go out to look for grass for our cattle. My daughter is in her sixth year of high school, and my son is now in his second year. They are both doing very well in school. The only thing I am now concerned about is how to ensure that my daughter will be able to attend university next year. It will be hard to pay for her tuition fees. University is very expensive.

We are happy with the house where we live. We have three rooms, two corridors and a sitting room. Both the inside and outside of the house are made of a mixture of cement and sand, so the house is sturdy. The floor is not yet done properly, and the roof could also be more solid. Although the house is not yet finished, we feel at home in it.

We live in a safe area and we have nice neighbours. We visit each other regularly, and because I am the community nurse, I see my neighbours quite often to advise them on health issues. I am proud to be a community nurse. In 2008, our neighbours selected me for this position. It showed me that they trust and love me. I love doing this work; it empowers me. I did not attend nursing school but completed a training program to prepare for this position. It is a voluntary job without payment, and it takes me about two hours every day. I see patients in the mornings at my house before I start my other work. In the evenings, I visit patients in their homes. In cases where I am not in a position to treat patients, I give them a transfer letter, which they can use to go to the local hospital. The hospital would then send me a report from the doctor, and I continue to care for the patient, if necessary.

I specialize in healthcare for young children and pregnant women. For example, I give medicine to young children if they have diarrhea or malaria. I teach people about hygiene. I also give parents advice on family planning, especially to ensure they take enough time between pregnancies and dedicate time to each child. I advise mothers to breastfeed in order to protect their babies from illnesses. And I tell parents to only have as many children as they can care for; it is preferable not to have more children than you have the means to raise well.

Of course, even though I am a community nurse, I also get sick from time to time. Recently I felt very ill, and I went to different hospitals for an assessment, but the doctors could not figure out what was wrong. Even now I am not feeling very well. I feel weak, I have back pain, and I have an ulcer and heart problems. I still take my HIV medication regularly, and my viral load levels have decreased over the years. The doctor assured me that my current problems are not connected to HIV. I have had other illnesses over the past ten years, but overall I still feel strong.

I also feel well mentally. It has taken me years, but I feel that my head is settled now. Whenever I struggle, I tend to focus on my work. The leaders of our community encourage us to work hard in order to become economically independent, but it was the Mukomeze Foundation that first made this possible. This organization supported me for several years, and through their generosity I was able to buy land, build my house, buy clothes and livestock, and invest in cultivating crops. I have always worked hard and engaged in many different kinds of income-generating activities. I am not one to just sit in the house from morning to evening, letting the day pass by without doing anything. I am always up and down, looking for something to do.

During the one hundred days of genocide commemoration period, I do not let it slow me down. Of course, I remember, but it does not stop me from doing my work. It makes me happy that the Lord has given me the strength to work for myself, so that I do not have to resort to begging on the streets. I thank God for the strength I have had over the past ten years to reach where I am now.

Over the past decade, my feelings toward the *gacaca* have really changed. In hindsight, the *gacaca* proceedings were very good for me. Although I was frightened to testify in front of an audience at the *gacaca* court, telling the truth gave me a sense of recognition for the harms that I had experienced in the genocide. But it can be said that *gacaca* was both good and bad. A positive outcome was that the *génocidaires* had to compensate survivors and ask for forgiveness, and they were sentenced or forgiven. Unfortunately, the *génocidaires* who destroyed and took our property never returned the goods or paid us back, even if the *gacaca* courts ordered them to do so.

As for forgiveness, I still feel that I cannot forgive the killers, rapists and looters of the genocide. I do not think you can simply forgive someone who has never come before you to ask for forgiveness. I cannot forgive someone who cannot even accept what he has done.

In general, I do not experience any problems in my community, but seeing the *génocidaires* is never easy. They are not always happy to see survivors, especially when we ask them to pay us back for the belongings that they destroyed and stole. Generally, I do not feel isolated or stigmatized as a survivor of sexual violence. Of course, when people see me going to the hospital, I feel that they may think the reason I am there is because I have HIV. But they do not harm me. In the past, some people destroyed our banana plants, but this had nothing to do with me being a survivor of sexual violence. My daughter also does not experience stigma, but she also rarely goes out. She is either at school or at home.

Participating in the first edition of *The Men Who Killed Me* only brought me positive things. First of all, it allowed me to tell my story. It also helped me to meet other genocide survivors of sexual violence, and we were able to share our stories and sorrows. We felt strengthened by this. At the same time, I believe the book helped the world to understand what had taken place in our country. I know that people who read my testimony know now what happened to me.

I never told my daughter that she was conceived from genocidal rape, but she always reads the book. Maybe she has also read my story, but just kept quiet about it. Sometimes I think about telling her, but then I find it difficult and I hesitate. Maybe one day I will tell her.

From everything I have learned in life, the lesson I wish to pass on to my children is to love one other and to love others. I hope they learn to work hard, because it is not good to be dependent on others. My wish for other genocide survivors of sexual violence is that they accept what has happened to them and be productive. When you do not work and just ruminate about the past all the time, you can lose weight, you can even have a heart attack, and your inner body parts can rot because you feel so lonely. When you work, your mind is not focused on the past, but on the future.

Based on where I am in my life now, all I know is that there is no going back. I am only moving forward. Even my children are growing up. They are working hard to have good jobs so that one day they will be able to take care of themselves.

ANNE MARIE WISHAVURA

BORN: 1973
TESTIMONIAL: Kigali, 2008

IT IS HARD for me to accept the fact that I am HIV positive. I live in awful conditions. I owned a bakery after the genocide, but in 2007 I was robbed and I could not continue my business. I lost one sister and one brother during the 1994 genocide. As the oldest of my surviving family, I have to take care of my three sisters and my cousin and pay for all their things, including their school supplies and clothes.

Before the genocide in 1994, I had only completed primary school. My father worked at a tea manufacturing plantation, and my mother was a farmer. In 1959, years before I was born, discrimination against Tutsi began, and my father and his sister left the country to go to Burundi. In Rwanda, houses that belonged to Tutsi were burned, and Tutsi were killed. My father returned in 1970, because he wanted to start his own life in Rwanda and no longer wanted to live with his sister, who had gotten married. Although there was still discrimination against Tutsi, he made a vow to himself never to flee Rwanda again, even if Hutu tried to kill him.

My parents married in 1971 and started a large family. I had, in all, eight brothers and sisters. When I was born, my father called me Mukandahunga, which means "the daughter of the one who fled the country." He called one of my sisters Nshutininka, which means "a friend is a cow," because every time Hutu were jealous of my father's land or his cows, he would give a cow to those who had the power to protect him. Cows are a sign of deep friendship in our culture.

There were many Hutu in our community, which was called Mata. In April 1994, when I was still living with my parents, Hutu started burning Tutsi houses. In my community, the rampaging started on April 8, at my uncle's house. Because my uncle had nine strong sons, the one *Interahamwe* militiaman who went there could not overpower them with his machete. That man left to round up some friends, and my uncle's family took the opportunity to flee to the Catholic church of Kibeho, which was about two hours away from my uncle's house in Gikongoro.

On April 10, a Hutu named Innocent came to our house and warned us not to seek refuge at the church in Kibeho or at schools in our area, because we would be killed if we did so. This was not the first time a Hutu had helped us. In 1992 and 1993, another Hutu man warned us that the killing of Tutsi was about to begin. He helped us because my family had given him some cows. So on April 10 my entire family except for one sister, who decided to stay at Kibeho thinking it would be safer, spent the night in a sorghum field. Early the next morning, we walked to Butare. The genocide had not yet started there. Although we considered walking to Burundi, we decided to stay in Butare, since it seemed safe. We tried our luck with a rich Tutsi man who lived in Butare. He welcomed us into his house, and we believed that his wealth would spare him and us. But two days later, the *Interahamwe* militia came and killed the rich Tutsi man and his son.

There were many Tutsi at the rich man's house, and when the *Interahamwe* attacked, we all ran away in separate directions. Except for two of my brothers, my family spent the night at the home of my aunt, who was also Tutsi and who lived in Butare. Although the genocide had still not really started yet in Butare, *Interahamwe* militia from Gikongoro had been sent to begin the killings, and we left my aunt's house the next day, since we thought we would not be safe there. My father and uncle stayed on, believing they could fight the *Interahamwe*. I never saw them again and I do not know how or where they were killed.

We fled to a nearby church in Karama. Only a few minutes after we got there, a bus full of FAR soldiers and *Interahamwe* arrived. The rest of us wanted to flee, but my mother refused, believing we would not be killed. When the shooting started, we insisted that we should leave. My mother said she wanted to stay, as she would die anyway, but when we told her we would stay too and die with her, she agreed to leave with us.

As we fled, we got separated from each other because of the shooting. Still, I was not FAR behind my mother and my younger sister. Together with many other Tutsi, we ran through a small alley. My mother was one of the first to arrive at a roadblock set up by *Interahamwe*, and she was hacked to death. Since she was wearing nice clothes, they stole those from her body. My sister, also in the front line of the fleeing Tutsi, was wounded by machetes at this roadblock, too. I was able to escape the horrors at that roadblock because of the chaos. I ran towards the centre of Butare town, because I had heard it was safe there. Others fled in the direction of Burundi.

I arrived at the Anglican church of Butare, where many Tutsi from Gikongoro were hiding. There I was approached by some FAR soldiers from ESO, a training centre for FAR soldiers in Butare, who were hand-picking young girls to abuse. The soldiers were looking for girls who already had breasts, since they considered them old enough to rape. Girls in the church were cutting off their hair so that the soldiers would not think they were old enough. The FAR soldiers took some other girls and me to their small houses in the ESO compound near the church. We were mostly teenagers.

I was raped all night long. The soldier who first raped me told me to cooperate; he said otherwise it would be much worse, as he would use more force against me. He told me it was the end of all Tutsi, but if I cooperated, he might help me survive. He raped me three times that night. Over the following days, I did not care what those soldiers were doing to me, because I wished to die. Six of us girls were raped by those soldiers day and night. There were many different men who raped me on different days. After the rapes, some girls were sent back to the church. Others were swapped between soldiers to be raped further, and some were even killed. Although I was in so much pain when I was first raped, I didn't feel anything afterward. It didn't matter any longer, since I felt I was going to die anyway.

Minister Pauline Nyiramasuhuko, who was the minister of Family and Women's Affairs in Rwanda and lived near the church in Butare, oversaw the "work" of the genocide at the church some of the time. She said she did not want to see "dirt" in the fields. We overheard one soldier reporting this to another soldier on his walkie-talkie. On the order of the minister, buses arrived to take us to Nyaruhengeri, just outside Butare, to be killed there. The girls on the first two buses did not survive the ride. I was on the third bus. When we arrived in Nyaruhengeri, the *Interahamwe* militia said they were exhausted from killing. They told Minister Nyiramasuhuko that there were too many dead bodies already, and that the smell of the corpses was so disgusting that she would have to send people to take the corpses back to Butare before they would agree to continue their "work." The minister said she could not promise them that, so we were taken back to Butare in order to be killed there.

The bus then took us to Rango forest, near Butare. There we were "welcomed" by a group of *Interahamwe* militia who raped us again and again for one week. There was a big ditch where they planned to throw us after they were done with us, and where many dead bodies from previous killings already lay. I was raped three times, by different men. Two girls, named Kantarama and Francine, died after enduring more sexual and other abuse than they could handle. We were raped, day after day, until the day the *Inkotanyi* arrived in Butare. A white priest had informed the RPF of our location. As soon as the *Interahamwe* heard that the RPF were on their way to the forest, they fled.

The RPF took us from the forest to a refugee camp in Butare. I stayed there for one week, until the conflict was over, and then for another week in a school called Groupe Scolaire Officiel de Butare. Some time later, I met my younger sister and a cousin who had survived the genocide, and we chose to live together. We lived in Butare for one year and after that we moved to Kigali.

After the genocide, I hated all Hutu, hated churches and hated praying. I wanted to hurt the Hutu, but I could not, because they were much stronger than I was. I learned that I was HIV positive in 2005, when I was about to get married. When I found out, I lost all hope, and none of the spiritual healing I had experienced since 1994 helped. The man I was about to marry did not want to marry me when he found out about my HIV status. I have now decided that I will marry only if the man is also HIV positive. I have no children, but I do not want to die before I have them. Even with my health status, I could have a baby without infecting the baby with HIV.

My sisters don't know that I am sick. They are very traumatized themselves, and I don't want to shock them. I have never asked them whether they were also raped during the genocide, but they are married and not sick like me. I don't want any pity or gossip. If people find out I am HIV positive, they might change their manner towards me. They might not greet me any more or might reject me completely.

I decided to share my testimony so that every country in the world knows genocide took place in Rwanda. I hope that everyone who hears my story helps us to find treatment for our sicknesses. I have forgiven those who hurt me. I do not remember them, and I would not recognize even one of them if I met him on the street. I don't go to the *gacaca* courts, because there is no justice in *gacaca* courts. The thought of those courts disturbs me. The courts are FAR away from where I live, and I have no money for bus tickets to go there. I also do not feel safe there. When I started praying and started to forgive the rapists, I felt no need to go to *gacaca* courts any longer. I actually don't really have a choice: it is hard to hate someone you don't even know. I just wish to have a normal life.

ANNE MARIE WISHAVURA

TESTIMONIAL: Kigali, 2018

BEFORE SHARING MY story for the first edition of *The Men Who Killed Me*, I could not speak openly about what had happened to me during the genocide. It was eating away at me. But once I started to speak up, I felt that I could start loving other people again. It helped me so much. It gave me an extended family at Solace Ministries, where we are all genocide survivors.

After the genocide, as the eldest of our surviving family, I felt the responsibility to take care of my relatives. For many years, it was very difficult to take care of them, to get us shelter and something to eat, but I tried my very best. I received some support from Solace Ministries and the government's FARG programme, but it was not easy because there was not enough funding to support all genocide survivors. Sometimes I was able to pay the rent, but then we had nothing left for food. Life was a constant struggle. I even reached a point where I thought it would be better to leave my young relatives at an orphanage. But Jean Gakwandi, the director of Solace Ministries, helped us with counselling and advice. He was like a father to us.

Even though it was extremely difficult to take care of my relatives after the genocide, I still felt blessed. After all, I still had family. There were many genocide survivors without any family left. Sometimes I could hear those survivors crying. Imagine a woman who had lost her children. These people had no words left.

Most of my siblings are married and have moved out of the house. Only three relatives are still living with me: my brother, nephew and niece. They are grown up now and doing well. I wish they could continue their studies at university, but I have no means to support them. My other siblings also could not afford to go to university, but I am very happy with what they have managed to achieve. My brother obtained his driver's licence so that he could become a taxi driver, even though he still dreams of going to university. My niece wrote a letter to FARG asking for funding for university, and we are waiting for a response.

We now live in a nice house that was given to me by World Vision, although the roof is not solid and it leaks when it is raining. We live in a safe neighbourhood. I do not have any problems with my neighbours or community; we greet each other in the streets. But I generally avoid visiting my neighbours. I prefer to keep to myself. The families I do visit are also survivors, and they know my story. I feel more comfortable with them. Even when I visit Solace Ministries, I avoid telling my neighbours and friends that I am going there; they do not need to know I am a genocide survivor. Sometimes when I pass people on the street, I think they may know about my past, but perhaps it is only in my own mind. Some men even proposed to me, and I don't think they would have done so had they known about my past.

Three years ago, the sponsorship that I had been receiving for about six years from the Mukomeze Foundation stopped. I had reached a certain level of financial security and stability. Through the sponsorship I was able to buy a small house with two rooms and a salon. I rented the house out and used the rent money to pay my own rent and food. The sponsorship did not only help me materially; I felt that my sponsors showed me love, even if they were living FAR away and had not known me before. There are so many beautiful people who deserve to be loved, but my sponsors decided to love me, and I am forever grateful for that. Today I feel fortunate, especially when I see how other genocide survivors are faring, although I realize that I still have a long way to go when I compare my situation with other Rwandans. When the Mukomeze support stopped, Solace Ministries continued to support my relatives as much as possible, and this has been very helpful as well.

In July 2017, I broke my wrist. I did not go to the hospital immediately after breaking it because I think at the time I did not love myself enough. The injury still prevents me from doing work that involves heavy lifting. After this accident, I received a loan from Solace Ministries, and I opened up a business called 'mobile money'. People would pay me to add credit to their cellphones. But in July 2018, a customer did not pay me after I had already added a large sum of credit to his cellphone, and this ruined my business completely. I was devastated but there was nothing I could do, so for the past few months I haven't been able to work. If I could manage to get some funding, I would consider starting up another 'mobile money' business. But it is difficult to compete because there are many young people doing this work, and at my age I struggle to go everywhere to find new customers. I think that it would be better for me to set up a small canteen, where I could sell milk and snacks.

Over the past ten years, I have been doing very well psychologically. I only developed a memory problem; I forget things easily. The genocide-related trauma does not come up often, and when it does, I prefer to stay at home alone. In those situations, I still try to make it to Solace Ministries so that I can be with other genocide survivors, and that strengthens me. I visit Solace Ministries regularly; usually I attend the group counselling sessions. We pray and worship and this changes something inside of me. It comforts me. I also go to church regularly; praying makes me feel whole.

I told two of my sisters about the sexual violence I endured during the genocide. I felt I needed to inform them so that I could rely on them to help me get my medication from the hospital when I am sick. When they first heard my story, my sisters were very hurt and shocked, and they comforted me in different ways. They reassured me that God did not protect me from death for nothing, and that I would stay alive and grow old with them.

Over the past decade, my sense of justice has also changed. In the past, I didn't feel compelled to participate in *gacaca* because I felt that it would not help me. But later, I agreed to support my relatives at their *gacaca* proceedings by providing evidence against those who killed our family. Now the perpetrators have already served their sentences and they are out of prison. When I see them on the streets, I greet them. What else can I do? On some level, I feel that justice has been done because they admitted their crimes, asked for forgiveness and we forgave them. Besides serving their sentences, they also had to perform community service and compensate victims. I think that, ultimately, *gacaca* had a positive impact on my life and it brought me a sense of justice; this is a different view from ten years ago. I am also happy that Pauline Nyiramasuhuko is in prison. The International Criminal Tribunal for Rwanda sentenced her for participating in the genocide, as the then Minister of Family and Women's Affairs in Rwanda. Among other things, she ordered the sexual violence in Butare—the place where I was raped. It is good she is in prison for the crimes she committed; not only for me but for everyone in this country.

Despite my difficulties over the past decade, I feel physically healthy; I haven't been severely sick, not even with malaria. I am still taking my HIV medication and I have been able to manage my health.

I have also been happy to benefit from the generosity of the people around me. Several years ago, I worked as a cleaner in a man's office, and one day he invited me to have dinner at his home with his big family. I never imagined that I could be welcomed in such a nice family. When I was about to go home, he gave me a gift: an envelope with 100,000 Rwandan francs. It was such a big surprise, and I felt loved.

Although so many years have passed, I am still alone. How could a man love me after he finds out that I am HIV positive? For the past four years, I have had a good friend in my life, but I never told him that I am living with HIV. I want to tell him the truth so that he could look for another woman. Maybe it could work out for us if he has HIV too, but I have never come across a man who is HIV positive. Now I do not know if I will ever get married, although around ten people have come to me at different times and told me that God informed them that I will get married soon. So I am waiting for God's wishes to come true. Some time ago, a man showed interest in me, but he is Hutu, and I don't know if I could marry him; maybe, if he is a good man and can recognize what happened in 1994, to me and to others.

I still have a dream to have children of my own, even though I am now older. I know that if I get married, I will have children; God cannot give you a man and then fail to give you children. I have to keep my faith. In any event, in ten years time, I will be an *Umukecuru*, an old lady. Although I do not like to age, I do wish to develop myself some more. I will try and maybe I will fail, but change is important and always a first step. My wish is to become a stronger woman.

Other genocide survivors of sexual violence should avoid thinking that their life is over. Although we were raped during the genocide, we did not die. We are still alive today. We should fight for all that we are and all that we have. Our future is bright, and I live on; we all will.

FRANÇOISE KAYITESI

BORN: 1962 (date and month unknown)
BIRTHPLACE: Bicumbi, near Kigali
DIED: February 19, 2010

TESTIMONIAL: Kigali, 2008

MY MOTHER AND father left Rwanda when I was just two years old. My father was a secretary in the royal court and therefore an important personality. When the discrimination against Tutsi began, he was in great danger, because Hutu believed he held the secrets of the court. The year my parents fled Rwanda, Tutsi were being burned alive in their houses. My parents had not planned to leave, but some kind Hutu warned them about the dangers of staying. My father fled to Uganda, and my mother, who was also Tutsi, to Burundi. My mother, my uncle and I began the journey to Burundi together, but my mother grew too tired to take me along. My uncle decided to stay with me in Rwanda, because he was not really wanted by the killers. My parents planned to return for me at some later stage, but I never saw my father again.

When I was a bit older, I moved from my uncle's house in Bicumbi, just outside Kigali, to Gatsata quarter in Kigali. I lived in a community where Tutsi were a minority, but this situation didn't seem to influence our relationships. We had friends among Hutu as well as Tutsi, though the discrimination was more visible in our schools. Tutsi students did not have the right to perform better than Hutu students did. For example, our teachers would switch the names of Tutsi who had received better marks with the names of Hutu who had not performed as well. I was a good student but did not continue my studies as I had hoped, because my place in secondary school had already been taken by a Hutu. Instead, I learned how to sew, cook and take care of children. I also studied auto mechanics and learned French by taking a language course. After I finished this training, I studied management, which included courses on how to use a typewriter.

I went to work in a garage in Gatsata called Amesorwa, owned by a Hutu from Gisenyi, where I did the typing and sold car parts. My husband and I met on the streets in Kigali, where he traded clothes for a living. We realized later that our parents had once been neighbours, though we didn't recognize each other at first. We got married in 1980.

I managed to see my mother twice while she was in exile in Burundi. In 1989, right after I had returned from a visit to see her, people came to my home to interrogate me about whether I had cooperated with the *inyenzi*. I had already burned my *laisser passer* card, which stated my ethnicity, so that they could not accuse me of being an RPF spy. The owner of the garage where I worked occasionally chauffeured *Interahamwe* to their meetings. But when the militia came to humiliate the Tutsi who worked in his garage, the owner was always by our side. He did not protect us out of compassion, but because he could not afford to lose hard-working people.

The owner of the apartment we rented in Kigali used to persecute us as well. My husband and I did not have a key to the front gate, whereas other renters did. The apartment owner used to tell my younger brother, who lived with us, that he would cut off his long nose, which was considered a typical Tutsi feature. We always had to return home earlier than others so that we could enter the apartment before the owner locked the front gate.

In 1991, Tutsi could not walk the streets, because there was a lot of hostility towards us. There were Congolese soldiers who had supposedly come to help the FAR soldiers protect Rwandans from an RPF invasion, but all they did was enter houses to rape Tutsi women. During that period, there were many barricades on the streets, and identity cards were checked for ethnicity. While my husband and I contemplated going to Burundi, we did not have the money to leave.

When I learned about the death of Habyarimana on the radio, I thought it would be our time for peace and justice, because Habyarimana was a dictator. But I realized I was wrong when I heard people screaming and shouting in the streets early in the morning. After several hours, a group of *Interahamwe* militia came to our home with guns, machetes, swords and other weapons. They beat my housemaid, who was Tutsi, after she showed them her identity card. I gave them money and begged them to let us live. They accepted and left. Because we knew they would return, my three sons

and I ran from our home as soon as the militia were out of view and went to the home of our neighbours. My husband ran to hide in the bushes because our neighbours did not want to hide him. It was much more dangerous to help a Tutsi man than a Tutsi woman.

After three days, my neighbours heard that the RPF were getting closer, and they ordered us to leave their house. I decided to walk with my sons to Gitarama. We travelled with another neighbour, a beautiful twenty-three-year-old girl. On our way to Gitarama, we were stopped by *Interahamwe* and FAR soldiers positioned at a roadblock before the bridge crossing the Nyabarongo River. They were asking people for their identity cards and killing the Tutsi. In the large crowd of people at the roadblock, I saw my husband. I believe the *Interahamwe* threw him into the river moments after, though I am not sure. Some people managed to escape when the *Interahamwe* and FAR soldiers were arguing with each other and not paying attention. I escaped with my children, who were small enough to pass through the legs of the militia and the soldiers.

My sons, our neighbour and I continued on our way, cutting through small forests until we finally arrived in Nyanza, my husband's birthplace. There, we hid on a cassava plantation until three *Interahamwe* found us. As soon as I saw them I completely lost my mind and could no longer think. They said that they wanted to kill us but first they wanted to "taste" a Tutsi woman. They raped me one after the other, in front of my children. They also raped my neighbour. While they were raping us, the *Interahamwe* kept saying that we Tutsi should have stayed in Ethiopia. After they were finished, they tied me to a tree, beat my children, calling them the sons of cockroaches, and abandoned us. The next morning I felt very ill, and my belly hurt. I drifted constantly in and out of consciousness. I was tied to the tree for three days before my neighbour had the strength to untie me.

As we continued our journey, hiding along the way, my three-year-old son became ill and eventually fell into unconsciousness. An old lady I didn't know gave us some milk. When I fed that to him, he started breathing normally again. But with the aid of their dogs, the *Interahamwe* who had raped us found us hiding in the forest. Two of them took me to a muddy area in a clearing and shouted at me to lie down. Many militiamen raped me, while holding their weapons beside them, yelling that my friends the Tutsi and the *Inkotanyi* should come and save me if they wanted to. My neighbour was also raped many times. Fortunately, my children were FAR away from the clearing and could not hear or see what was happening.

After the *Interahamwe* finished raping me, they left me, and I reunited with my children in the forest. A girl passed by and offered to help by taking my two older children to a nuns' orphanage. The girl gave my sons some girls' clothing to wear, so that they would have a better chance of survival. My youngest son stayed with me, because I could still pretend he was a girl.

In May, my youngest son and I arrived in Gikongoro. For several weeks, we hid in bushes and empty houses, never for longer than two days at a time. We would flee whenever we heard footsteps, and we managed to conceal ourselves before the *Interahamwe* noticed us. Weeks later, the RPF reached that area and helped us to return home to Kigali. When they first arrived, I was afraid of them, because I was not sure whether they were RPF or government soldiers. After a few days, as I saw them distributing clothes and food and speaking to other Tutsi in a nice way, I realized that they were really there to help us.

Back in Kigali, I learned that my brother had not survived. He had been killed on the first day he returned to our apartment. The *Interahamwe*, who included one of our former neighbours, had stabbed my brother with a sword. His blood was splashed all over the walls of our apartment. He had been able to run as FAR as the main road before they caught him and buried him alive.

Shortly after the genocide ended, I realized that I was pregnant. Everyone told me to abort the pregnancy, because I didn't know if the father was my husband or one of the men who had raped me. But I couldn't bring myself to do it. Something stopped me. I prayed that the baby belonged to my husband and not an *Interahamwe*. When my son was born, in January 1995, I counted back the days and realized that he was conceived during the time I was still with my husband. A few months after my son's birth, I saw that he looked like my husband, too.

In 2003, I found out that I was HIV positive. I was always ill and I experienced severe pains in my private parts. Because I tested HIV positive, my doctor advised me to bring my four children in to be tested, too. My youngest son tested HIV positive. When I first found out that I had HIV, I completely lost hope. I thought it would be my last few days on Earth. I prayed a lot. No one knew but my sons, who survived the genocide with me. I have no one else. My husband, his family and most of my own family were killed during the genocide.

After the genocide, I could not return to the garage to work, because my boss had fled the country. I started typing letters for people on a rented typewriter. That provided me with some income to care for nine children, including five orphans I had adopted—my four nephews and one niece, as well as my mother, who had returned to Rwanda in the fall of 1994.

Since the genocide, I have headaches and feel permanently ill. I am constantly afraid. I hallucinate and see knives in front of my eyes all the time. When I go to buy meat, I sometimes imagine that the butcher is going to kill me with his knives. Every time I try to fall asleep, I see the men who raped me, telling me to take off my clothes. I feel like I can never experience joy, and I do not wish to speak about what I experienced. I can't even write down what happened to me. When I try, I stop after one page and burn the writing. Worst of all, I have been rejected by my community because my neighbours know that I am HIV positive. They always insult me about my HIV status. Maybe they would stop rejecting me if they knew I was infected from the rapes I endured during the genocide. I keep on praying, because prayers have helped make my life worth living. I also discovered from other survivors that if I take antiretroviral treatment, together with enough food, I will be able live longer.

I don't feel that I forgive the *Interahamwe*, not yet. No one has asked for my forgiveness, and no one wants to talk about it. I still live among them, and the very best I can do is ignore them. I wouldn't have the courage to accuse those who raped me in the *gacaca* courts, but I know that even if I did, they would not receive the punishment they deserve. I couldn't accuse the ones who raped me even if I wanted to, since those rapes happened FAR from Kigali, and I don't know who those men are. When killers confess to their crimes, they are quickly released. I would rather see them in prison for the rest of their lives. Although I have attended *gacaca* three times, each time I go I become very traumatized, seeing myself being raped in the forest again. I think that the people who are now released from prison should help the survivors of the genocide by building them houses and digging their fields. If I was a judge, I would sentence them to carry out general works to help the community.

Today, I wish to find a job so that I will have a regular income and can live in better conditions. My eldest son still remembers what happened during the genocide, though he hardly talks about it and he never speaks about the rapes he saw perpetrated against his mother. I do not wish for my face to be recognizable for the portrait in this book—not to protect myself, but for my children, because I do not want to create more wounds in their hearts. I decided to share my testimony so that the world may know what happened to us in 1994. We must never let this happen again and must build a better world for our children.

BIBILIYA
NTAGATIFU

FRANÇOISE'S SON JANVIER UWIMANA

TESTIMONIAL: Kigali, 2018

AT FIRST, I felt ashamed to see my mother in *The Men Who Killed Me*—a book that is read all over the world. Although I respected her decision to share her story, as a child I felt ashamed. I felt that this story should be kept in our own hearts, our own home, and not go any further. It is not in our culture to speak about this so openly.

But now, my feelings are changing. When you speak your truth, it can help others to understand what happened. I cannot say that I am always comfortable with it; sometimes I still feel shame. But other times, I think that maybe it would be a good idea to make a film out of the book, as it may help others to understand what happened during the genocide against the Tutsi. There are still people suffering from the consequences of the genocide and people should know about that.

My mother passed away in 2010. The HIV medication was not working for her. My three brothers and I were devastated. Suddenly, we became orphans. There was no one else to support us. Apart from our sorrow, my mother's death left us with many challenges. We struggled to find food. It is difficult to explain how grim our situation became overnight. I was twenty-two years old at the time, and my older brother and I had to take on a parental role in order to care for our two younger brothers. It was very difficult. I had never been in that position before. But God helped us, and we found the strength to help ourselves.

Eight years have passed since my mother's death, and life has improved. I have a family of my own, and I can somehow support my wife and children.

My youngest brother is still struggling. He is now twenty-two, and he is still living in our former house. He has HIV, and he does not understand why. This is very traumatic for him, and my brothers and I find it extremely difficult to talk to him about his condition. I think it is time to tell him my mother's story, so that he understands why he is living with HIV. We have started to talk about my brother's struggles with Mama Lambert, the counsellor of Solace Ministries, but we need more counselling in order to alleviate my brother's trauma.

Although things are better now than they were eight years ago, we still have a very hard time paying for my youngest brother's education. We had to stop his education at some point because we simply could not afford it. My hope is for him to have a good future, just as my mother wished. I am tired of taking care of all my parental duties and I wish someone could support me in that.

Thinking about my mother makes me sad and happy at the same time. Sad, because she was taken away from us FAR too early. She was only forty-eight years old. And happy, because she was such a beautiful, honest and wonderful person. She taught me so many things. She taught me the importance of praying and of having God in your life. She also taught me the importance of understanding a person who is struggling in life. She taught me to be humane. Despite her trauma, my mother was able to forgive the *génocidaires*. For me, this is still hard at times. I feel angry thinking about what they did in 1994, but there is nothing I can do. The only thing I can do as a Christian, is to forgive. When *génocidaires* confess, I forgive them. Another lesson my mother taught me is to always think ahead, for a good future. I am passing on these lessons to my own children now.

I cherish the moments I had with my mother. Especially Sundays, when she used to cook fresh food. Those were my happiest moments. And all the times she told us stories about her youth. There were so many happy moments with her. My mother also had big dreams for all her children. She wanted us to study and do well in life. She wanted us to become good men. My mother was very proud of us and we felt so happy about that.

Many people tell me that I look like my mother because I have dark skin, like she did. I still remember her smile. She had such a beautiful smile. Sometimes at night, I still dream of her smile.

ERNESTINE NYIRANGENDAHAYO

BORN: 1981 (day and month unknown)
BIRTHPLACE: Muyira sector, Butare

TESTIMONIAL: Kigali, 2008

MY FATHER WAS a Tutsi my mother was seeing while she was still married to a Hutu man. Because I was illegitimate, my Tutsi mother sent me to live with my grandparents in Muyira sector, near Butare, as soon as I was born. The rest of my family also lived there. I had two half brothers who were Hutu, but I didn't get along with them, because I was Tutsi and grew up in a Tutsi family. After my mother divorced her husband, she came to live with my grandparents and me, but she never ended up marrying my father.

I spent my childhood helping to shepherd my grandparents' cattle. The Tutsi were in the minority in our area. The Hutu could do anything they wanted, like "asking" Tutsi for cattle to slaughter. If a Tutsi refused, the Hutu would take the cattle anyway and never be held accountable for it. I remember an incident in 1993 when a Tutsi man refused to give one of his cows to a Hutu. Later that evening, the Hutu went to the man's house with a machete and killed the man and his entire family. That was before the genocide.

When the genocide began in our neighbourhood, I was in the pasture taking care of my cows. After I witnessed *Interahamwe* burning Tutsi alive in their houses, I left the cows in the pasture and ran to Nyamure Mountain, only a few minutes from where I was. Many Tutsi families had gathered at Nyamure Mountain, and the *Interahamwe* approached with machetes and guns. They shot so many people that I was covered in blood and the *Interahamwe* thought I was also dead. I fell unconscious. When I woke up, there were dead bodies all over the mountain, but the *Interahamwe* were no longer there. I was covered with the blood of my aunt, uncle and grandmother, but I was not wounded myself.

Everywhere I looked I saw dead bodies, thousands of bodies. I felt nothing and thought that I would die anyway.

I couldn't stay there because of those bodies. Late in the night, I left Nyamure Mountain and hid in a nearby cornfield. The next morning, an old Hutu man—I think he owned the field—found me hiding and took me with him. He told me that he would not hurt me but would hide me. I trusted him and followed him to his house.

The old man had two sons, who were about twenty-three and twenty-six years old and were both *Interahamwe*. When the sons saw me coming, they exchanged a look, but at the time it did not occur to me that the look was not normal. I took a shower and went to bed immediately. Two days later, when I woke up, the old man was already out, occupied with stealing Tutsi property. His sons, who were still at home, asked me if I was a boy or a girl. I knew that boys were killed immediately, so I didn't object when they asked me to take off my clothes to see if I was lying about being a girl. One of them then said that I was too young to be raped—I was only thirteen years old at the time—but the other one said that even if I was too young, my vagina would not be. They told me that they would kill me after raping me. I saw that they had knives, so I begged them to stab me to death immediately. I wanted to die, but they said they would kill me only after they were finished with me.

One of the men pushed me onto the bed and told me that my shouting wouldn't save me. I screamed very hard, because I was in so much pain, but when he finished, his brother came on me and raped me too. Fortunately, when their mother, a Tutsi, came home, they left me in the room. She did not reprimand her own sons, because she was afraid they would kill her too. When she saw me bleeding, she took me to some sort of cave just outside the house, where the family stored their bananas. My vagina smelled very bad, and she washed me with warm water and gave me some food. She said that this was every Tutsi's destiny and that she was afraid for her own life, too. She told me not to go back to the house, because her sons would kill me. I spent four days in that cave and decided to leave only when I heard that the *Inkotanyi* were approaching. I feared the fighting that would probably ensue. I waited for the Hutu family to leave the house and then I left the cave.

While I was fleeing, I met one of my aunts, who was with her three-year-old son. We continued on together. There were also many *Interahamwe* fleeing. There was panic everywhere, but we finally reached the Nyanza football stadium. We crossed paths with a group of *Interahamwe* in the stadium, and one of them told my aunt to dig three holes, which would be our graves. She started digging, and after she finished, the *Interahamwe* beheaded my cousin with a machete. They ordered my aunt to sit in the hole and they beat her with nailed clubs before one of them chopped her head off, too. While they were beating her, an old Hutu lady I didn't know pushed me into a nearby tent, where the *Interahamwe* did not find me.

The old lady said that she was going to help me escape and that I might be the only Tutsi survivor. It was no longer safe to stay at the stadium, because many Tutsi were being killed. I went with the old lady. She told me that I was too young to die, and she felt compassion for me. She herself was married to a Tutsi man. She hoped that someone would do for her own relatives what she was doing for me. We didn't know where we were going, but when we finally arrived in Gikongoro, we spent two weeks there. We were living in horrible conditions. We slept outside, we had nothing to eat, and we were always begging for food.

After the RPF liberated the country, I tried to reach my home. I travelled with the old lady, who happened to live near the mountain where my family members had been killed. I found out that my mother was still alive. The rest of my family had died.

After the genocide, I lived in terrible conditions and experienced many ailments in addition to the trauma. In 2002, I married a man named Emmanuel. He was a friend of a relative of mine, and he first came to my house in 2001. He liked me and came more often. He knew what had happened to me during the genocide, but he comforted me and decided to marry me anyway. He was also a Tutsi who had experienced the genocide, and that is why he understood what had happened to me.

I gave birth to our first child, a boy, in 2003. I continued feeling ill after that, and I went for an HIV test, which came back positive. I was tested for HIV many times and in many different places, because I wanted to verify whether I was truly HIV positive, especially since I was pregnant at the time. I believe I was infected with HIV when I was raped during the genocide. When my husband found out I was HIV positive, he did not leave me, which is a miracle. I have several tumours on the outside of my private parts and I don't know what to do. Because of the antiretroviral treatments I'm taking, I feel slightly better. I gave birth to a second child, a daughter, in 2005. Luckily, neither of my children is HIV positive.

The men who raped me are all dead. They were killed by the *Inkotanyi*. I don't know if I would have forgiven them if they were still alive, but I don't think so. The fact that the *Interahamwe* are being released makes me feel bad, but we don't have any choice but to accept it. I would have preferred to know that they were still in prison or even dead. I hope that my testimony will open some human hearts and make people feel there is something they can do. Even if they don't have material things to offer, their presence or their thoughts would be a nice thing. It helps us to know that people are thinking of us.

ERNESTINE NYIRANGENDAHAYO

TESTIMONIAL: Kigali, 2018

I AM VERY happy to be a mother of four beautiful children: I have a teenaged son and daughter, a seven-year-old son, and my baby girl is just one. After the sexual violence I suffered during the genocide, I lost hope that I would ever be able to have children. And although I am very sick now and sometimes think that I may die soon, I feel so happy when I see my children. I am happy that I can feed them rice, sweet potatoes and occasionally even meat, and that they go to bed happily with full stomachs. We villagers rarely do special things with our children, but having food delights us. On Sundays, I always attend Catholic church with my children, where they participate in a children's group and learn about the word of God. I am also happy when the children can go to school. The older two have finished their six years of primary school, and my third child is still in primary school. My children are my greatest joy.

My former partner Emmanuel is father to my two older children. After they were born, he moved to another region, and has no interest in the children at all. My younger two are with my husband, Paul. We met in 2008, married two years later and I moved in with him. I am very proud of Paul; he is a farmer and grows crops like maize, cassava and beans. When I talk about him, I feel my face start to glow. He is five years younger than I am. He is very strong and luckily he does not have HIV. I am the only one in our family who is living with HIV; fortunately, I have HIV medication. Paul knows what happened to me in the genocide, and I told him that I was HIV positive when we met.

I am very proud of my family and we are generally doing well. But what worries me is that I cannot afford my children's secondary education. Not only do I have to pay the school fees, but I must also buy them school materials and uniforms. My daughter is at home now that she has completed her primary school education, and she likes to help out around the house; she takes care of her siblings and cooks for us. My older son, who also finished primary school, is staying with my elderly mother to take care of her; he fetches water for her and tends to her cow. My mother still lives in the same house where we lived together before I married Paul. My older son loves my mother so much, and I am fine with him living with her because they live very close by so we see each other all the time.

We feel safe in the area where we live. Our house is in the centre of the village, and we also have a plot of land. We do not have permanent electricity in my house, but I do have a cash power meter, so when I want to use electricity, I just add credit to the machine.

We are close to our neighbours; we visit each other regularly and there are no problems between us. But our neighbours and my husband's family do not know that I suffered sexual violence during the genocide. Sometimes they hear rumours from my former neighbours, but they do not really believe it. They do not ask me about it; they only ask my husband. And I like his answer. He simply tells them: "It's not your responsibility to know my wife, I'm the one who loves her. You do not need to know about how we are living as a family. It's only for us to know, and that is enough."

My children know the whole story of what I experienced during the genocide. They were eager to find out because they know that I am HIV positive and their father does not have HIV. So, I tried to explain everything to them. The children also heard other people's stories because survivors and perpetrators speak publicly about the genocide during the one hundred days of commemoration every year. So they know the truth. Sometimes my children also read *The Men Who Killed Me* at home, although it is challenging for them to read English because they have only attended primary school. They still ask me all kinds of questions. The children do not blame me for what happened; they just thank God and tell me: "You know, mama, there is a reason why you survived and it is because then you could take care of us. If you would have died, who would have protected us?" They love me and support me so much.

The love and support of my family has strengthened me and enabled me to support others. Our neighbours chose me to be the community nurse. In this role, I advise people on health issues, like good hygiene and reproductive health. As a community nurse, I also have the opportunity to gain many insights into my community. I have seen positive changes within families as a result of my work, and I am proud of myself for that. Many women who were experiencing conflicts with their husbands or children were able to settle their disputes after I gave them advice.

Some women come to see me because their husbands are violent towards them. The men spend their money—not on food or clothes for the family—but on beer, and then they get drunk and become violent. If these women tell their husbands to stop drinking, they just refuse; in fact, these men even feel that they are being disrespected because their wives are trying to be leaders of their family. In villages, a man who refuses to join other men in drinking alcohol is accused of being under the control of his woman; the other men will not respect him. I listen to these women and advise them to take on small businesses, to pray, and to go to the local security leaders and to the police. The laws in our country support women in these kinds of situations, so we should not keep quiet. Luckily, we already have some good examples of men who do not drink, like the leader of our community. My husband drinks a lot, but fortunately, he always ensures that the family has enough to eat and he does not spend all the money on alcohol.

Besides my volunteer work as a community nurse, I have also managed to work and earn an income over the past decade. The proceeds I received from *The Men Who Killed Me* and the subsequent support I received through the Mukomeze Foundation helped me to get back on my feet again. And now I can say that I am economically independent. I am proud of what I have accomplished; it makes me feel strong. I have a house and my own plot of land with over one hundred coffee trees. With the income I earn from selling coffee beans, I can take care of my family. I can now buy clothes, soap and food for my children.

It was not always like this. After the genocide I was very traumatized; my neighbours knew I was HIV positive, and I got so sick that sometimes I fainted. Once I even fell into a coma. When I met Mama Lambert, the counsellor at Solace Ministries, for the first time, I cried a lot. I did not have any hope left. I tried to run away from my past, and I even wanted to commit suicide several times. But when Mama Lambert comforted me, I began to feel positive changes within myself, until I finally felt that I could love again and even get married. Of all the people who have supported me since the genocide, I am most grateful to Mama Lambert. She is such a good person. She gave me life again after the genocide. Nowadays I always pray: "Please, God, protect me so that I can face tomorrow." And, of course, we still face hardship, but I am so thankful that we genocide survivors have each other.

The *gacaca* courts have also been helpful in our healing. During the trials, the perpetrators told us survivors where they had left the dead. This made it possible for us to find them and give them a proper burial. It was also important to see a perpetrator stand in front of others and tell the truth; that he had killed your mother, your child. Those who murdered my family asked me for forgiveness, and I found the courage to forgive them. As for those who raped me, I believe they passed away, so I could not confront them in *gacaca*. If they would have confessed and asked for forgiveness, I would have been able to forgive them. Many perpetrators were honest in *gacaca*; what they said was really the truth. *Gacaca* made people feel free again; it allowed us to live side-by-side again. The only difficulty with *gacaca* is that our children heard many details, and it could really traumatize them. For me, I was very happy with *gacaca*, but it was more difficult for my children.

I used to also speak in public during the annual commemoration, but I stopped in 2011 because by then people already knew my story. I always used to talk about everything, including the sexual violence, even though it is very difficult to talk about this. Afterwards, people know everything, including your HIV status, and they may gossip about you. I never cared about that. I always felt I needed to talk about everything I had experienced during the genocide. I just wish to speak the truth because it gives me a sense of peace and it takes away my burdens.

For a while, my health was improving and I felt strong. In 2012, I was very happy when I weighed ninety kilograms; back then I was so beautiful and healthy. It was one of my best moments in life. But now, as I said, I am very sick. The doctor told me that I have ulcers in my uterus, and that they are growing and will eventually burst. They might develop into cancer. The doctors still need to find out what the exact problem is; they might remove the ulcers, but if the disease has already spread and progressed into cancer, they will not be able to remove my uterus. I need to go to the hospital to find out what they can do to help me, but we cannot afford the necessary transport, medication and surgery; it is very expensive. We are thinking of selling a piece of our land to save money.

I am not as worried as I was when I first heard about my health condition. I only found out about it in August 2018, but I already had pain around my genitals before then. I started to use pads because pus and blood were leaking from my vagina. So I decided to go to the hospital. The doctor told me that even if I must undergo surgery, life would go on. I think the problem was caused by an infection in my genitals that may have been the result of the sexual violence I endured during the genocide. I received injections to clean my private parts, so that the infection would subside.

Judging by how I feel now, I am not sure whether I will be able to survive for a few more years. Maybe I will have a miracle. If I die of cancer, my children will inherit my possessions. That is why it is important to me to have a house and land; my children will have shelter and a source of income even if I am gone. Although I have done everything I could to ensure that my children will be supported, they are still very young, and I am not sure if my inheritance will be enough. I believe Paul will take care of our children, but it might be difficult for him if he remarries.

I have also tried to prepare my children for whatever may come. I always tell my children to pray; that is the first thing: love God. I also tell my children to make sure they are self-reliant, and to avoid depending on other people. Even if I die very soon, I tell them to always have hope and to work very hard. Another thing I always tell them is that their father is young, so if I die he might marry another woman; I tell them to please love this new woman and their children.

Looking back over the past decade, I realize that participating in *The Men Who Killed Me* made it possible for me to share with everyone the truth about what I suffered during the genocide. People need to accept the reality. What happened to me in the genocide is the truth, and I do not need to hide myself, not even my face. This second book will illustrate the challenges that survivors continue to face, but also the positive changes in our lives. This book will show the world that we are not dead; we are still alive and we strive for a better future.

3

THE ENDURING IMPACT OF SUPPORT

Mama Lambert providing support to a survivor after she was tested f

"A person who has suffered a lot has a story to tell. They need to tell it to someone who is willing to listen and who will empathize. Otherwise, it can be more damaging to tell your story to someone who doesn't want to listen. This is what we have been experiencing in the course of doing this work. When [survivors] trust you, and share their story, the heavy load and burden that they are carrying is somehow lifted a bit. And I think this is the first contribution leading to the process of healing."

JEAN GAKWANDI
Founder and Director of Solace Ministries

THE SURVIVORS FEATURED in this book are current or former beneficiaries of Solace Ministries and the Mukomeze Foundation.* Solace Ministries is a Rwandan ecumenical non-governmental organization dedicated to meeting the needs of widows and orphans of the 1994 genocide against the Tutsi in Rwanda. Jean Gakwandi, a genocide survivor, established the organization in December 1994, and it continues to be run by genocide survivors today. The sorrow that plagued Jean during and following the genocide, as well as the love he felt for his fellow survivors and his devout Christian faith, motivated him to dedicate his life to comforting others.

Solace provides its members with counselling, community development programs, medical care, education and employment support. Those who have the capacity to work also receive micro-credits for agricultural or business endeavours. These services are uniquely tailored to the needs of genocide survivors. The organization's holistic approach is informed by the belief that the first step in the healing process requires survivors to feel that they are truly being heard. Trauma counselling, in both individual and group sessions, is vital. In Solace's experience, survivors are generally unable to adequately care for themselves or resume other activities without this crucial first step. Even after survivors have received

* This chapter is based on interviews with Solace Ministries staff: Jean Gakwandi (Founder and Director), Mama Lambert (Head of Counselling) and Agnes Mukankusi (Sponsorship Programme). Their perspectives and insights have also been integrated in the chapter, "Life after death." For more information about the work of Solace Ministries, see: Jean Gakwandi and Karin Heidrich, *Solace: The Story of Solace Ministries* (Stiftung Bethel-prowerk, 2015); Mama Lambert, *For Those Who Do Not Believe in Miracles: The Resilience of a Rwandan Woman Who Survived the Genocide* (Wolf Legal Publishers, 2015); Solace Ministries, online: <www.solacem.org>. For more information about the Mukomeze Foundation, see: <www.mukomeze.nl/en>.

counselling, trauma related to the genocide is deep-rooted, enduring and may affect subsequent generations. The healing process unfolds over many years.

Solace has five regional centres around Rwanda, with a total of sixty-two staff. Solace supports more than eight thousand families (about forty thousand people) across Rwanda, in sixty Solace communities ranging in size from fifty to several hundred members. The organization strives to become an alternative family for survivors, to restore survivors' sense of dignity and to create support networks for those who are traumatized, isolated, poor and crave hope in the face of an uncertain future.

In 1999, at the initiative of a group of women within the organization, Solace began providing specific services for survivors of sexual violence. It was soon evident that there were many more genocide survivors of sexual violence, most of them living with HIV, who had feared speaking up about their experiences. They were afraid of the reactions of their relatives and community members. Within the year, Solace had set up specialized individual and group counselling sessions with Mama Lambert as the main counsellor. Mama Lambert, Jean Gakwandi and other Solace staff listened to survivors' stories and provided them with comfort and advice.

In 2002, Solace established a private clinic in Kigali, where women could be tested for and counselled about HIV in a safe and private environment. In 2011, Solace converted the private clinic into a public one. At the public clinic, twenty-nine Solace staff now serve tens of thousands of people from the region, and continue to provide crucial individual counselling to genocide survivors of sexual violence.

By 2004, Solace Ministries had documented among their membership more than eight hundred survivors who were subjected to sexual violence during the genocide, and this number continues to grow. Even today—25 years after the genocide—Solace continues to encounter survivors who have never spoken about their experiences of sexual violence during the genocide.

Throughout the years, Solace has supported survivors as they faced a myriad of consequences related to their experiences of sexual violence. After 25 years, numerous psychological, health and socio-economic impacts of the genocide persist, and Solace provides crucial, long-term services and support to survivors. Among other things, the organization has helped survivors grapple with medical complexities associated with HIV, as well as other illnesses linked to the sexual violence they suffered; in some cases, survivors succumbed to their illnesses. Solace also created a safe space for male survivors of sexual violence, who faced—and continue to face—significant challenges in recounting their experiences. Moreover, the organization has helped to heal dysfunctional relationships between mothers and their children who were conceived from sexual violence inflicted during the genocide. Over the years, Solace has grown to accommodate survivors' needs, as they navigate the devastating ramifications of genocide.

Thousands of genocide survivors of sexual violence have benefited from Solace's comprehensive, compassionate and dedicated approach to healing. Despite a host of often-debilitating obstacles, survivors of sexual violence are active and many have taken on leadership positions in their communities. The survivors are proud of their accomplishments.

"I have been working at Solace Ministries for so many years because I see the positive developments in genocide survivors. When I see someone hopeless, but I can encourage her and tell her that she has value, that she is created in God's image, this makes me think that I am perhaps in this world to do this kind of work. When I see how these survivors go from one level to the next, I believe that even I can overcome anything."

AGNES MUKANKUSI
Sponsorship Programme at Solace Ministries

SOLACE PARTNERS WITH different organizations, both inside and outside of Rwanda. One of these organizations is the Mukomeze Foundation, based in the Netherlands. Mukomeze supports genocide survivors of sexual violence, in an effort to help them regain their sense of dignity, hope and economic independence. Most of Mukomeze's beneficiaries live in southern Rwanda, where fewer services and facilities are available.

Mukomeze coordinates individual sponsorships and group projects, intended to support beneficiaries in rebuilding their lives. Survivors spend their sponsorship funds in different ways, including by repairing or purchasing their own homes, paying for their children's school materials and fees, supporting their own post-secondary education, setting up small businesses (e.g., handicraft-making and sewing), and engaging in livestock farming or agriculture.

To date, seventy-five women and one man have benefited from the Mukomeze sponsorship program, and several hundred Rwandans have also received support through a variety of projects. Mukomeze regularly coordinates meetings between Rwandan survivors and sponsors, donors and others. By raising awareness of survivors' living conditions, resilience and strength, and by promoting cross-cultural exchange, the Mukomeze Foundation strives to provide a global platform for genocide survivors of sexual violence.

Mama Lambert embracing a woman during a group counselling session in Kigali

4

LIFE AFTER "DEATH"

IN THE IMMEDIATE aftermath of the 1994 Genocide against the Tutsi in Rwanda,[1] the profound impact on survivors was difficult to fathom. This was particularly so for survivors of sexual violence, who felt obliged to hide their pain because of the stigma associated with sexual violence, and were left to wrestle with illness, poverty and trauma in isolation.[2] While women and girls were the primary targets of the rape campaign, boys and men also suffered brutal sexual violence during the genocide.[3] Of course, "rape was invariably only one element in a succession of traumatic episodes, including other forms of abuse, terror, betrayal, bereavement and displacement."[4] By the tenth anniversary of the genocide, one report noted:

> For some victims, there is no life after rape; they lose their health and happiness. Women raped during the 1994 genocide in Rwanda lead a uniquely troubled existence and many feel their survival is its own form of torture. They are desperately impoverished, commonly infected with [HIV] and are responsible for several children. They see their lives as "finished" or "another form of martyrdom"; one woman described herself as "a living dead person."[5]

Twenty-five years later, the devastating consequences of sexual violence on survivors remain palpable. At the same time, tremendous strides have been made in addressing survivors' many needs. The Rwandan government, non-governmental organizations (NGOs), and the international community have undertaken a host of initiatives and programs to support survivors, many with promising and impressive outcomes.

In this edition of *And I Live On: The Resilience of Rwandan Genocide Survivors of Sexual Violence*, we explore some developments in the lives of genocide survivors of sexual violence over the past decade, focusing on the realms of HIV and healthcare, justice and reconciliation, socio-economic support, and survivors' healing process.

1. HIV AND HEALTHCARE

FOLLOWING THE GENOCIDE, there was "an HIV pandemic among those who had survived the conflict."[6] An estimated 70% of survivors of sexual violence were infected with HIV,[7] which was "among the weapons of choice calculated to destroy while inflicting maximum pain and suffering."[8] In rural areas of Rwanda, HIV prevalence increased dramatically, from 1% before the genocide to 11% in 1997.[9]

Survivors experienced significant gaps in access to healthcare and HIV treatment, particularly in the years following the genocide; by 2006, only 53% of adults and 41% of children in need of antiretroviral treatment were receiving it.[10] Ironically, while HIV-positive survivors of sexual violence struggled to access healthcare and a basic standard of living in the years following the genocide, those accused of orchestrating the genocide who were awaiting trial at the International Criminal Tribunal for Rwanda (ICTR) were receiving antiretroviral treatment in prison.[11] Even where treatment was available, HIV-related stigma often discouraged survivors from accessing healthcare services.[12] A 2004 report by African Rights summarized medical care for genocide survivors of sexual violence as "too little, too late"; without a real sense of hope, many survivors preferred to "remain in the dark about their HIV status."[13] As a result, AIDS-related deaths peaked about ten years following the genocide, with an upper estimate of 22,000 deaths per year.[14]

Over the past decade, however, Rwanda has made strides in its response to HIV and AIDS.[15] In 2011, the President of Rwanda, Paul Kagame, was the first African leader to convene a UN General Assembly meeting about the global AIDS response.[16] Between 2010 and 2017, annual rates of new HIV infections declined by 20% to 7,400 from 9,300, and annual rates of AIDS-related deaths decreased by almost 50%, to 3,100 from 6,000.[17] By 2017, 83% of individuals living with HIV were receiving treatment as a result of a robust government program called "Treat All."[18] In the same year, with near universal coverage of services to prevent vertical HIV transmission (i.e., the

Adela (centre) with other survivors during a gathering at Solace Ministries in Kigali

transmission of HIV from a mother to her child during pregnancy, labour, delivery or breastfeeding),[19] 92% of pregnant women living with HIV had accessed treatment, which prevented 1,900 new infections among their children.[20] Since 2015, the rate of vertical HIV transmission has been under 2%,[21] and as of 2017, HIV prevalence is at 3.4% among women and 1.9% among men.[22] According to a 2017 report of the Joint UN Programme on HIV/AIDS (UNAIDS), HIV prevalence in Rwanda is highest among women aged 40-44 years (8%) and men aged 45-49 years (9%), while residents of Kigali have the highest HIV prevalence compared to the rest of the country at 6%.[23]

NGOs have been invaluable in lobbying domestically and internationally to improve supports, channelling funding and providing programs for people living with HIV in Rwanda, including through the provision of free antiretroviral treatment for genocide survivors.[24] Rwanda-based organizations, such as Solace Ministries,[25] the Association of Genocide Widows (Avega)[26] and Imbuto Foundation[27]—among others—stand out in bringing genocide rape survivors together, many of whom are living with HIV, and offering them unique assistance and a safe space.[28] One vital measure that some organizations offered to survivors was the establishment of medical clinics where women could be tested for HIV without the need to visit public hospitals.[29] Many survivors avoided public hospitals because of HIV-related stigma, and to minimize the possibility that they might encounter their perpetrators' families.[30] Survivors who tested positive received HIV counselling, medical advice and information about antiretroviral treatment, and comfort in an environment free of stigma and shame.[31] As the Rwandan government adopted different measures to address stigma and discrimination against people living with HIV, it directed patients living with HIV to public hospitals. Today, many genocide survivors of sexual violence no longer have concerns about going to public hospitals.[32]

While antiretroviral treatment allows survivors to manage their HIV infection and generally improves their long-term health,[33] many HIV-positive survivors have more comprehensive medical needs because of HIV-related co-morbidities and other illnesses that resulted from their experiences of sexual violence during the genocide.[34] These related health conditions—so-called "secondary diseases"—have a major impact on the lives of survivors, and include tuberculosis,[35] a range of infection-related cancers,[36] hepatitis B and hepatitis C.[37] The lasting health impacts of genocidal sexual violence is evident among the seventeen survivors featured in *The Men Who Killed Me*, four of whom died from illnesses related to the sexual violence they endured.[38] Several others continue to suffer from these sexual violence-related health conditions.

Rwanda's government has facilitated access to healthcare through a near-universal health insurance program called "Mutuelle de Santé."[39] The program is financed by tax revenue, foreign aid and voluntary premiums scaled by income.[40] Access to Mutuelle de Santé has significantly improved in recent years, reaching 84% of the population in 2016.[41] The government's commitment in the realm of healthcare is also evident in the "substantial expansion of health sector resources, which has improved health access across the country," including in the form of more national hospitals, provincial hospitals, health centres and health posts.[42]

For genocide survivors living with HIV who may not be able to work consistently, accessing Mutuelle de Santé can be difficult.[43] Although the government covers the cost of health insurance for the poorest households in Rwanda,[44] the program remains less accessible to poor households that do not qualify for this subsidy.[45] This is particularly so for large households who are required to pay a fee for every family member upon registration; if they cannot pay the entire fee in one lump sum, they are denied coverage.[46] With

39% of Rwandans living below the poverty line,[47] many must prioritize food and shelter to the detriment of healthcare and other future planning.[48]

In order to supplement health insurance, the government has made efforts to improve access to healthcare for genocide survivors. In 1998, the government established the Genocide Survivors Support and Assistance Fund (FARG) to promote survivors' social welfare and facilitate their reintegration and social development,[49] although there are no specific provisions prioritizing support for genocide survivors of sexual violence.[50] Over the past twenty years, under this program the government has provided healthcare coverage to treat over two million medical cases in domestic hospitals, and a further 398 complex medical cases abroad.[51]

Despite these essential supports for genocide survivors, many health-related challenges remain and new difficulties are emerging, both for the aging generation of survivors and the younger generation that relies on them. In recent years, development aid to Rwanda has declined significantly, including funds for HIV treatment.[52] Stigma associated with HIV persists,[53] and survivors continue to require better access to healthcare and counselling, including a wider range of HIV treatment, and nutritious food to maintain health.[54] Many elderly survivors, particularly those without immediate family, require home-based care.[55] Gender-based violence also continues to plague the country: the latest available data indicate that in 2015, 21% of women had experienced physical or sexual violence from their intimate male partner over the previous twelve-month period, and 34% of women had experienced this at least once in their lifetime.[56] Rates of domestic violence are also higher among women who are between the ages of 40-49 years (43%), women who are poor (44%), women who do not have an education (41%), women who are divorced, separated or widowed (54%), and those who have more children (43% of women with three or four children, and 46% of women with five or more children).[57] A "culture of silence" around domestic violence continues to affect reporting,[58] and "deeply rooted patriarchal stereotypes regarding roles and responsibilities of men and women" endure in Rwanda.[59] According to UNAIDS, gender-based violence and gender inequalities, combined with physiological factors, place women and girls at "a huge risk of HIV infection."[60]

II. JUSTICE AND RECONCILIATION

IN ORDER TO address over one million individuals suspected of crimes during the genocide, the Rwandan government established the *gacaca* courts and launched its proceedings in 2001.[61] The *gacaca* were traditional tribunals where "the community historically came together to deal with family or neighbourly disputes," and they were "adapted as a mix of both customary law and classical penal state justice to deal with cases of genocide."[62] Without the *gacaca* courts, Rwanda's ordinary courts would have taken more than one hundred years to complete legal proceedings addressing all of the accused persons; the *gacaca* courts were established to expedite these proceedings.[63] As outlined in the preamble of the Rwandan law establishing the *gacaca* courts, their objectives were to:

(1) Uncover the truth of what happened during the genocide;
(2) Address a culture of impunity by prosecuting the genocide's perpetrators;
(3) Reconcile Rwandans and support their unity; and
(4) Prove that Rwandans had the capacity to settle their own problems through a system of justice based on Rwandan custom.[64]

The *gacaca* courts were structured to allow communities "to work together in order to judge those who had participated in the genocide, to identify the victims and to rehabilitate the innocent."[65] These institutions were designed to be "at the basis of collaboration, reconciliation and unity among Rwandans."[66]

Initially following the genocide, ordinary courts maintained jurisdiction over the most severe genocide crimes, or "category one" crimes, including approximately 8,000 cases of rape.[67] These crimes carried sentences of life imprisonment.[68] However, in 2008, cases involving sexual violence were transferred to *gacaca* courts in order to expedite the remaining trials and to provide justice long overdue for survivors of sexual violence, many of whom were very ill; the transfer also helped mitigate resource constraints.[69] Because of the difficult and potentially traumatizing nature of the cases, *gacaca* judges, called *Inyangamugayo* (meaning "people of integrity" in Kinyarwanda, and who were lay judges in the community), received training on the legal and psychological components of cases involving rape and sexual torture.[70] Legal amendments were also incorporated to implement several procedural rules to protect survivors and their families.[71] For example, cases involving sexual violence were heard in closed sessions (i.e., only in front of *Inyangamugayo*, as opposed to the general public).[72] This way, survivors of sexual violence testified against their perpetrator(s) in a confidential setting, where trauma counsellors were allowed to accompany them for support, whenever possible.[73] Between mid-2008 and mid-2009, approximately 7,000 cases of sexual violence were tried before 1,900 *gacaca* courts.[74]

In spite of the above procedural protections, several obstacles continued to prevent genocide survivors of sexual violence from participating in *gacaca* courts,[75] some of which were described by the individuals featured in *The Men Who Killed Me*. Some survivors did not know who had raped them, including those who were assaulted by French soldiers stationed in southern Rwanda.[76] Many survivors had also passed away from AIDS-related illnesses or other traumas,[77] and numerous perpetrators had died or escaped the country by the time the *gacaca* proceedings began.[78] Survivors also feared attending *gacaca* courts because of threats from relatives of accused *génocidaires*. Indeed, according to the Rwandan government's Victim and Witness Support Unit, during the 15 years following the genocide, an estimated 168 individuals—mostly genocide survivors, but also *gacaca* witnesses—were killed because of their ethnicity or participation in *gacaca* proceedings.[79] The murder rate more than quintupled during the operation of *gacaca*, with the highest number of deaths reported in 2006 when proceedings began across the country.[80] Some survivors chose not to participate in the *gacaca* proceedings because they felt it would be too difficult to testify and were concerned that community members would find out they had been raped, despite the special procedures in place to protect confidentiality.[81] Finally, the designation of sexual violence offences as a 'category one' crime that carried a sentence of life imprisonment, coupled with the shame of being labelled a rapist in Rwanda, likely had the counterproductive effect of deterring perpetrators from confessing to these crimes.[82] Of the seventeen survivors featured in *The Men Who Killed Me*, two women testified against some of their rapists in *gacaca*.

The *gacaca* courts officially closed on May 4th, 2012,[83] having adjudicated a total of nearly two million cases involving over one million accused persons.[84] In many ways, the *gacaca* courts were unprecedented: by integrating "Rwanda's customary conflict resolution method and modified aspects of the ordinary criminal justice system," *gacaca* reflected an innovative judicial approach to address "insurmountable challenges in pursuit of justice for Rwanda."[85] *Gacaca* was unique in prioritizing, on such a large scale, accountability for perpetrators of international crimes, including conflict-related sexual violence.[86]

Survivors' experiences in and perceptions of the *gacaca* courts vary considerably and are difficult to generalize, but are largely positive.[87] The interviews we conducted with the survivors featured in this book also provide some insight. In 2008, survivors generally expressed a sense of skepticism about the *gacaca* courts' potential to achieve justice for survivors. A decade later, however, most of these same survivors felt that *gacaca* proceedings provided them, and Rwandans in general, with a real prospect of reconciliation and unity. *Gacaca* proceedings enabled a public airing of the events that occurred during the genocide, and the expedient proceedings paved the way for survivors to move forward with their lives. In particular, some perpetrators' confessions allowed survivors to locate the remains of their loved ones, thus providing an opportunity for closure. By prosecuting a significant number of suspected perpetrators, *gacaca* courts helped to address the culture of impunity in Rwanda following the genocide. Importantly, while the *gacaca* court proceedings were often deeply re-traumatizing, many survivors felt that the process unburdened their hearts and allowed them to heal and reintegrate into society. The passage of time, better understanding of the workings of the *gacaca* courts, an improved security situation, increased access to the most basic (e.g., material and psychological) needs, and teachings about the role of forgiveness in individual and societal reconciliation all seem to have influenced the way survivors evaluate *gacaca* today.[88]

Despite these positive aspects of the *gacaca* proceedings, survivors consistently expressed disappointment in not having received reparations from their perpetrators, as per court orders.[89] A 2001 report by the International Crisis Group estimated that close to USD$100 million had been awarded after only 4,000 people had been tried, but none of the reparations had been paid.[90] *Gacaca* courts tried a total of over one million cases involving Category 3 offences, which included looting or destroying property, and 96% resulted in convictions with orders to pay reparations.[91] By mid-2017, thousands of reparation orders had yet to be executed, but the government has instituted measures to enforce payments to survivors.[92] This is significant not only because many survivors remain indigent, but also because reparations form a cornerstone of the reconciliation process. As one editorial in Rwanda's major news publication explained:

> Perpetrators who are intentionally refusing to pay their reparations are only fuelling the pain of survivors. It stifles the healing process for the survivors, and defeats the whole purpose of the unity and reconciliation efforts. ... This is another form of genocide denial ... Paying reparations is a symbol that the perpetrators are remorseful and regret what they did. It is not an equivalent of compensation of what survivors lost. No compensation can equate to what survivors went through or lost.[93]

The Rwandan government and others have also suggested that the United Nations should take part in compensating survivors, given the international community's failure to protect victims during the genocide.[94] As one genocide survivor of sexual violence stated, "Tell the world that the international community has a debt because they didn't come to our rescue. They should now come to support us as we deal with the legacy of genocide."[95]

BEYOND THE *GACACA* courts within Rwanda, in 1994 the United Nations Security Council also established the ICTR in Arusha, Tanzania.[96] The ICTR indicted 93 individuals, including "high-ranking military and government officials, politicians, businessmen, as well as religious, militia, and media leaders," who were alleged to have committed the most serious violations of international humanitarian law—crimes of genocide, crimes against humanity and war crimes.[97] The Tribunal was officially closed on December 31st, 2015, having sentenced sixty-two individuals and referred ten indictments to national jurisdictions for trial (two referrals to France, and eight to Rwanda).[98]

The ICTR was the "first institution to recognize rape as a means of perpetrating genocide"[99]—effectively singling out sexual violence from the obscurities of conflict, and reframing it as among the most heinous crimes requiring prosecution at the highest courts. The Court recognized in the 1998 *Akayesu* case that sexual violence may contribute to the destruction of the group, such that it would constitute genocide:

> These rapes resulted in physical and psychological destruction of Tutsi women, their families and their communities. Sexual violence was an integral part of the process of destruction, specifically targeting Tutsi women and specifically contributing to their destruction and to the destruction of the Tutsi group as a whole.[100]

Among those indicted of crimes relating to sexual violence, forty-three proceeded to trial and fourteen were convicted,[101] five of them for genocide.[102] The evolution of international law and practice in this respect is an immense achievement for survivors of sexual violence, and it was fuelled in large part by the courage of survivors to testify as witnesses.[103]

Despite its achievements, the ICTR was not without shortcomings in its prosecution of crimes of sexual violence during the 1994 genocide. The court did not adequately investigate cases of sexual violence, including cases involving male victims and female perpetrators, and prosecutors also failed to charge crimes in the way that victims perceived them to have been carried out—that is, as genocide.[104] At times, these shortcomings led to great disappointment among survivors, as a 2005 United Nations report indicated:

> Even as Rwandan rape survivors continue to recognize the value and potential of an international court set up to deliver justice to them, the overwhelming sentiments expressed by them are a burning anger, deep frustration, dashed hopes, indignation and even resignation. Justice moves slowly for all at the ICTR, but even more slowly for rape victims.[105]

In 2014, the ICTR prosecutor published the "Best Practices Manual for the Investigation and Prosecution of Sexual Violence Crimes in Post-Conflict Regions," a valuable tool of lessons-learned paving the way for future accountability with respect to these crimes.[106] In recent years, international institutions and governments around the world have reaffirmed through various initiatives that conflict-related sexual violence is not simply an inevitable by-product of war, but constitutes a crime that is preventable and punishable under international law.[107]

In addition to legal proceedings, survivors have also found other avenues towards a sense of justice to be valuable. These include symbolic gestures to commemorate and memorialize the genocide, such as the Kigali Genocide Memorial[108] and dozens of other memorial sites across the country.[109] Some of these memorial sites commemorate the rampant sexual violence that took place, such as the Nyamata Genocide Memorial, where a coffin displays the body of Annonciata Mukandoli, a young woman who was raped by multiple assailants and viciously murdered during the genocide.[110] Several films and documentaries have also provided important insight into the scale of sexual violence during the genocide, and the complexity and extent of its impact on survivors.[111] However, conflict-related sexual violence is by and large still frequently neglected in initiatives for commemoration and memorialization, to the detriment of survivors.

III. SOCIO-ECONOMIC SUPPORT

IN THE IMMEDIATE aftermath of the genocide, it was estimated that 70% of the population was female, and women headed 50% of all households.[112] In practical terms, this meant that rebuilding efforts were dependent on women. Nearly one decade after the genocide, the majority of women who were the heads of their households were widowed.[113] In some urban centres, such as Huye and Kibuye, female-headed households constituted 84% and 72%

of all households, respectively, and were generally more impoverished than their male counterparts.[114]

Poverty remains a pervasive and significant constraint on survivors' capacity to reclaim their lives.[115] Severe illness and psychological trauma left many survivors unable to work, and those who were widowed are deprived of family income and support.[116] Added responsibilities of caring for surviving family members or children born of rape plunged many survivors into extreme poverty.[117] Even those survivors who were able to work often faced stigma because of their HIV status, which in turn led to loss of employment.[118] Insecure living conditions and inadequate access to shelter also rendered survivors vulnerable to sexual advances from neighbours and passers-by, further increasing the risk of unwanted pregnancies and HIV.[119]

While healthcare support and *gacaca* proceedings contributed to the process of healing and reconciliation, socio-economic assistance over the past decade has also been crucial for survivors to move forward with their lives. This has included several initiatives implemented by the Rwandan government, such as the construction of housing and the provision of cows to indigent families.[120] Through the FARG program, the government paid orphans' school fees, built shelter for homeless genocide survivors, and supported income-generating activities.[121] With the support of UNICEF, the government set up in 2009 the *Isange One Stop Centre*, which provides free services for survivors of child domestic abuse and gender-based violence.[122] Contraception has also become widely promoted and freely distributed at all public health facilities.[123]

In the years following the genocide, the government also implemented essential legislative reforms in support of gender equality.[124] For example, criminal law amendments in 2008 acknowledged sexual violence as a serious offence, carrying heavy jail sentences for perpetrators, spanning from ten years to life imprisonment depending on the consequences of the attack.[125] In 1999, women were granted the right to own land and property, and they could now choose to maintain their assets separately from their husbands'.[126] In 2016, inheritance laws were also passed so that a man's property must be split equally between his wife and both his female and male children.[127]

Women in Rwanda are also better represented in government and the courts; in fact, Rwanda is a world leader in women's political representation.[128] In 2003, the government amended the Rwandan Constitution to require "at least 30% of posts in decision making organs" to be occupied by women, but in many areas, women are even better represented.[129] By 2017, Rwanda had the world's highest proportion of women in parliament.[130] As of 2018, 61% of Rwanda's members of parliament are women, as are 50% of the country's Cabinet[131] and judges.[132] Rwanda's trajectory in this regard is in direct contrast to the general trend worldwide: in recent years, women's political representation around the world has stagnated, with a global average of 23% women in parliament.[133] Rwanda is also at the forefront of deploying female peacekeepers for United Nations missions, thereby acknowledging the important role women play in peace processes.[134]

Despite Rwanda's commitment to women's representation in government, the "reality of gender advancement is different among grassroots populations."[135] Women's political power does not necessarily extend to their private lives; as one commentator observed: "a female politician could stand up in parliament, advocating for issues like stronger penalties for sexual violence and subsidized maxi-pads for the poor, but find herself scared to speak out about the oppression in her own home."[136] According to 2015 figures, over one-third of women in Rwanda have experienced intimate partner violence.[137] Nevertheless, among the younger generation, there are recent indications of an "openness to rectify the gap between women's representation and [their] daily lived experiences." In 174 schools across the country, adolescent boys and young men are learning how to stop domestic violence in all forms and to address power imbalances between the sexes—"a re-education that stands in opposition to cultural norms."[138]

Marie Louise feeding her cow. Milk and manure used as fertilizer have helped her become more financially self-sufficient

An important aspect of women's advancement at the grassroots level is financial independence, particularly for survivors.[139] Many NGOs provide survivors with entrepreneurship training, as well as income-generating support through micro-credit loans that allow survivors to start their own businesses.[140] In addition to enhancing survivors' material status and helping to tackle the widespread poverty into which the genocide plunged many survivors, these initiatives contribute to survivors' sense of personal agency and wellbeing by helping to restore their sense of dignity as breadwinners and providers for their children.[141] Women in Rwanda have earned recognition as agents of change and reconciliation, with meaningful roles in the recovery and reintegration of their families and communities following the genocide.[142]

NGOs, such as the Mukomeze Foundation, also coordinate sponsorships to support survivors and orphans in their educational aspirations, covering school fees and materials. These programs not only alter children's life trajectories, but also fuel their motivation and bestow them with hope for the future. According to one survivor, these sponsorships make children "feel secure and confident to go to school, knowing that somebody cares for them. They feel like they can begin to live."[143]

Notwithstanding these developments, genocide survivors of sexual violence continue to face severe challenges. Many survivors face challenges finding income-generating activities and securing stable housing.[144] Some survivors living with HIV are chronically ill, and even if they are able to obtain formal employment or start a business, they often experience significant income loss because of their episodic and often debilitating illnesses, which force them to stop working.[145] Survivors living with HIV also fear that they will succumb to their illness without being able to leave a sufficient inheritance for their children.[146] Survivors express a need for better support for their children's school fees and materials.[147]

Moreover, unique challenges persist for a new generation of children born of rape. Local NGOs estimate that, "the widespread campaign of rape and torture during the Rwandan genocide led to the births of an estimated 20,000 children."[148] These children are often disparaged as "children of killers," and they "tend to live in poverty, facing higher rates of HIV and domestic abuse than their peers."[149] Many of the survivors who struggled to raise and support these children have become weak and ill due to HIV and related health conditions.[150] Children of this generation are also often unaware of how they were conceived, do not understand the source of the hostility that they face, and do not know of the trauma that they have come to symbolize.[151] Families in such situations require extensive counselling and ongoing support.[152] However, efforts to extend FARG support to children born of genocidal sexual violence[153] ultimately failed and these children continue to be dependent on the support of NGOs.[154]

IV. HEALING PROCESS

"In our culture, talking about sex is very private. That is why it was very hard for survivors to come up and reveal that they were raped. Some even killed themselves following the genocide. But nowadays things are changing slowly. We believe that we should not keep quiet; we should speak the truth so that justice could take its course. If you speak out, it can be a lesson to others. When you release your burden, you release your heart."

MAMA LAMBERT
Head Counselling Department at Solace Ministries

THE GENOCIDE TORE apart the fabric of Rwandan society. Hundreds of thousands of victims were left to grapple with their agonizing memories and new realities, and to recover from paralyzing trauma. By sheer perseverance, survivors have a restored sense of dignity and an identity that transcends their experiences of the genocide. As one survivor and trauma counsellor described, "Empowerment is a process."[155]

NGOs have played an invaluable role in supporting survivors following the genocide. By 1997, more than 15,000 grassroots women's organizations and fifty national associations for women were established, most of them multi-ethnic.[156] These groups have created unique and responsive programming, and an accepting environment that addresses survivors' trauma and suffering. These programs include, among other things, comprehensive individual and group counselling, spiritual healing, medical clinics for survivors living with HIV or AIDS, material support, income-generating and capacity-building activities, educational support and sponsorship initiatives.[157] Having lost so many loved ones in the genocide, many survivors find a safe space within these organizations, where they can heal and gradually re-establish their community.[158] Survivors find comfort in sharing their challenges and joys with each other, and forging new bonds within an enduring and mutually reinforcing support system.

Pascasie sharing her story during a group counselling session at Solace Ministries in Kigali

For some survivors, counselling and prayer were essential first steps towards healing, as it freed them to "accept to live on."[159] According to a Solace Ministries staff, for genocide survivors who were left feeling like "insects or snakes—not humans," the opportunity to "tell their story and be heard restored their dignity."[160] Group counselling sessions have been particularly helpful because they allowed survivors to feel accepted by others, and sharing mutual vulnerabilities has strengthened these bonds.[161] Notably, in a country such as Rwanda where religion plays an important social role, religious aspects of group meetings have been vital to the healing process; as one Solace Ministries staff observed, these meetings have helped survivors "to restore their relationship with God."[162] Once survivors are able to recover a sense of self-worth, they can resume "activities they had abandoned," and feel that "they are really human."[163]

Most remarkable is survivors' capacity to forgive: the majority of survivors featured in this book reported that they had forgiven their perpetrators, although it was generally more difficult for survivors whose perpetrators failed to admit to their crimes or apologize. This was mitigated, to a certain degree, for survivors who had the unconditional support of their new families. Forgiving was a crucial step for many survivors to enable them to move forward with their lives.

WITHOUT EXCEPTION, SURVIVORS' inspiring resilience continues to fuel their determination to heal and live on.

NOTES

1. On January 26, 2018, the United Nations (UN) General Assembly designated April 7 as the "International Day of Reflection on the 1994 Genocide against the Tutsi in Rwanda," amending the title of the annual observance. The General Assembly took note that the new title "captured the historical facts of what happened in 1994—genocide against the Tutsi in Rwanda—and left no room for ambiguity." (UN, "General Assembly Designates April 7 International Day of Reflection on 1994 Genocide against Tutsi in Rwanda, Amending Title of Annual Observance," 26 January 2018, online: <https://www.un.org/press/en/2018/ga12000.doc.htm>.)
2. See UN Commission on Human Rights, *Report on the Situation of Human Rights in Rwanda Submitted by Mr. Rene Degni-Segui, Special Rapporteur of the Commission on Human Rights* (29 January 1996) E/CN.4/1996/68; Human Rights Watch, *Shattered Lives, Sexual Violence During the Rwandan Genocide and its Aftermath* (September 1996) [Human Rights Watch, *Shattered Lives* 1996]; African Rights, *Rwanda: Death, Despair and Defiance* (August 1995).
3. Anne-Marie de Brouwer and Usta Kaitesi, "Sexual Violence" in *The Elgar companion to the International Criminal Tribunal for Rwanda*. Eds. Anne-Marie de Brouwer and Alette Smeulers (Edward Elgar Publishing, 2016), at page 174 [de Brouwer & Kaitesi, "Sexual Violence" (2016)]. See also, Usta Kaitesi, *Genocidal Gender and Sexual Violence: The Legacy of the ICTR, Rwanda's Ordinary Courts and Gacaca Courts*. Cambridge, Antwerp, and Portland (Intersentia, 2013) [Kaitesi, *Genocidal Gender and Sexual Violence* (2013)]; Usta Kaitesi & Roelof Haveman, "Prosecution of Genocidal Rape and Sexual Torture before the Gacaca Tribunals in Rwanda," in *Victimological Approaches to International Crimes: Africa*. Eds. Rianne Letschert et al. (Intersentia, 2011) [Kaitesi & Haveman, "Prosecution of Genocidal Rape and Sexual Torture before Gacaca Tribunals in Rwanda, (2011)].
4. African Rights, *Rwanda: Broken Bodies, Torn Spirits – Living with Genocide, Rape and HIV/AIDS*, (April 2004) at page 9 [African Rights, *Rwanda: Broken Bodies, Torn Spirits* 1996].
5. *Ibid* at page 6.
6. UN, "Press conference on women living with HIV/AIDS from sexual violence during genocide in Rwanda" (31 May 2006), online: <https://www.un.org/press/en/2006/060531_Rwanda.doc.htm>.
7. Amnesty International, "Rwanda: 'Marked for Death,' rape survivors living with HIV/AIDS in Rwanda" (5 April 2004), at page 3 [Amnesty International, "Marked for Death" (2004)].
8. Paula Donovan, "Rape and HIV/AIDS in Rwanda," *The Lancet* (1 December 2002), online: <https://www.thelancet.com/journals/lancet/article/PIIS0140-6736(02)11804-6/fulltext?_eventId=login#>.
9. World Health Organization (WHO), "Sexual violence in conflict settings and the risk of HIV," *Information Bulletin Series Number 2* (May 2005), online: <http://data.unAIDS.org/gcwa/gcwa_fs_vaw3_who_01may05_en.pdf>.
10. Republic of Rwanda, "Country Progress Report—Rwanda (January 2006—December 2007)" *United Nations General Assembly Special Session on HIV/AIDS* (2008), online: <http://data.unAIDS.org/pub/report/2008/rwanda_2008_country_progress_report_en.pdf>.
11. Amnesty International, "Marked for Death" (2004), *supra* note 7, at page 20.
12. African Rights, *Rwanda: Broken Bodies, Torn Spirits* 1996, *supra* note 4, at page 47.
13. *Ibid* at pages 51 and 47.
14. Joint UN Programme on HIV/AIDS (UNAIDS), "Rwanda Factsheet 2017: HIV and AIDS Estimates" (2018), online: <http://www.unAIDS.org/en/regionscountries/countries/rwanda> [UNAIDS, "Rwanda Factsheet 2017" (2018)].
15. UNAIDS, "Rwanda's leadership provides model for advancing global agenda towards ending AIDS" (10 December 2018), online: <http://www.unAIDS.org/en/resources/presscentre/featurestories/2018/december/rwanda-leadership> [UNAIDS, "Rwanda's leadership

provides model for advancing agenda towards ending AIDS" (2018)]. See also, Republic of Rwanda Ministry of Health, "National HIV/AIDS Targets 2018-2020-2030" (2015), online: <http://www.rbc.gov.rw/IMG/pdf/rwanda_hiv_AIDS_2020_and_2030_targets.pdf> [Rwanda Ministry of Health, "National HIV/AIDS Targets" (2015)]; UNAIDS, "2018 Data" (2018), online: <http://www.unAIDS.org/sites/default/files/media_asset/unAIDS-data-2018_en.pdf> [UNAIDS, "2018 Data"].

16. UNAIDS, "Rwanda's leadership provides model for advancing agenda towards ending AIDS" (2018), *supra* note 15.
17. *Ibid*. See also UNAIDS, "Rwanda Factsheet 2017" (2018), *supra* note 14.
18. *Ibid*; UNAIDS, "Rwanda 2017 Country Report" (2018), online: <http://www.unAIDS.org/sites/default/files/country/documents/RWA_2017_countryreport.pdf> [UNAIDS, "Rwanda 2017 Country Report" (2018)]. See also, Sabin Nsanzimana et al., "Phased implementation of spaced clinic visits for stable HIV-positive patients in Rwanda to support Treat All," *Journal of the International AIDS Society* (21 July 2017), online: <https://www.ncbi.nlm.nih.gov/pmc/articles/PMC5577720/>.
19. United Nations International Children's Emergency Fund (UNICEF), "Situation Analysis of Children in Rwanda: Summary Report" (2018), at page 10, online: <https://www.unicef.org/rwanda/RWA_resources_sitansummary.pdf> [UNICEF, "Situation Analysis of Children in Rwanda" (2018)].
20. UNAIDS, "Rwanda's leadership provides model for advancing agenda towards ending AIDS" (2018), *supra* note 15.
21. UNICEF, "Situation Analysis of Children in Rwanda" (2018), *supra* note 19, at page 10. See also, Rwanda Ministry of Health, "National HIV/AIDS Targets" (2015), *supra* note 15, at page 11.
22. UNAIDS, "Rwanda Factsheet 2017" (2018), *supra* note 14.
23. UNAIDS, "Rwanda 2017 Country Report" (2018), *supra* note 18.
24. Lindsey Hilsum, "Rwanda genocide survivors denied AIDS treatment" BMJ (17 April 2004) 328(7445): 913, online: <https://www.ncbi.nlm.nih.gov/pmc/articles/PMC390156/>.
25. Solace Ministries, online: <http://www.solacem.org/>.
26. Avega – Agahozo, online: <http://avega.org.rw/>.
27. Imbuto Foundation, online: <http://www.imbutofoundation.org/>.
28. Interview with Mama Lambert, Solace Ministries, Rwanda (Nov 2018) [Mama Lambert interview (2018)].
29. *Ibid*.
30. *Ibid*.
31. *Ibid*.
32. *Ibid*.
33. Juvenal Biraguma, Eugene Mutimura, Jose Frantz, "Health-related quality of life and associated factors in adults living with HIV in Rwanda," *Journal of Social Aspects of HIV/AIDS* (10 September 2018), online: <https://www.ncbi.nlm.nih.gov/pmc/articles/PMC6136357/>. See also, Sabin Nsanzimana et al., "Life expectancy among HIV-positive patients in Rwanda: a retrospective observational cohort study," *The Lancet: Global Health* (March 2015) Vol. 3, Issue 3, pages 169-177, online: <https://www.sciencedirect.com/science/article/pii/S2214109X1470364X>.
34. *Ibid*; Mama Lambert interview (2018), *supra* note 28. See also, Rafael Maciel et al., "Comorbidity is more common and occurs earlier in persons living with HIV than in HIV-uninfected matched controls, aged 50 years and older: A cross-sectional study," *International Journal of Infectious Diseases* (May 2018) Vol. 70, pages 30-35, online: <https://www.ijidonline.com/article/S1201-9712(18)30045-6/fulltext>.
35. In 2017, 22% of tuberculosis patients in Rwanda were also HIV-positive: WHO, "Rwanda Tuberculosis profile" (2018) online: <https://extranet.who.int/sree/Reports?op=Replet&name=%2FWHO_HQ_Reports%2FG2%2FPROD%2FEXT%2FTBCountryProfile&ISO2=RW&LAN=EN&outtype=html>.

36. According to a 2018 study, HIV was significantly associated with Kaposi Sarcoma, lymphoma and cancers of the cervix, vulva, penis and eye (Tharcisse Mpunga et al., "A case-control study of HIV infection and cancer in the era of antiretroviral therapy in Rwanda," *International Journal of Cancer* (15 September 2018) Vol. 143, Issue 6, pages 1348-1355, online: <https://www.ncbi.nlm.nih.gov/pmc/articles/PMC6099235/>).
37. A 2016 study found that, among patients living with HIV in Rwanda, the prevalence of hepatitis B and hepatitis C (HCV) was 4.3% and 4.6%, respectively (Justine Umutesi et al., "Prevalence of hepatitis B and C infection in persons living with HIV enrolled in care in Rwanda," *BMC Infectious Diseases* (May 2017) Vol. 17, online: <https://bmcinfectdis.biomedcentral.com/articles/10.1186/s12879-017-2422-9>). According to the WHO, one of the assumed causes for hepatitis C transmission in Rwanda is "exposure to contaminated blood during the Rwandan genocide. ... Repeated rape and penetrating trauma under torture exposed thousands of survivors to potential contact with HIV or HCV." (Aimable Mbituyumuremyi, "Controlling hepatitis C in Rwanda: a framework for a national response," *Bulletin of the World Health Organization* (2018) Vol. 96, pages 51-58, online: <https://www.who.int/bulletin/volumes/96/1/16-183772/en/>).
38. According to Jean Gakwandi, founder and director of Solace Ministries in Rwanda: "People need to know the consequences. Yes, we all die, but those survivors who died because of secondary diseases all died because of the mistakes and sins of other people. These were not natural deaths. They were assassinations. The ones who raped them, wanted them to die. To die slowly. And in this way – they killed them. As Marie Louise [one of the women who was interviewed for the book] said, [her assailants] killed her. She is dying little by little. They have all been killed. And the title—*The Men Who Killed Me*—reflects this fact. They were killed." (Interview with Jean Gakwandi, Solace Ministries, Rwanda (Nov 2018)).
39. Andrew Makaka, Sarah Breen, and Agnes Binagwaho, "Universal health coverage in Rwanda: a report of innovations to increase enrolment in community-based health insurance," *The Lancet* (21 October 2012) Vol. 380(S7), online: <https://www.thelancet.com/journals/lancet/article/PIIS0140-6736(13)60293-7/fulltext>.
40. Eduardo Porter, "In Health Care, Republicans Could Learn From Rwanda" *New York Times* (18 July 2017), online: <https://www.nytimes.com/2017/07/18/business/economy/senate-obamacare-rwanda.html>.
41. UNICEF, "Situation Analysis of Children in Rwanda" (2018), *supra* note 19, at pages 9-10 and 27.
42. *Ibid*, at page 8. Health posts provide access to primary healthcare services in rural areas. Health posts "follow a Public-Private Partnership model and operate as a franchise, with each Health Post being owned, operated and managed by a nurse as a small business. Start-up loans are provided at affordable rates, and the Ministry of Health designates available infrastructure and chooses the location for the Health Post, with a bursary account also established for continued financial and business training of the nurses." (HANSHEP, "Increasing Access to Primary Care Services through Health Posts in Rwanda," online: <https://www.hanshep.org/our-programmes/increasing-access-to-primary-care-services-through-health-posts-in-rwanda>.)
43. Mama Lambert interview (2018), *supra* note 28.
44. UNICEF, "Situation Analysis of Children in Rwanda" (2018), *supra* note 19, at pages 9-10 and 27.
45. Janviere Uwimana, "Saving a Few Cents Every Day, Some Rwandans Manage to Pay Health Insurance Premiums," *Global Press Journal* (14 September 2017), online: <https://globalpressjournal.com/africa/rwanda/saving-cents-every-day-rwandans-manage-pay-health-insurance-premiums/>.
46. *Ibid.*
47. UNICEF, "Situation Analysis of Children in Rwanda" (2018), *supra* note 19, at page 7.
48. Janviere Uwimana, "Saving a Few Cents Every Day, Some Rwandans Manage to Pay

Health Insurance Premiums," *Global Press Journal* (14 September 2017), online: <https://globalpressjournal.com/africa/rwanda/saving-cents-every-day-rwandans-manage-pay-health-insurance-premiums/>.

49. Republic of Rwanda, "FARG registering big milestones in improving survivors' welfare," (accessed 21 December 2018), online: <http://www.farg.gov.rw/index.php?id=18&tx_ttnews%5Btt_news%5D=36&cHash=a99dc451e93a82c15b282d92940f9a8b> [Republic of Rwanda, "FARG registering big milestones in improving survivors' welfare"]. The program was originally called, "Assistance to the Needy Genocide Survivors."

50. Coalition for Women's Human Rights in Conflict Situations, "Women's Rights to Reparation" (background paper, Nairobi Meeting, March 19-21, 1997), at page 61.

51. Republic of Rwanda, "FARG registering big milestones in improving survivors' welfare," *supra* note 49.

52. Rwanda Ministry of Health, "National HIV/AIDS Targets" (2015), *supra* note 15, at page 12.

53. *Ibid*, at page 13; "Stigma still barrier to AIDS fight – activists," *The New Times* (3 March 2018), online: <https://www.newtimes.co.rw/section/read/229238>.

54. Mama Lambert interview (2018), *supra* note 28.

55. *Ibid*.

56. UN Women, "Global Database on Violence Against Women: Rwanda," online: <http://evaw-global-database.unwomen.org/en/countries/africa/rwanda#1>. Despite this high prevalence of physical and sexual violence against women, Rwanda has made a great deal of progress over the past few years. The proportion of women in Rwanda who experienced physical or sexual violence from their intimate partner over the previous 12-month period in 2010 was 44.3% – over double that in 2015 (UNAIDS, "2018 Data," *supra* note 15, at page 54).

57. National Institute of Statistics of Rwanda, "Rwanda Demographic and Health Survey 2014-2015," (2015), at page 270, online: <http://evaw-global-database.unwomen.org/-/media/files/un%20women/vaw/vaw%20survey/rwanda%20vaw%20survey.pdf?vs=411>.

58. *Ibid*, at page 267.

59. UN Office of the High Commissioner for Human Rights, "Concluding observations on the second and fourth periodic report of Rwanda," Committee on Economic, Social and Cultural Rights (10 June 2013) E/C.12/RWA/CO/2-4, at para 9.

60. UNAIDS, "2018 Data," *supra* note 15, at page 22.

61. *Organic Law No 40/2000 Setting Up "Gacaca Jurisdictions" and organizing prosecutions for offences constituting the crime of genocide or crimes against humanity committed between October 1, 1990 and December 31, 1994* (26 January 2001), online: <https://www.refworld.org/cgi-bin/texis/vtx/rwmain/opendocpdf.pdf?reldoc=y&docid=52f2349c4>. The *gacaca* laws were amended several times thereafter – in 2001, 2004, 2006, 2007 and 2008 – to adapt to new and changing realities and difficulties in trial proceedings.

62. Anne-Marie de Brouwer and Etienne Ruvebana, "The Legacy of the *Gacaca* Courts in Rwanda: Survivors' Views," *International Criminal Law Review* 13 (2013) 937-976, at page 939 [de Brouwer & Ruvebana, "The Legacy of *Gacaca* Courts in Rwanda" (2013)]. See also, Roelof Haveman, "Gacaca in Rwanda: Customary Law in Case of Genocide," in J. Fenrich, P. Galizzi and T. Higgins (eds.), *The Future of Customary Laws in Africa* (Cambridge University Press, Cambridge, 2011) pages 387-422.

63. *Ibid*.

64. *Organic Law No 40/2000 Setting Up "Gacaca Jurisdictions" and organizing prosecutions for offences constituting the crime of genocide or crimes against humanity committed between October 1, 1990 and December 31, 1994* (26 January 2001), online: <https://www.refworld.org/cgi-bin/texis/vtx/rwmain/opendocpdf.pdf?reldoc=y&docid=52f2349c4>.

65. de Brouwer & Ruvebana, "The Legacy of *Gacaca* Courts in Rwanda" (2013), *supra* note 62, at page 942.

66. *Ibid*. For more in-depth analysis of the pros and cons of the *gacaca* courts, see: Felix Ndahinda and Alphonse Muleefu, "Revisiting the Legal, Socio-Political Foundations and (Western)

Criticisms of *Gacaca* Courts," in Tom Bennett et al (eds.), *African Perspectives on Tradition and Justice* (Intersentia, Antwerp, 2012) pages 149-173; Gerald Gahima, *Transitional Justice in Rwanda: Accountability for Atrocity* (Routledge, Oxon, 2013); Roelof Haveman, "Doing Justice to Gacaca," in Alette Smeulers and Roelof Haveman (eds.), *Supranational Criminology* (Intersentia, Antwerp, 2008, Vol. 6) pages 359-400; Roelof Haveman and Alphonse Muleefu, "Gacaca and Fair Trial," in Dawn Rothe et al (eds.), *State Crimes* (Ruggers University Press, New Brunswick, NJ, 2010) pages 219-244; Bert Ingelaere, "Does the Truth Pass Across the Fire Without Burning? Locating the Short Circuit in Rwanda's Gacaca Courts," *The Journal of Modern African Studies* 47 (2009) pages 507-528.

67. *Ibid*, at page 940.
68. Anne-Marie de Brouwer and Sandra Ka Hon Chu, "*Gacaca* Courts in Rwanda: 18 years after the genocide, is there justice and reconciliation for survivors of sexual violence?" (3-part series) *IntLawGrrls* (April 2012), online: <http://www.intlawgrrls.com/2012/04/gacaca-courts-in-rwanda-18-years-after.html>; <http://www.intlawgrrls.com/2012/04/survivors-views-on-gacaca.html>; <http://www.intlawgrrls.com/2012/04/as-end-of-gacaca-nears-looking-toward.html> [de Brouwer & Chu, "*Gacaca* Courts in Rwanda" (2012)].
69. de Brouwer & Ruvebana, "The Legacy of *Gacaca* Courts in Rwanda" (2013), *supra* note 62, at page 940.
70. For more details on training of the *Inyangamugayo*, see Kaitesi, *Genocidal Gender and Sexual Violence* (2013), *supra* note 3.
71. de Brouwer & Chu, "*Gacaca* Courts in Rwanda" (2012), *supra* note 68. See also, de Brouwer & Ruvebana, "The Legacy of *Gacaca* Courts in Rwanda" (2013), *supra* note 62.
72. *Ibid*.
73. *Ibid*.
74. *Ibid*.
75. *Ibid*.
76. *Ibid*.
77. *Ibid*.
78. de Brouwer & Ruvebana, "The Legacy of *Gacaca* Courts in Rwanda" (2013), *supra* note 62, at page 947.
79. Leslie Haskell, "Justice Compromised: The Legacy of Rwanda's Community-Based Gacaca Courts," *Human Rights Watch* (31 May 2011), online: <https://www.hrw.org/report/2011/05/31/justice-compromised/legacy-rwandas-community-based-gacaca-courts#>, citing interview with Théoneste Karenzi, Coordinator of the Victim and Witness Support Unit (VWSU) in the National Prosecutor's Office, Kigali, November 16, 2010. In 2009, the Rwandan government reported 6 killings of genocide survivors and *gacaca* witnesses, while Ibuka (a survivors' organization) reported 24 killings: US State Department, Bureau of Democracy, Human Rights, and Labor, "Country Reports on Human Rights Practices – 2009: Rwanda" (March 2010), online: <https://www.state.gov/j/drl/rls/hrrpt/2009/af/135971.htm> [Haskell, "Justice Compromised" *Human Rights Watch* (2011)].
80. *Ibid*.
81. de Brouwer & Chu, "*Gacaca* Courts in Rwanda" (2012), *supra* note 68.
82. de Brouwer & Ruvebana, "The Legacy of *Gacaca* Courts in Rwanda" (2013), *supra* note 62, at page 947-948.
83. United Nations, "Background Information on the Justice and Reconciliation Process in Rwanda," *Outreach Programme on the Rwanda Genocide and the United Nations* (March 2014), online: <https://www.un.org/en/preventgenocide/rwanda/about/bgjustice.shtml>.
84. de Brouwer & Ruvebana, "The Legacy of *Gacaca* Courts in Rwanda" (2013), *supra* note 62, at page 950, citing "Summary of the Report Presented at the Closing of *Gacaca* Courts Activities" (18 June 2012).
85. Kaitesi, *Genocidal Gender and Sexual Violence* (2013), *supra* note 3, at page 48. See also Kaitesi & Haveman, "Prosecution of Genocidal Rape and Sexual Torture before Gacaca Tribunals in

Rwanda, (2011), *supra* note 3, at page 409.

86. *Ibid*, at page 59. See also Preamble, *Organic Law No. 16/2004 of 19/6/2004 establishing the organization, competence and functioning of gacaca courts charged with prosecuting and trying the perpetrators of the crime of genocide and other crimes against humanity, committed between 1 October 1990 and 31 December 1994* (19 June 2004), online: <https://repositories.lib.utexas.edu/bitstream/handle/2152/4582/3677.pdf?sequence=1>.
87. *Ibid*; de Brouwer & Ruvebana, "The Legacy of *Gacaca* Courts in Rwanda" (2013), *supra* note 62; de Brouwer & Chu, "*Gacaca* Courts in Rwanda" (2012), *supra* note 68; Kaitesi & Haveman, "Prosecution of Genocidal Rape and Sexual Torture before Gacaca Tribunals in Rwanda, (2011), *supra* note 3; Phil Clark, "Bringing the peasants back in, again: state power and local agency in Rwanda's *gacaca* courts," *Journal of Eastern African Studies* (April 2014) 8(2), pages 193-213, online: <https://journals-scholarsportal-info.myaccess.library.utoronto.ca/details/17531055/v08i0002/193_btpbialairgc.xml>; Phil Clark, *The Gacaca Courts, Post-Genocide Justice and Reconciliation in Rwanda: Justice without Lawyers* (Cambridge Studies in Law and Society, 2010).
88. See also, de Brouwer & Ruvebana, "The Legacy of *Gacaca* Courts in Rwanda" (2013), *supra* note 62.
89. Mama Lambert interview (2018), *supra* note 28.
90. International Crisis Group, "International Criminal Tribunal for Rwanda: Justice Delayed," *Report No. 30* (7 June 2001), at page 33.
91. Netherlands Ministry of Foreign Affairs, "Country Report on Human Rights and Justice in Rwanda" (18 August 2016), at page 31. *Gacaca* laws never provided direct reparations for victims of Category 1 and 2 crimes, although the 1996 and 2001 *Gacaca* Laws required judges to draw up lists of damages suffered by victims, which would be passed on to a government compensation fund that had yet to be established. The 2004 *Gacaca* Law contemplated other forms of compensation for victims that would be provided by another law, which was ultimately never enacted. For further details, see Haskell, "Justice Compromised" *Human Rights Watch* (2011), *supra* note 79.
92. At the time of writing, it remained unclear how many reparation orders had yet to be executed, as reports provided vastly different figures, from 8,445 cases to 64,000: "Editorial: Genocide reparation defaulters should be given a deadline to pay up," *The New Times* (11 April 2017), online: <https://www.newtimes.co.rw/section/read/210485>; Nasra Bishumba, "Government seeks to wind down Gacaca reparation cases by 2018," *The New Times* (15 June 2017), online: <https://www.newtimes.co.rw/section/read/214265>.
93. "Editorial: Genocide reparation defaulters should be given a deadline to pay up," *The New Times* (11 April 2017), online: <https://www.newtimes.co.rw/section/read/210485>.
94. Republic of Rwanda, National Unity and Reconciliation Commission, "Unity and Reconciliation Process in Rwanda" (December 2016), online: <http://www.nurc.gov.rw/index.php?id=70&no_cache=1&tx_drblob_pi1%5BdownloadUid%5D=98>; Jean Paul Mugiraneza, "Rwanda genocide: why compensation would help the healing," *The Guardian* (7 April 2014), online: <https://www.theguardian.com/global-development-professionals-network/2014/mar/04/rwanda-genocide-victims-compensation>; James Karuhanga, "Will there ever be reparations for Genocide survivors?" *The New Times* (7 April 2018), online: <https://www.newtimes.co.rw/rwanda/will-there-ever-be-reparations-genocide-survivors>. A major criticism of the Tribunal was its failure to provide reparations to survivors: Human Rights Watch, "Rwanda: International Tribunal Closing Its Doors" (23 December 2015), online: <https://www.hrw.org/news/2015/12/23/rwanda-international-tribunal-closing-its-doors>.
95. "Intended Consequences," *MediaStorm* (October 2008), at minute 12:12 – 12:27, online: <https://mediastorm.com/publication/intended-consequences> ["Intended Consequences" (2008)].
96. UN Security Council, Resolution 955 (8 November 1994) S/RES/955, online: <http://www.

irmct.org/specials/ictr-remembers/docs/res955-1994_en.pdf?q=ictr-remembers/docs/res955-1994_en.pdf>.

97. UN International Residual Mechanism for Criminal Tribunals, "The ICTR in Brief," *Legacy website of the International Criminal Tribunal for Rwanda* (accessed 22 December 2018), online: <http://unictr.irmct.org/en/tribunal> [UN, "The ICTR in Brief"].
98. *Ibid*; International Criminal Tribunal for Rwanda, "Complementarity in Action: Lessons Learned from the ICTR Prosecutor's Referral of International Criminal Cases to National Jurisdictions for Trial," (February 2015) at page 7, online: <https://reliefweb.int/sites/reliefweb.int/files/resources/150210_complementarity_in_action.pdf>.
99. UN, "The ICTR in Brief", *supra* note 97.
100. *The Prosecutor v. Akayesu* ICTR-96-4-T (Judgment, 2 September 1998), at para 731. The ICTR also made important contributions to acknowledging that sexual violence constitutes crimes against humanity and war crimes.
101. de Brouwer & Kaitesi, "Sexual Violence" (2016), *supra* note 3, at page 177.
102. *The Prosecutor v. Sylvestre Gacumbitsi* ICTR-2001-64-T (Judgment, 17 June 2004), paras 291–293; *The Prosecutor v. Mikaeli Muhimana* ICTR-95-1B-T (Judgment, 28 April 2005), paras 513, 517–519; *The Prosecutor v. Bagosora et al.* ICTR-98-41 (Judgment and Sentence, 18 December 2008) (confirmed on appeal: *Theoneste Bagosora and Anatole Nsengiyumva v. The Prosecutor* ICTR-98-41-A (Judgment, 14 December 2011), para 721); *The Prosecutor v. Edouard Karemera and Matthieu Ngirumpatse* ICTR-98-44-T (Judgment and Sentence, 2 February 2012), paras 1670–1671 (confirmed on appeal: *Édouard Karemera and Matthieu Ngirumpatse v. The Prosecutor* ICTR- 98-44-A (Judgment, 29 September 2014), paras 587–636).
103. de Brouwer & Kaitesi, "Sexual Violence" (2016), *supra* note 3, pages 171-201; Kaitesi, *Genocidal Gender and Sexual Violence* (2013), *supra* note 3. See also the documentary film, "The Uncondemned" (2016), online: <http://www.theuncondemned.com/about/> ["The Uncondemned" (2016)].
104. *Ibid*.
105. Binaifer Nowrojee, "'Your Justice is Too Slow': Will the ICTR Fail Rwanda's Rape Victims?" *United Nations Research Institute for Social Development* (November 2005), at page 4, online:<http://www.unrisd.org/80256B3C005BCCF9/(httpAuxPages)/56FE32D5C0F6DCE9C125710F0045D89F/$file/OP10%20Web.pdf>. See also, de Brouwer & Kaitesi, "Sexual Violence" (2016), *supra* note 3, pages 171-201.
106. International Criminal Tribunal for Rwanda, "Best Practices Manual for the Investigation and Prosecution of Sexual Violence Crimes in Post-Conflict Regions" (30 January 2014), online: <http://unictr.irmct.org/sites/unictr.org/files/legal-library/140130_prosecution_of_sexual_violence.pdf>. See also, Linda Bianchi, "The Prosecution of Rape and Sexual Violence: Lessons from Prosecutions at the ICTR," in Anne-Marie de Brouwer *et al.* (eds.), *Sexual Violence as an International Crime: Interdisciplinary Approaches* (Intersentia, Cambridge/Antwerp/Portland, 2013), pages 141-172.
107. For example, see UN Security Council Resolution 1888 (2009), which created the *United Nations Team of Experts on the Rule of Law and Sexual Violence in Conflict* to assist national authorities in strengthening the rule of law to ensure criminal accountability for perpetrators of conflict-related sexual violence, as well as the *Women's Protection Advisors* in the context of UN peacekeeping missions (Office of the Special Representative of the Secretary-General on Sexual Violence in Conflict, online: <https://www.un.org/sexualviolenceinconflict/our-work/team-of-experts/>; United Nations Peacekeeping, "Conflict-related Sexual Violence," online: <https://peacekeeping.un.org/en/conflict-related-sexual-violence>). UN Security Council Resolution 1888 also led to the appointment of a Special Representative of the Secretary-General on Sexual Violence, who provides strategic leadership and coordination through UN Action, and compiles an annual report on conflict-related sexual violence around the world (online: <https://www.un.org/sexualviolenceinconflict/>). See also, UN Security Council Resolutions 1889 (2009), 1960 (2010), 2106 (2013), and 2122 (2013) (United Nations,

"Background Information on Sexual Violence used as a Tool of War," online: <http://www.un.org/en/preventgenocide/rwanda/about/bgsexualviolence.shtml>). Several campaigns were also launched in an effort to eliminate violence against women, including the UN Women's *UNiTE to End Violence Against Women*, and the UN Action Against Sexual Violence in Conflict's *Stop Rape Now* (UN Women, "UNiTe to End Violence Against Women," online: <http://www.unwomen.org/en/what-we-do/ending-violence-against-women/take-action/unite>; UN Action Against Sexual Violence in Conflict, "Stop Rape Now", online: <http://www.stoprapenow.org/>). In 2014, the Global Summit to End Sexual Violence in Conflict was a milestone as the largest gathering ever on this subject, and it culminated with the UN's Declaration of Commitment to End Sexual Violence in Conflict (Gov.UK, "2014 Global Summit to End Sexual Violence in Conflict," online: <https://www.gov.uk/government/collections/2014-global-summit-to-end-sexual-violence-in-conflict>). In 2018, the Nobel Peace Prize was awarded to Denis Mukwege and Nadia Murad for their efforts to end the use of sexual violence as a weapon of war and armed conflict (The Nobel Peace Prize (2018), online: <https://www.nobelpeaceprize.org/The-Nobel-Peace-Prize-2018>).

108. Kigali Genocide Memorial, online: <https://www.kgm.rw/>.
109. Genocide Archive of Rwanda, "Genocide Memorials," online: <http://genocidearchiverwanda.org.rw/index.php/Category:Memorials>. See also de Brouwer & Chu, "*Gacaca* Courts in Rwanda" (2012), *supra* note 68.
110. *Ibid.*
111. See "The Uncondemned" (2016), *supra* note 103; "Intended Consequences" (2008), *supra* note 95. See also, "100 Days" (2001) and "A Sunday in Kigali" (2006).
112. Human Rights Watch, *Shattered Lives* 1996, *supra* note 2.
113. Republic of Rwanda, "A Synthesis of the Analysis of the 2002 Census of Rwanda" *Ministry of Finance and Economic Planning* (15 August 2002), page 109.
114. *Ibid.*
115. Amnesty International, "Marked for Death" (2004), *supra* note 7, at pages 4-5 and 9.
116. African Rights, *Rwanda: Broken Bodies, Torn Spirits* 1996, *supra* note 4.
117. *Ibid.*
118. Amnesty International, "Marked for Death" (2004), *supra* note 7, at page 2.
119. *Ibid*, at page 4.
120. de Brouwer & Chu, "*Gacaca* Courts in Rwanda" (2012), *supra* note 68.
121. Republic of Rwanda, *National Action Plan 2009-2012* (May 2010).
122. United Nations International Children's Emergency Fund (UNICEF), "The Isange one stop centre: transforming the lives of survivors of violence in Rwanda" (May 2010), online: <https://www.unicef.org/rwanda/reallives_8374.html>.
123. Sarah Boseley, "Rwanda: A revolution in rights for women," *The Guardian* (28 May 2010), online: <https://www.theguardian.com/world/2010/may/28/womens-rights-rwanda>[Boseley, "Rwanda: A revolution for Women" *The Guardian* (2010)]. See also, Rwanda Ministry of Health, "National HIV/AIDS Targets" (2015), *supra* note 15, at page 17; Republic of Rwanda Ministry of Health, "National Guidelines for Prevention and Management of HIV and STIs" (2016) at pages 41-42, online: <https://AIDSfree.usaid.gov/sites/default/files/rw_national_guidelines_hiv.pdf>.
124. See Republic of Rwanda, "National Gender Policy," *Ministry of Gender and Family Promotion* (July 2010), online: <https://www.ilo.org/dyn/natlex/docs/ELECTRONIC/94009/110188/F-1576743982/RWA-94009.pdf>; Republic of Rwanda, *National Action Plan 2009-2012* (May 2010).
125. Official Gazette of the Republic of Rwanda, *Law No. 59/2008 of 2008 on Prevention and Punishment of Gender-Based Violence*, (6 April 2009), online: <https://www.refworld.org/docid/4a3f88812.html>. See also, Boseley, "Rwanda: A revolution for Women" *The Guardian* (2010), *supra* note 123.
126. Official Gazette of the Republic of Rwanda, *Law No. 22/99 of 12/11/1999: Law to supplement*

book one of the civil code and to institute part five regarding matrimonial regimes, liberalities and successions, (15 November 1999), online: <https://repositories.lib.utexas.edu/bitstream/handle/2152/5448/2740.pdf?sequence=1&isAllowed=y>. See also, Boseley, "Rwanda: A revolution for Women" *The Guardian* (2010), *supra* note 123.

127. Official Gazette of the Republic of Rwanda, *Law No. 27/2016 of 08/07/2016: Law governing matrimonial regimes, donations and successions*, (8 July 2016), online: <http://www.minijust.gov.rw/fileadmin/Law_and_Regulations/Official_Gazette_no_31_of_01.08.2016.pdf>. See also, Boseley, "Rwanda: A revolution for Women" *The Guardian* (2010), *supra* note 123.
128. UN Women, "Women in Politics: 2017" (2017), online: <http://www.unwomen.org/-/media/headquarters/attachments/sections/library/publications/2017/femmesenpolitique_2017_english_web.pdf?la=en&vs=1123> [UN Women, "Women in Politics" (2017)].
129. Republic of Rwanda, *National Action Plan 2009-2012* (May 2010).
130. UN Women, "Women in Politics" (2017), *supra* note 128.
131. Ignatius Ssuunal, "Rwanda unveils gender-balanced cabinet with 50% women," *Independent* (19 October 2018), online: <https://www.independent.co.uk/news/world/africa/rwanda-cabinet-women-gender-balance-government-africa-ethiopia-a8592461.html>. See also, Republic of Rwanda Parliament, "Fourth Parliament sworn in," (19 September 2018), online: <http://parliament.gov.rw/index.php?id=218&tx_news_pi1%5Bnews%5D=1519&tx_news_pi1%5Bcontroller%5D=News&tx_news_pi1%5Baction%5D=detail&cHash=76643ec1fd6d62a7f8d7ba1866efc5c4>.
132. UN Women, "Revisiting Rwanda five years after record-breaking parliamentary elections" (13 August 2018), online: <http://www.unwomen.org/en/news/stories/2018/8/feature-rwanda-women-in-parliament>.
133. UN Women, "Press Release: New IPU and UN Women map shows women's representation in politics stagnating" (15 March 2017), online: <http://www.unwomen.org/en/news/stories/2017/3/press-release-new-ipu-and-un-women-map-shows-womens-representation-in-politics-stagnating>.
134. United Nations Peacekeeping, "Female Rwandan police officers empower the vulnerable women and children in UN protection site" (1 October 2018), online: <https://peacekeeping.un.org/en/female-rwandan-police-officers-empower-vulnerable-women-and-children-un-protection-site>; United Nations Peacekeeping, "Service born of sacrifice: Rwanda's commitment to UN peacekeeping" (11 May 2018), online: <https://peacekeeping.un.org/en/un-news/service-born-of-sacrifice-rwandas-commitment-to-un-peacekeeping>; Elisée Mpirwa, "Rwanda makes case for greater women's role in peacekeeping," *The New Times* (7 May 2018), online: <https://www.newtimes.co.rw/news/rwanda-makes-case-greater-womens-role-peacekeeping>. For statistical breakdowns, see: United Nations Peacekeeping, "Monthly Strength Report" (December 2018), online: <https://peacekeeping.un.org/sites/default/files/msrs_december_2018_0.pdf>.
135. Anne Bouleanu, "The Rwandan school turning boys into feminists," *BBC News* (26 September 2018), online: <https://www.bbc.com/news/world-africa-45496335>.
136. Gregory Warner, "It's The No. 1 Country For Women In Politics – But Not in Daily Life" *NPR* (29 July 2016), online: <https://www.npr.org/sections/goatsandsoda/2016/07/29/487360094/invisibilia-no-one-thought-this-all-womans-debate-team-could-crush-it>. See also, Justine Uvuza, "Hidden Inequalities: Rwandan Female Politicians' Experiences of Balancing Family and Political Responsibilities," Doctoral Thesis at Newcastle University School of Geography, Politics and Sociology (April 2014), online: <https://theses.ncl.ac.uk/dspace/bitstream/10443/2475/1/Uvuza,%20J.%2014.pdf>.
137. UN Women, "Prevalence Data on Different Forms of Violence Against Women" (2015) online: <http://evaw-global-database.unwomen.org/en/countries/africa/rwanda>.
138. Anne Bouleanu, "The Rwandan school turning boys into feminists," *BBC News* (26 September 2018), online: <https://www.bbc.com/news/world-africa-45496335>.
139. Mama Lambert interview (2018), *supra* note 28; Jean Gakwandi interview (2018), *supra* note 38.

140. See, for example, Solace Ministries, online: <http://www.solacem.org/>; Avega – Agahozo, online: <http://avega.org.rw/>; Imbuto Foundation, online: <http://www.imbutofoundation.org/>.
141. Mama Lambert interview (2018), *supra* note 28; Interview with Agnes Mukankusi, Solace Ministries, Rwanda (Nov 2018) [Agnes Mukankusi interview (2018)].
142. Elizabeth Powley, "Strengthening Governance: The Role of Women in Rwanda's Transition – a Summary," UN Office of the Special Advisor on Gender Issues and Advancement of Women (19-22 January 2004, Expert Group meeting, New York).
143. Mama Lambert interview (2018), *supra* note 28.
144. *Ibid.*
145. *Ibid.*
146. *Ibid.*
147. *Ibid.*
148. Foundation Rwanda, online: <http://www.foundationrwanda.org/thegenocide.aspx>.
149. Danielle Paquette, "Turning Pain into Hope," *The Washington Post* (11 June 2017), online: <https://www.washingtonpost.com/sf/world/2017/06/11/rwandas-children-of-rape-are-coming-of-age-against-the-odds/?noredirect=on&utm_term=.137a62caac38>[Paquette, "Turning Pain into Hope" *The Washington Post* (2017)].
150. Emmanuel Ntirenganya, "The plight of children born of rape during Genocide," *The New Times* (17 April 2018), online: <https://www.newtimes.co.rw/news/plight-children-born-rape-during-genocide> [Ntirenganya, "The plight of children born of rape during Genocide," *The New Times* (2018)].
151. Paquette, "Turning Pain into Hope" *The Washington Post* (2017), *supra* note 149. See also, "Intended Consequences" (2008), *supra* note 95; Survivors Fund (SURF), "Born of Rape" (11 January 2019), online: <https://survivors-fund.org.uk/news/born-of-rape/>.
152. For example, Survivors Fund (SURF), a UK-based charity, provides children born of genocidal sexual violence in Rwanda with psychological services, small business aid and tuition assistance (Survivors Fund (SURF), "Born of Rape" (11 January 2019), online: <https://survivors-fund.org.uk/news/born-of-rape/>).
153. Jean de la Croix Tabaro, "The dilemma of children born of rape in the 1994 Genocide," *The New Times* (1 July 2013), online: <https://www.newtimes.co.rw/section/read/67119.">. See also Ignace Nikwivuze, "Supporting Children Born of Rape from the Tutsi Genocide," *Samuel Centre for Social Connectedness* (17 August 2018), online: <https://www.socialconnectedness.org/supporting-children-born-of-rape-from-the-tutsi-genocide/>.
154. Ntirenganya, "The plight of children born of rape during Genocide," *The New Times* (2018), *supra* note 150. The United Nations has highlighted "The Plight and Right of Children Born of War" in the 2018 theme of the third annual International Day for the Elimination of Sexual Violence in Conflict (United Nations, "2018 Theme: 'The Plight and Right of Children Born of War'" (2018), online: <http://www.un.org/en/events/elimination-of-sexual-violence-in-conflict/>).
155. Mama Lambert interview (2018), *supra* note 28.
156. Cameron Macauley, "Women After the Rwandan Genocide: Making the Most of Survival," *Journal of Conventional Weapons Destruction* (April 2013) Vol. 17, Issue 1, online: <https://commons.lib.jmu.edu/cisr-journal/vol17/iss1/9/?utm_source=commons.lib.jmu.edu%2Fcisr-journal%2Fvol17%2Fiss1%2F9&utm_medium=PDF&utm_campaign=PDFCoverPages>.
157. See, for example, Solace Ministries, online: <http://www.solacem.org/>; Avega – Agahozo, online: <http://avega.org.rw/>; Imbuto Foundation, online: <http://www.imbutofoundation.org/>.
158. Mama Lambert interview (2018), *supra* note 28. Several studies conducted in post-genocide Rwanda found that understanding the roots of violence can contribute to both healing and reconciliation. According to one study: "As participants in the various seminars/workshops

came to see the genocide they suffered as one of a number of genocides, the perpetrators' actions as psychologically and culturally understandable, even though horrible, and genocide as not an incomprehensible evil but the outcome of understandable human processes even if extreme and terrible in their consequences, they seemed to feel humanized or 're-humanized.' They expressed the newfound belief that they were not the victims of blind evil or God's punishment, and the hope that through understanding the roots of violence, they can act to prevent it" (Ervin Staub, "Reconciliation after Genocide, Mass Killing, or Intractable Conflict: Understanding the Roots of Violence, Psychological Recovery, and Steps toward a General Theory," *Political Psychology* (2006) 7(6), pages 867-894 at 878).

159. Mama Lambert interview (2018), *supra* note 28; Agnes Mukankusi interview (2018), *supra* note 141; Jean Gakwandi interview (2018), *supra* note 38. See also, Mama Lambert, *For Those Who Do Not Believe in Miracles* (2015); Doreen Umutesi, "Emotional wounds can heal," *The New Times* (12 April 2012), online: <https://www.newtimes.co.rw/section/read/101997>.
160. Jean Gakwandi interview (2018), *supra* note 38. See also, Mama Lambert, *For Those Who Do Not Believe in Miracles* (2015).
161. *Ibid.*
162. *Ibid.*
163. *Ibid.*

WHAT YOU CAN DO

MANY SURVIVORS OF the 1994 genocide against the Tutsi in Rwanda are still struggling to make ends meet. Here is a list of organizations that make a difference in the lives of sexual violence survivors in Rwanda and elsewhere around the world. All of these organizations welcome donations, and some have (sponsorship) programs that allow donors to support individual survivors or groups of survivors.

SOLACE MINISTRIES is an ecumenical, survivor-run organization that supports widows, orphans and survivors of sexual violence. The survivors featured in this book are all beneficiaries of Solace Ministries.
Solace Ministries
P.O. Box 6090, Kigali, Rwanda
Tel. +250-738-305-094 (Jean Gakwandi, Director)
solaceguesthouse@gmail.com
www.solacem.org

MUKOMEZE ("empower her") offers a sponsorship program for Rwandan genocide survivors of sexual violence. Mukomeze partners with Solace Ministries in Rwanda.
Mukomeze
Cimburgalaan 72, 4819 BD, Breda, The Netherlands
Tel. +31-6-14282748
info@mukomeze.nl
www.mukomeze.nl/en

IBUKA ("remember") is the umbrella organization for Rwandan organizations supporting survivors of the genocide. As such, it can also provide information about organizations that specifically support survivors of sexual violence.
Ibuka
P.O. Box 625, Kigali, Rwanda
info@ibuka.be
ibuka.org.rw

SURVIVORS FUND (SURF) helps survivors of the Rwandan genocide deal with and recover from the tragedies of 1994, supporting a wide range of services.
SURF
35 Westholm, London, UK NW11 6LH
Tel. +44-20-7617-7121
enquiries@survivors-fund.org.uk
www.survivors-fund.org.uk

AIDS HEALTHCARE FOUNDATION RWANDA provides health services to over 23,000 people with HIV in Rwanda, including HIV testing, counselling, condom distribution and community-outreach.
AHF Rwanda
M&M Plaza – 3rd floor Plot 17, KG 8 Avenue 6, Gishushu, Remera, Kigali, Rwanda
Tel. +250-252-584-834
brenda.asiimwe@aidshealth.org (Dr. Brenda Asiimwe-Kateera)
www.aidshealth.org/global/rwanda

ELIZABETH GLASER PEDIATRIC AIDS FOUNDATION provides technical and financial support for HIV clinical services in Rwanda, with a specific focus on maternal and pediatric health.
Elizabeth Glaser Pediatric AIDS Foundation (Rwanda)
Avenue des Mille Collines, 5432 KN60 Street Chadel Building, B.P.: 2788, Kigali, Rwanda
Tel. +250-252-570-583
info@pedaids.org
www.pedaids.org/country/rwanda

THE IMBUTO FOUNDATION, first established as a project of the Office of the First Lady of Rwanda, offers support to families affected by HIV in the form of family planning, nutritional balance, psychosocial support and more.
The Imbuto Foundation
Office of the First Lady, Kacyiru, Kigali, Rwanda
Tel. +250-252-552-064
info@imbutofoundation.org
www.imbutofoundation.org

WE-ACTX (WOMEN'S EQUALITY IN ACCESS TO CARE AND TREATMENT) is a community-based HIV/AIDS initiative in Rwanda that provides access to HIV testing and treatment, nutritional and psychosocial services, as well as HIV prevention education, with a focus on survivors of sexual violence.
WE-ACTx
Dorona House, Avenue Karisimbi, P.O. Box 5141, Kigali, Rwanda
us@we-actx.org
www.we-actx.org

RWANDA WOMEN'S NETWORK is dedicated to the promotion and improvement of socio-economic welfare of the women of Rwanda, with a focus on genocide survivors and survivors of sexual and gender-based violence.
Rwanda Women's Network
Kagugu, Mucyo Estate KG 54, off KG 482 – Kinyinya Sector, P.O. Box 3157, Kigali, Rwanda
Tel. +250-788-334-257
info@rwandawomennetwork.org
www.rwandawomennetwork.org

HAGURUKA is an advocacy group that provides access to counselling and legal services for vulnerable women and children in Rwanda, particularly victims of gender-based violence.
Haguruka
KG 11 AV 95, P.O. Box 3030, Kimironko, Kigali, Rwanda
Tel. +250-788-300-834
info@haguruka.org.rw
www.haguruka.org.rw

PRO-FEMMES/TWESE HAMWE is a Rwandan civil society umbrella organization aimed at women's empowerment and socio-economic development, peace building, and promotion of gender equality.
Pro-Femmes/Twese Hamwe
Gahanga Sector, Kicukiro District, Kigali, Rwanda
Tel. +250-788-521-600
info@profemmes.org
www.profemmes.org

AERG (ASSOCIATION DES ETUDIANTS ET ÉLEVES RESCAPÉS DU GENOCIDE) advocates for the ongoing needs of university and secondary school students whose parents and relatives were killed during the Rwandan genocide. AERG is dedicated to ensuring that students overcome trauma, homelessness and financial issues.
AERG
Nyanza Kicukiro Memorial Site, Kigali
Tel. +250-788-306-930
aergcoordination@gmail.com
www.aerg.org.rw

DR. DENIS MUKWEGE FOUNDATION is dedicated to ending rape as a weapon of war worldwide through national and international advocacy.
Dr. Denis Mukwege Foundation
Laan van Meerdervoort 70, 2517 AN, The Hague, The Netherlands
Tel. +31-70-364-8814
info@mukwegefoundation.org
www.mukwegefoundation.org

IMPACT: CENTER AGAINST HUMAN TRAFFICKING AND SEXUAL VIOLENCE IN CONFLICT is an independent expertise center that aims to prevent and address human trafficking and conflict-related sexual violence, through advocacy and empowerment projects, research and advice, education and awareness-raising, and training and capacity-building.
Impact: Center against Human Trafficking and Sexual Violence in Conflict
Ericssonstraat 2, 5121 ML, Rijen, The Netherlands
Tel. +31-6-18804890
info@impact-now.org
www.impact-now.org

WOMEN FOR WOMEN INTERNATIONAL provides women survivors of war, civil strife and other conflicts with tools and resources to move from crisis and poverty to stability and self-sufficiency.
Women for Women International
2000 M Street NW, Suite 200, Washington, D.C., USA 20036
Tel. +1-202-737-7705
general@womenforwomen.org
www.womenforwomen.org

WOMEN'S INITIATIVES FOR GENDER JUSTICE advocates for accountability and prosecution of crimes of sexual and gender-based violence before the International Criminal Court and domestic courts and mechanisms, as well as supports survivors and builds a gender justice field.
Women's Initiatives for Gender Justice
Noordwal 10, 2513 EA, The Hague, The Netherlands
Tel. +31-70-302-9911
info@iccwomen.org
www.4genderjustice.org

THE CANADIAN HIV/AIDS LEGAL NETWORK promotes the human rights of people living with, at risk of or affected by HIV or AIDS, in Canada and internationally, through research and analysis, litigation and other advocacy, public education and community mobilization.
Canadian HIV/AIDS Legal Network
1240 Bay Street, Suite 600, Toronto, ON, Canada M5R 2A7
Tel. +1-416-595-1666
info@aidslaw.ca
www.aidslaw.ca

THE STEPHEN LEWIS FOUNDATION funds community-based initiatives in Africa focusing on women, orphans, grandmothers and people living with HIV or AIDS.
Stephen Lewis Foundation
260 Spadina Avenue, Suite 100, Toronto, ON Canada M5T 2E4
Tel. +1-416-533-9292
info@stephenlewisfoundation.org
www.stephenlewisfoundation.org

V-DAY is a global movement dedicated to ending violence against women and girls.
V-Day
4104 24th Street, #4515, San Francisco, CA USA 94114
Tel. +1-212-645-8329
info@vday.org
www.vday.org

DIGNITAS INTERNATIONAL is a medical and research organization dedicated to improving health care for people facing a high burden of disease, including HIV, and unequal access to services.
Dignitas International
550 Queen St. East, Suite 335, Toronto, ON Canada, M5A 1V2
Tel. +1-416-260-3100
info@dignitasinternational.org
www.dignitasinternational.org

GLOSSARY

Abazungu: Kinyarwanda for "white people." The term is commonly used to refer to all people from outside Rwanda, irrespective of their racial identity.

AIDS: Acquired Immune Deficiency Syndrome. AIDS is a set of symptoms and infections resulting from the damage to the human immune system caused by the Human Immunodeficiency Virus (HIV). The most serious stage of HIV infection is often referred to as AIDS.

Antiretroviral treatment: Also called ARV treatment. Treatment for people living with HIV that works by reducing the replication and amount of HIV in the body.

Bourgmestre: Term used in 1994 for the mayor of a commune. The *bourgmestre* was the most powerful figure in the commune, subject to the authority of the prefect.

Cockroach: Term used by Hutu to insult Tutsi.

Commune: In 1994, Rwanda was divided into twelve regional prefectures that were further subdivided into communes.

Conseiller: Term used in 1994 for the head of a sector.

DRC: The Democratic Republic of the Congo, also commonly referred to as the Congo, formerly known as Zaire.

FAR: Forces Armées Rwandaises, or Rwandan Armed Forces, the national army of Rwanda until July 1994.

FARG: Fonds d'Assistance aux Rescapés du Génocide, or Fund for Assistance for Genocide Survivors, established by the Rwandan government to assist survivors of the genocide in obtaining housing, education and health care.

Gacaca: Kinyarwanda for "on the grass," referring to the traditional courts of Rwanda. Their mandate evolved after 1994 to adjudicate crimes committed during the genocide.

Gender-based violence: Violence targeted specifically at a person because of their gender. Includes but is not limited to sexual violence.

Genocide: The deliberate and systematic destruction, in whole or in part, of an ethnic, racial, religious or national group. The term was first used in the 1948 UN Convention on the Prevention and Punishment of the Crime of Genocide.

Génocidaire: A person who commits or has committed the crime of genocide.

HIV: Human Immunodeficiency Virus. HIV is a virus that weakens the body's immune system and can lead to AIDS. Someone who is diagnosed with HIV is said to be HIV positive.

ICTR: The International Criminal Tribunal for Rwanda based in Arusha, Tanzania. Established in 1995 by a UN Security Council resolution to prosecute the main perpetrators of the Rwandan genocide. The Tribunal was officially closed on December 31st, 2015.

Inkotanyi: Kinyarwandan term used to refer to the Rwandan Patriotic Front, or RPF. Hutu extremists often used this term to refer to alleged Tutsi spies.

Interahamwe: Kinyarwanda for "those who attack together." Refers to a Hutu militia group, composed mainly of Hutu youth, that was active during the genocide.

Inyenzi: Kinyarwanda for "cockroach." A term used by Hutu to insult Tutsi.

Inyangamugayo: Kinyarwanda for "people of integrity," the lay judges of the *gacaca* courts.

Irondo: Kinyarwandan term used to refer to a neighbourhood patrol.

Kangura: Kinyarwanda for "wake others up," and the title of a magazine, established in 1990 and published in Kinyarwanda and French, that stoked ethnic hatred in the run-up to the genocide.

Kinyarwanda: The national language of Rwanda, spoken by all Rwandans.

Laisser passer card: Travel document used in Rwanda in lieu of a passport.

Muzehe: Kinyarwanda for "old man."

Opération/Zone Turquoise: Opération Turquoise was a French military operation in Rwanda under the mandate of the United Nations. During the genocide, Zone Turquoise was the French-controlled "safe zone" in the southwest of Rwanda. The French have been accused of assisting Hutu *génocidaires* during the genocide.

Prefect: Term used in 1994 for the head of a prefecture.

Prefecture: In 1994, Rwanda was divided into twelve regional prefectures, each governed by a prefect. On January 1, 2006, the twelve prefectures of Rwanda were abolished and replaced with five provinces.

Presidential Guards: Elite force under the command of the Rwandan president.

Radio Muhabura: A pro-Tutsi RPF radio station, created in 1991 that broadcast from RPF-occupied territory, including Uganda.

RPF: Rwandan Patriotic Front, a political and military movement formed in 1987 by the Tutsi refugee diaspora in Uganda. Beginning in 1959, Tutsi refugees fled to Uganda to escape ethnic purges. In 1994, the RPF invaded Rwanda and halted the genocide.

RTLM: Radio Télévision Libre des Mille Collines. A Hutu-controlled radio station famous for broadcasting propaganda against the Tutsi.

Rwandan franc: Currency used in Rwanda. At the time of writing, one U.S. dollar was equivalent to approximately 900 Rwandan francs.

Sector: A subdivision of a commune.

Sexual violence: Violence encompassing various forms of sexual abuse, such as rape, gang rape, sexual mutilation and sexual slavery. Sexual violence is a form of gender-based violence.

Snake: Term used by Hutu to insult Tutsi.

Umuganda: Kinyarwanda for "performing community work one day each month by all Rwandans."

Umukecuru: Kinyarwanda for "old lady."

Umuzungu: Kinyarwanda for "white person." The term is commonly used to refer to all people from outside Rwanda, irrespective of their racial identity.

UNAMIR: United Nations Assistance Mission for Rwanda, established in October 1993 to help implement the peace agreement between the Rwandan government and the RPF. UNAMIR's mandate and strength were adjusted several times during the genocide. Its mandate ended in March 1996.

ACKNOWLEDGEMENTS

TO THE SEVENTEEN survivors and their families featured in the first and second editions of this book, and to the countless others who have shared their stories with us in Rwanda, there are no words to express our appreciation for your courage and our admiration for your perseverance and dignity. You are our partners in this book, our teachers and friends in life, and forever in our hearts and minds.

Both editions would not have been possible without the many wonderful people and organizations who have assisted us along the way. These include the staff at Solace Ministries, who welcomed us with open arms. Despite their many commitments in providing assistance to survivors of the genocide and others in need, each staff member made time for us. In particular, director Jean Gakwandi believed in this project from the beginning and did everything in his power to guarantee its success. During the project's inception, Denise Uwimana was instrumental in having the survivors recount their stories. Mama Lambert, who became our mentor and our inspiration, empowered the survivors to share their experiences and performed a miracle or two to rectify derailed plans. Agnes Mukankusi was an indispensable coordinator and source of positive energy. Our translators, Jessie Gakwandi, Doris Uwicyeza, Alina Tuiyishime and Christine Mukantaganda, displayed sensitivity, professionalism and endless patience and endurance, and for this we thank them.

Our research and editorial assistants Hanna Gros, Yolanda Song, India Annamanthadoo and Mehak Kawatra from the International Human Rights

Program (IHRP) at the University of Toronto's Faculty of Law provided invaluable transcription of the interviews, editorial finesse and meticulous fact-checking support. Volunteers Milena Adamczewska and Chiun Min Seah from IMPACT: Center against Human Trafficking and Sexual Violence in Conflict, the Netherlands, helped to raise awareness of and crowdfund for the project.

For the first version of this book, Cordaid provided us with the resources to forge ahead on schedule, and we thank Sanne Bijlsma for making this possible. For the 2019 update, our thanks to IHRP, IMPACT, Mukomeze and the crowdfunders for supporting the project.

Thanks to our publishing teams at D&M Publishers Inc. and Wolf Legal Publishers for their professionalism. At D&M, we are tremendously grateful to Scott McIntyre, who believed in this project and shared our vision, and to Barbara Pulling for her expertise and wisdom in helping to mould our final product. At Wolf Legal Publishers, we are indebted to Willem-Jan van der Wolf, who helped shepherd this project over the span of almost a decade, publishing the first edition in 2011 in Dutch, and now the second edition. Thanks also to Stephen Lewis, Eve Ensler, Patrick Cammaert, Patricia Viseur Sellers, James Orbinski, Romeo Dallaire, Jan Pronk and Neelie Kroes for agreeing to support this project so wholeheartedly in spite of their harried schedules.

A special thanks to Kim Siedel and Shaima Al-Khalili for their photography mentorship and editorial wizardry, to Jen Sookfong Lee for her insight and encouragement and to Bernice and Christian Paul for their passionate, enthusiastic promotion of the book.

Finally, we thank our families Freek, Liese, Jef, Leonie, Vanessa, Nick, Daan, Saar, Ria, Hans, Oi, Ho-Ming, So-Ching, Hui-Tong, Vincent, Angie, Karen, Zadie, Mika, Siham, Zaki, Sina, Najat, Jawad, Najat, Abdul-Hussein, Marcello, Marvis and Cees for their generosity, unconditional love and support.

ANNE-MARIE DE BROUWER works in the field of international criminal justice, conflict-related sexual violence, human trafficking and victims' rights at Impact: Center against Human Trafficking and Sexual Violence in Conflict. She is the co-founder of Mukomeze.

SANDRA KA HON CHU is the Director of Research and Advocacy at the Canadian HIV/AIDS Legal Network, where she works on HIV-related human rights issues concerning prisons, drug policy, sex work, women and immigration.

EEFJE DE VOLDER is an anthropologist and lawyer working in the field of human trafficking, victims' rights and conflict-related sexual violence at Impact: Center against Human Trafficking and Sexual Violence in Conflict.

SAMER MUSCATI is a Canadian lawyer, documentary photographer and former journalist. As a senior researcher for Human Rights Watch, he focused on women's rights in conflict zones. He runs the International Human Rights program at University of Toronto's Faculty of Law.

Please visit www.impact-now.org for photographs, videos, news and events related to this book.